WANTED: *An Asian Policy*

WANTED:

An
Asian
Policy

by Edwin O. Reischauer

GREENWOOD PRESS, PUBLISHERS
WESTPORT, CONNECTICUT

Library of Congress Cataloging in Publication Data

Reischauer, Edwin Oldfather, 1910-
  Wanted: an Asian policy.

  Reprint of the 1st ed. published by Knopf, New York.
  1. Asia--Foreign relations--United States.
2. United States--Foreign relations--Asia. 3. Asia--
Politics. I. Title.
[DS518.8.R44 1973]   327.73'05   73-2341
ISBN 0-8371-6843-0

Originally published in 1955
by Alfred A. Knopf, New York

Reprinted with the permission
of Alfred A. Knopf

Reprinted in 1973 by Greenwood Press,
a division of Williamhouse-Regency Inc.

Library of Congress Catalogue Card Number 73-2341

ISBN 0-8371-6843-0

Printed in the United States of America

For Ann, Bob, and Joan

Preface

There is an urgent need for us in America to develop a sound and comprehensive Asian policy, but to do this we must first devote more and deeper thought to our problems in Asia than we have in the past. This book has been written in the hope that it will contribute to this end. Its size alone will show that it is not a complete survey of the situation in Asia nor a definitive formulation of our relationship with that part of the world. My purpose has not been to add to the known facts about Asia or to supply ready-made the policy called for in the title. Instead of attempting to say the last word, I am more interested in saying a first word in helping to stimulate the free debate that is necessary if we are to develop an adequate Asian policy.

Although I am by profession a scholar, this is not, strictly speaking, a scholarly book. I have written it less as a dispassionate student of Japanese and Chinese history than as an American citizen deeply concerned about our nation's future. While I have drawn on my background in Far Eastern studies as much as possible, the greater part of this book extends far beyond my professional competence. It is made up largely of opinion and conjecture— well-founded opinion and reasonable conjecture, I trust— but not scholarship. No one man's specialized knowledge could cover more than a small portion of the huge field of our relations with Asia, and the collective knowledge of all our specialists would still leave the most difficult problems in the realm of speculation. That is no reason, however, for ignoring this vastly important subject or for leaving it entirely in the hands of those who have no specialized competence whatever.

I have attempted first to explore, within the context of the present world situation, the basic nature of our interests in Asia, and then to assess within a broad historical framework the recent course of internal developments there. Finally, I have attempted to draw from a balanced consideration of these two sets of factors some principles that should guide us in our dealings with Asia. The result is a series of hypotheses, and the many facts and historical examples with which I have supported them should be regarded more as illustrations of their meaning than as positive proof of their validity.

Few who read this book will find it an entirely satisfactory formulation of the problems of our relationship with Asia. Each of us inevitably has a somewhat different area of knowledge and experience and therefore a slightly different point of view. I trust that in time our increasing knowledge and understanding of the problems dealt with here will make this particular statement of them no longer adequate for me either. But my chief hope is that the hypotheses set forth will, through either stimulation or irritation, induce others to examine more deeply the basic assumptions on which we are conducting our relations with Asia, so that we shall become more aware of these fundamentals when we face specific issues there.

While the many imperfections of this book fall entirely on my own shoulders, I owe a great debt to many friends of divergent political views, who through their criticisms of the manuscript eliminated from it many errors of fact, inaccuracies of statement, and obscurities of expression. Their generous contributions, however, in no sense imply concurrence on their part in all the views expressed here. Among these friends I wish to express my particular thanks to Dr. Francis W. Cleaves; my father-in-law, Dr. George H. Danton; Lt. Col. Trevor N. Dupuy; Dr. Alexander Eckstein; Dr. John K. Fairbank; Dr. Richard N. Frye; Mrs. Susan Guttman; Dr. James R. Hightower; Dr. Daniel H. H. Ingalls; Mrs. Robert Treat Paine; Dr. John C. Pelzel; my father, Dr. A. K. Reischauer; Dr. Benjamin J. Schwartz; Mrs. Anne Thomson; and to my wife. I also am deeply indebted to Mr. Harold Strauss for many invaluable suggestions which have helped to shorten the length of this book while bringing its contents into sharper focus.

E. O. R.

Cambridge
October 1954

Contents

WANTED: *An Asian Policy*

PART ONE:

1. *Asia in the World Today*

In recent years we Americans have often been in violent disagreement over our relations with Asian countries, but there is one point on which all of us seem to be in accord: the present state of our relationship with Asia is certainly not satisfactory. Most of us would go beyond this statement and describe our contacts with Asia as profoundly disturbing and extremely dangerous. Our batting average in Asia is very low.

Something, we feel, is wrong, but when we try to define what that something is, extraordinary differences of

The Problem

opinion emerge. The same set of facts about Asia seems to mean one thing to some Americans and almost the opposite to others. And this despite the fact that the political differences between these same people on domestic issues are often not very great, especially when compared with the far wider range of political opinions in most other parts of the world.

We Americans, who see eye to eye on most major issues, obviously must be approaching our problems in Asia with some very different assumptions, or else we could not be reaching such sharply contradictory conclusions based on the same body of information. Of course, we are far from having an adequate knowledge of the multitudinous facts that bear on our specific problems in Asia. We face a prime need for more and better information. But beyond this we also need much greater agreement on the over-all meaning of the facts already available to us. In other words, we need to re-examine the various assumptions that have led to our conflicting interpretations.

We have often failed to see past the many distressing surface phenomena to underlying causes. We have approached problems piecemeal without adequately considering their relationship to one another or to the situation in the rest of the world. It can be said that we have had many Asian policies but not an Asian policy, and this lack is undoubtedly the primary reason for the very limited success we have had in meeting our greatest crises in Asia and our even more frightening inability to foresee them.

We have still to determine what are our basic interests in Asia—what are the dangers to be avoided and the hopes to be fulfilled in that part of the world. We have reached no agreement on what really is happening in Asia, how this may affect us, and what we should do about it. We all share the desire to stop communism from spreading farther in Asia and to roll it back if possible, but this is not in itself a full policy. Not only is it a dangerous oversimplification of our Asian problem, but it is inadequate even as far as it goes, for it tells us nothing about how communism spreads in Asia or how it can best be combated there.

Unless we have a more fully developed Asian policy than this, we cannot even judge with assurance the success or failure of our specific actions, until it is too late to modify them. So long as we do not know what we are dealing with or what we can reasonably hope to achieve, we are operating in the dark. Under such circumstances we need not be surprised when apparent success turns mysteriously into failure, as happened not so long ago when the fruits of victory over the Japanese in China were suddenly transformed into the bitter ashes of defeat. The whole problem of our Asian policy has in recent years become further obscured by the fogs of fear and suspicion. Mutual distrust and frenzied emotionalism have warped our thinking, and a virtual taboo has been built up against any serious consideration of the bases of our policies in Asia. These should instead be the central theme of a great debate.

The guideposts of our earlier policies toward Asia mark only a faint trail on the periphery of our problems of today, when man's new mastery over space and cosmic power has stripped us of our ocean defenses, and two terrible wars have destroyed much of what little order had once been achieved in the relations between nations. Today communism and democracy meet everywhere in open conflict for the minds of men, and the totalitarian slave-state prepares relentlessly for the destruction of free society. Asia, once so remote, has become the principal field of maneuver in a divided and precariously balanced world. It is there that we have experienced in recent years most of our major disappointments and failures in foreign policy. From this fact alone we can surmise that in Asia may lie our least understood and therefore, in the long run, possibly our most dangerous problems.

Certainly Asia was the scene of our clearest foreign-policy defeat in recent years, when the Chinese people, the largest single bloc of human beings in the world, shifted from friendship and co-operation with us to open hatred and, for a while, limited but costly warfare. In Asia in the past few years cold war has turned hot more often than elsewhere in the world and threatens to continue to do so in the future. In Asia lies the greatest no man's land between the tightly drawn lines of the divided world. Here are to be found the greatest masses of people who remain uncommitted or who abjure both sides, the greatest space for maneuver between contending political philosophies and also, for that matter, between contending armies, and the greatest room for the development of dangerous ambiguities.

From these failures and problems in Asia have also arisen the most bitter disagreements that have divided and weakened Americans in recent years. The great defeat in China has with some justice been termed a traumatic experience for the American public. Certainly our reactions to it have often been those of frustrated men. We have sometimes sought scapegoats for failures instead of remedies, and all too frequently intemperate accusations have smothered impartial inquiry and reasoned debate. The resultant atmosphere of suspicion and fear has narrowed the scope of our thinking and stifled the voices of the timid. Our relations with other Asian countries meanwhile have shown a growing tendency toward dangerous inflexibility. We have approached some of our problems hampered by the chip-on-the-shoulder attitude of the weak rather than with the breadth of vision and understanding tolerance of the strong. Worst of all, we seem to have lost confidence in ourselves, fearing our own ability to negotiate and mistrusting our own judgment. It would be hard to find a historical parallel either to the defeat we suffered in China or to the crippling aftereffects it has produced.

Our frustration over our relations with Asia is all the more puzzling because at the present moment Asia does not appear to be the most immediately dangerous area in our foreign policy. Our relations with the Soviet Union are obviously far more hazardous. Whatever the future may bring, it is only the Soviet Union at present which is capable of plunging the world into the type of war that could obliterate civilization. A failure in diplomatic relations with the Soviet Union or a failure on our part to provide an effective counterbalance to its military power could prove immediately disastrous to us and to the whole world. And Europe, of course, is the area in which such a failure in diplomacy or military preparation could most easily occur. With its industrial power and potential military might poised between the Soviet Union and the United States, it is obviously the area of balance today between peace and possible annihilation.

Actually the Russian betrayal of our hopes for lasting peace through mutual trust and a democratic world order was a far more serious policy defeat for the United States than the subsequent defection of China and one without which our defeat in China would have had little immediate significance and might never have occurred. But the Russian betrayal, while perhaps hard to believe at first in its full enormity, became in time all too clear-cut and obvious. The Russian position, however distressing, has come to be a known quantity that can be reckoned with, and Russian reasons for acting as they have, though fantastically unreasonable to us, are nevertheless no mystery.

There are, of course, many difficult and irritating aspects of our relationship with Europe, and nothing is satisfactory in our contacts with Russia. But despite the grave dangers of our foreign relations in these areas, they have brought no sense of frustration comparable to that we have felt over Asia. Our liberal distribution of economic aid has not prevented the admiration most Asians felt for us at the end of the Second World War from turning in a few short years into distrust or even hostility. Our tremendous investments in aid to China have only benefited our enemies. Our work to pull Japan down must now be matched by our efforts to build her up. The costly war in

Korea has perhaps prevented even more serious losses, but certainly has brought no appreciable gains. Our attempt to stem the flow of communism in Indochina has only succeeded in achieving a precarious balance between semidefeat and complete disaster. Our continuing efforts throughout Asia, when viewed against the perspective of past failures, give no greater prospect of success. Asia remains a fertile field for petty conflicts, each of which could be the spark that ignites a world conflagration. Asia is a source of friction between us and our European allies, impairing the goodwill and mutual confidence built up in other areas.

It is only natural that our relations with Asia have been much more perplexing than our relations with either Europe or Russia. Our relations with European countries are dealings between cousins, if not brothers, for we share a common cultural heritage and similar points of view on many vital matters. With Russia the relationship may be more distant, but the Russians nevertheless are cousins of a sort. Some observers, looking eastward from western Europe, have placed Russia beyond the pale of Western civilization. If one stands outside of Europe, however, in Asia, and looks westward toward Europe, it becomes at once evident that what unites Russia to the rest of the West is far more significant than what divides it. Most things Russian or Communist that appear important to Asians differ from those traditional in any part of Asia and are distinctly Western. More than a thousand years of cultural contacts with Byzantium and later with the rest of Europe have naturally left a far more lasting mark on Russia than a period of Mongol suzerainty, now many centuries in the past, or the continuing proximity of nomads of a distinctly different race and culture.

The Communist faith of the Russians, however odious, was born and nurtured in the heart of the Western world. Compare it with the traditional beliefs of the West and those of the various parts of Asia and it becomes amply clear that communism is indeed nothing more than a Western heresy. Unfortunately it does not even represent a unique perversion of Western ideals, for it is a doctrine that has found totalitarian counterparts elsewhere in the Occident. It would be gratifying to us of the West to be able through some semantic sleight of hand to lay the blame for communism and all totalitarianism on someone else, but to do so would be to indulge in a foolish self-deception that would blind us to half the danger that we face. Communism is a product of our Western civilization, and though it is for this reason all the more understandable to us, it is also all the more dangerous.

Whatever the differences between ourselves and the peoples of western Europe and Russia, the historical and cultural gap between us and the peoples of Asia is far greater. None of the civilizations of Asia is closely related to ours, even though they have felt the influence of the West in recent years. While in Russia we see an abhorrent system built on a substructure of Western civilization, in Asia we often find familiar Western superstructures resting on what are to us strange if not altogether unknown foundations. There is a vast gulf in backgrounds between Westerners and Asians, and the superficial similarities often serve to accentuate the differences. What seems familiar and known proves suddenly unfathomable. We expect friendship from the Chinese and they turn on us with hate. We expect hate from the Japanese, and they turn to us with admiration and trust. We expect sympathy and respect from the Indians, and they look upon us with suspicion and fear. In Asia at best we are skating on a very thin ice of mutual understanding over deep and often unknown waters.

These are, of course, broad generalizations with all

the inevitable inaccuracies and imperfections of generalized statements. Actually Asia, as I have used the term here, signifies the whole non-Western world, for the vast bulk of the non-Western peoples lives in Asia, just as the bulk of the Western peoples, except for ourselves, lives in Europe. The world around us naturally does not fall neatly into the three categories of Russia, Europe, and Asia. Some lands fall in between these generalizations, and many are hybrids of these worlds within the world. But these three names do identify the three major sectors of our foreign relations, and of the three, Asia is unquestionably the one we understand least well and therefore find most puzzling.

Once the gulf between ourselves and Asia made little difference to us. We lived in an as yet undivided Western world, which dominated Asia whenever and wherever the two met. But this is no longer true. Asia in terms of national strength is the fastest-growing part of the world. We have seen spectacular growth in the United States in recent times and also a rapid rate of development in Russia, but in both countries this was growth on top of a solid substructure of power and under most favorable physical conditions. In Asia the growth of national power has been more phenomenal because it started from almost nothing and has taken place under far from fortuitous circumstances. A century ago Japan lay defenseless before a single squadron from a Western land, but it rose so rapidly in military power that it defeated Imperial Russia on both land and sea and later challenged with extraordinary initial success the leading naval powers of the world. Three or four decades ago Western military men boasted, not altogether without reason, that a handful of European or American soldiers could march with impunity from one end of China to the other; today, through some alchemy of the national soul, the armies of China have become formidable adversaries not only at home but also beyond their frontiers. Not long ago the vast subcontinent of India could be held in colonial sway by a token force of British soldiers; today India, if not a world power in a military sense, is certainly a world force in international politics.

Half the people of the world live in geographic Asia, well over half in the broader Asia of the non-Western world. A century ago this more than half of humanity was a negligible factor in international relations, except as economic or political assets to be fought over by the great or even the small powers of the West. A half-century ago the non-Western peoples were still decidedly peripheral in world affairs. Today they are unquestionably important and often central in the gravest international problems of our age. No one can say what their role will be tomorrow or the next day, except that it is certain to be a far larger one than today.

It would be an exaggeration to say that Asia will decide the fate of the world. Rephrase the proposition but slightly, however, and it is probably true: the fate of the world will be that of Asia; for in a rapidly shrinking world it seems unlikely that there will be more than one destiny for humankind. Today the area of balance between democracy and totalitarianism is western Europe; tomorrow it may well be Asia. Today the cleavage between free and slave state within the Western world overshadows all human life; but it is not hard to imagine a tomorrow in which the even more fundamental cleavage between the Western minority and the non-Western majority of mankind is the most significant fact in human affairs.

2. *The Nature of the Problem*

To some people it may seem easier and more reasonable to attribute our errors in Asia to inexcusably inept and sometimes disloyal individual Americans, rather than to insufficient knowledge and understanding. Such a judgment would be a most comforting one if it were correct, for then our difficulties would be easy to remedy. We should only need to put wiser and more trustworthy men in charge of our contacts with Asia. But unfortunately this interpretation of our failures, though often put forth with vehemence, is so far from the truth that only our own frustration could have given it much credence.

There is no denying the vast ineptness of our handling of the Chinese problem, for example, but the ineptness was caused by misunderstanding rather than treachery—a misunderstanding that appears to have been almost nation-wide. If there has been treason, it was at most a minor factor, for anyone familiar with the ponderous and often cumbersome workings of our government can readily see that we simply are not susceptible to treachery in policy decisions. A democracy, as we know, can suffer seriously from the treachery of espionage or even of sabotage, but one of its greatest advantages over a totalitarian regime is that the large numbers of persons who participate in making decisions and still more the final check of popular approval make treason in policy decisions virtually impossible. Treachery of this sort may be a great danger in a totalitarian system, but for us it is little more than the imaginings of minds more attuned to totalitarianism than to democracy.

If one looks back briefly over what was said and done by all the diverse people who influenced policy decisions in the crucial days of the China debacle, from the President down to the State Department officials and the army officers in the field, one cannot but be appalled at how wrong most of them were in one way or another about what would or could happen in China. Few had a deep understanding of both China and communism, the two chief ingredients in the problem, and many knew little of either. As a consequence, some did not believe that the Chinese Communists could replace the Kuomintang, and many of those who did were not able to comprehend the full significance of this situation. And whatever may have been the bitter differences between the diverse and sometimes bizarre array of Americans involved in the formulation and execution of our policy toward China, there can be no doubt that almost all of them shared certain basic concepts that were not at all justified by the facts. The record of our relations with China during the war and early postwar years were, as Mr. Feis has well described it, "the tale of the wearing out of a conception that was not well enough aligned with reality." [1]

It would be a mistake to attribute the Communist triumph in China primarily to what Americans either did or did not do. Even if we had been blessed with unerring wisdom, it is not at all certain that we could have had much influence on the course of events there. At the same time, there were several grave misapprehensions on our part which certainly contributed to the completeness of the defeat of our policy. First was the assumption that China would play a large role in the defeat of Japan and that therefore immediate military considerations outweighed all others—and this despite the fact that each new phase of the war showed the dwindling validity of that point of view. Then came the determination that China should be made the stabilizing force of the Far East and

[1] Herbert Feis: *The China Tangle. The American Effort in China from Pearl Harbor to the Marshall Mission* (Princeton University Press, 1953), page 4.

one of the five major powers in the postwar world—and this despite the growing evidence that China was headed for open civil war and possible chaos. And finally, as the situation became increasingly desperate, all American factions held doggedly to the great illusion that a country which even in peacetime had been unable to run its affairs by democratic means could, through exhortation, be persuaded to do so when divided into two armed camps, both sworn to the complete destruction of the other.

In our relations with Korea we find an even more glaring case of ignorance leading to catastrophe. Before the outbreak of the Korean War scant attention was paid to our problems there by either the American public or our government. Limited interest was aroused in some circles over the advisability of co-operating with or, as some felt, supporting the regime of Syngman Rhee in South Korea instead of fostering the development of some possibly more dynamic or forward-looking group of leaders. There was some discussion in retrospect over the wisdom of having allowed a division of the country along the thirty-eighth parallel in the first place, though much of the debate was conducted by persons with no clear understanding of the circumstances under which the line had been drawn. There was some dispute over the nature of the weapons to be furnished the South Koreans, but because of our critical shortage in military manpower, there was a much more lively interest in withdrawing our own troops from Korea.

It was not until North Korea invaded the south and we, by Presidential decision but with almost unanimous approval, stepped in to stop this blatant act of aggression, that the public or even the American government began to pay much attention to Korea. The grave decision to cross the thirty-eighth parallel became a matter of serious disagreement, particularly after it had been made and the

Chinese Communists had entered the war. A bitter and prolonged dispute raged over the comparative advantages of a geographically limited war and the extension of hostilities by the aerial bombing of Chinese soil. Each phase of the truce negotiations and the subsequent political maneuverings became the subject of sharp differences of opinion.

Every one of these points of debate fully merited all the attention it was given, but they were merely the surface crises of a profoundly unsatisfactory relationship of much longer standing between ourselves and Korea. Until the outbreak of war our ignorance of Korea was only matched by our indifference. But Korea is not, nor was it a decade or two ago, a country of negligible importance. There are close to thirty million Koreans, making them perhaps the twelfth or thirteenth largest bloc of human beings in the world. Their land, lying between far larger and more powerful neighbors, was for long a bone of international contention, until it fell prey to Japan's imperialistic appetite. The day we went to war with Japan, we inevitably undertook to alter the status of Korea, for the defeat we envisaged for Japan could only mean the liberation of Korea. Because of our deep belief in the right of national self-determination and our strong hope for a democratic world order of truly independent national groups, no other end of the war with Japan was conceivable, so far as Korea was concerned. Indeed, as early as December 1943 our President at Cairo joined the leaders of Britain and China in promising that "in due course Korea shall become free and independent."

Although no one can doubt the rightness or the inevitability of this decision, it is impossible to condone what we did or, rather, failed to do next. The liberation of Korea was a military problem, and this we met squarely, but the establishment of a truly free and stable

Korea, without which liberation itself would mean little, was another and far more delicate matter, and for this we made no preparation whatsoever.

The Koreans had behind them no political tradition on which to build a stable regime that would be capable of playing a healthy role in a democratic world order. For forty years they had been cruelly dominated and exploited by their Japanese masters. Virtually all positions of leadership had been monopolized by Japanese. Very few Koreans had been allowed to gain any knowledge of problems of government, and these few were regarded as renegades by their compatriots. Only as the rank and file of a notoriously brutal police force had many Koreans gained much experience in controlling the affairs of their fellow men. Korea was in fact a police state, all the more vicious for being at the same time a colonial regime. The only memory of government before Japanese police rule was that of an outdated, degenerate, and enfeebled Oriental monarchy of a type entirely unfitted for the problems of the twentieth century, even if it had left behind it enough vestiges and sufficient prestige to make its resurrection feasible.

The lack of political experience among Koreans was serious enough, but their attitude toward government and the violence of their political sentiments were even more alarming. A generation and more of harsh Japanese oppression had left a legacy of suspicion and hatred for all authority. A patriot was almost by definition a man who defied the government. Nationalism burned all the more fiercely in Korean hearts because of its long and brutal suppression. Under the Japanese the Koreans had been forbidden any sense of national pride or even of national identity; they were to become second-class Japanese. They were prohibited the use of their own language in schools or in any public office. They were denied all freedom of opinion; nothing but complete and servile submission to Japan was tolerated. Physical mistreatment by the police regime was perhaps little worse than in some other colonial lands of the day, but the spiritual oppression of the Koreans was more terrible than anything we have known in modern times outside the barbed wire of the Nazi concentration camp or the iron walls of Communist imperialism. Korean bodies were of use to the Japanese militarists, but there were to be no Korean souls. Small wonder that tremendous pressures developed among the emotional and volatile Korean people beneath the heavy lid of Japanese rule—pressures that were bound to expand with explosive force once liberation had removed the lid.

In the economic field the situation was little better. Japan had made a great investment in Korea, developing her industry and her transportation system far beyond those of most Asian lands, but the Japanese were in complete control as owners, managers, and technicians. Koreans were not prepared to run the machine of their own economy. And in any case it was so carefully and fully integrated with the economy of Japan and of Japanese-dominated Manchuria that it was obvious that the collapse of Japan would be a profound blow to the Korean economy, no matter how skillfully the transfer from Japanese to Korean hands was effected.

Added to these domestic problems were those of Korea's vulnerable geographic position. In the past, rivalries between great powers over a weak or disrupted Korea had given rise to more than one war. There was every reason to fear that a feeble and chaotic Korea would be a weak spot in the postwar world order, if not a serious menace to world peace. And yet what did we do to prepare for this situation? Absolutely and literally nothing.

It is hard to imagine a more complex or delicate problem than the one posed by the liberation of Korea or a situation more fraught with dangers, but American preparation for Korean independence stopped with the simple promise of freedom. A group of soldiers reportedly was trained for a while in the Korean language in the somewhat remote eventuality that we should be engaged in land fighting on Korean soil, but when other manpower demands became more pressing, they were diverted to Europe. Japan's sudden but not altogether unexpected collapse in the summer of 1945 found us no more ready to face the Korean problem than we had been at the start of the war.

The United States government hastily drew a line across Korea at the thirty-eighth parallel to demarcate the zones in which the American and Soviet armies would receive the Japanese surrender. As Russian troops were already pouring across the borders into the northern fringes of Korea, the only choice we had was between a line drawn somewhere through Korea and one placed in the straits between Korea and Japan, leaving the whole of the peninsula, like Manchuria, within the area in which the Russian forces would take the Japanese surrender. Back of this situation lay our earlier misjudgment at Yalta in encouraging Russian participation in the war against Japan, though it seems probable that the Russians would have jumped safely into the war in its closing days and invaded Korea regardless of what had been said at Yalta. In any case there can be no doubt that the drawing of this line was one of the most fateful political decisions of the postwar world, not the minor military detail it seemed to us in our almost willful disregard of the looming problem of a liberated Korea.

The Russians, well equipped with detailed plans and a large number of trained, Russian-speaking Communists of Korean origin, marched into their zone and with their customary guile and force started molding the people of the region into an effective Communist regime. Meanwhile we improvised hastily and with little thought beyond the immediate problem of the Japanese surrender. An army corps poised on Okinawa for the projected autumn invasion of Japan was shunted to Korea, and its combat general, entirely unprepared by temperament or training for his delicate political mission and lacking anything but the most superficial guidance from Washington, stepped innocently ashore into a political situation that would have tried the wisdom of a sage. He scornfully brushed aside the scores of self-appointed committees and governments, which the most vigorous and able Koreans had started to form upon hearing of the Japanese surrender. They were not properly elected bodies, he felt, and therefore could not be tolerated. The decision was a reasonable one from the American point of view, but unrealistic in terms of the situation in Korea. It rebuffed the natural and in many ways healthy first steps toward self-rule in Korea and needlessly aroused the suspicion and anger of the potential leaders.

As it seemed obvious that the machine of government and industry could not run efficiently without the Japanese who knew its operation, it was blandly announced that, for the time being, the American forces would control South Korea through the Japanese. Imagine what would have happened in France if we had decided even temporarily to maintain Nazi rule. A lighted brand had been unwittingly tossed into the powder keg of Korean national pride. The resultant explosion forced an immediate revision of this ill-considered plan. It was decided to pack all Japanese off home, administrators and technicians alike. This was done with dispatch, and then, of course, the Korean administration and economy collapsed. The machine ground to a halt. Almost every index of economic well-being plummeted dangerously downward toward zero.

Although Korea had escaped the physical ravages of war almost entirely, this most unskillful transfer of its economic machine from Japanese to Korean hands, together with the damaging effects of the breaking of its economic ties with Japan and Manchuria and the division of the country into two halves, produced the same economic chaos and suffering that had resulted elsewhere in the world from aerial devastation.

While these well-intentioned blunders were being made in top policy, most of the other members of our army of occupation were doing little better at their individual levels. Steeled as they were for battle with the ruthless soldiers of Japan, they were ill-prepared to give sympathy or understanding to any Orientals. But sympathy and understanding the Koreans most certainly needed, with their wildly aroused national hopes and their woefully inadequate technical skills. Without any understanding of how Koreans felt and with scorn for their ignorance, our soldiers soon fell into the "gook" mentality. The liberator looked with contempt upon the man he had freed and received in return a well-earned measure of resentment.

It is all too easy to condemn those who represented American policy in Korea in the early postwar years, but the real blame lies with all of us Americans for having sent such ill-prepared and unguided men to a task that called for the highest degree of skill and tact. As the story continues, the blame falls all the more clearly on Washington and the rest of us at home.

For a while we lulled ourselves into believing that the agreement made in Moscow in December 1945 for a negotiated unification of Korea would solve our problem. This agreement looked toward a complicated series of negotiations, beginning with the consultation of "Korean democratic parties and social organizations" and leading eventually to the establishment for five years of a joint trusteeship over Korea by ourselves, the Soviet Union, the United Kingdom, and China. Naturally the Koreans reacted violently against the suggested delay of complete independence, but Communist discipline soon brought all Communist-dominated groups into line behind the proposals. The Russians then argued that all Korean groups that had not speedily accepted the decision could not be considered democratic and, through this deft verbal trick, sought to eliminate all non-Communist Koreans from any part in leadership.

It took a year and a half of intermittent and entirely fruitless debate over this one point to convince us that by negotiation the Russians had meant the complete surrender of our democratic ideals, and only then did we begin to take full stock of the situation. The Russians in North Korea had been rapidly building with characteristic harsh efficiency on the convenient foundations of the Japanese police state, and an effective Communist satellite was arising there, while we had made but little progress in the south in the far more difficult task of creating a working democracy from nothing but national enthusiasm. North Korea was a viable political unit, a success within the framework of Communist imperialism. South Korea was far from a success in any terms—a regime with only a small beginning toward true democracy, an economy that was still in a perilous condition, a mass of people whose future was most uncertain. We were far behind in a race, without even realizing that we had entered it.

The apathy of Congress and of the general public made a truly realistic approach to the problem out of the question. Instead we did what little we could on an entirely inadequate budget, saving a little today with no thought of what vast costs false economies might force

upon us tomorrow. Extricating ourselves from a dangerous position was a more attractive possibility than trying
to correct the situation itself.

Russian military withdrawal from the firmly established police state in North Korea by the end of 1948
made speedy American withdrawal from South Korea imperative. With loud sighs of relief, we pulled our soldiers
out the following June, trusting to luck that the shaky,
hybrid regime and the wobbly economy would not collapse of themselves and that a poorly equipped army
would prove adequate for defense. More arms, specifically
tanks, could easily have been given the South Koreans to
match those in the hands of the Communist regime. Because, however, of the boastful assertions of the South
Koreans that they could and would conquer the north, it
seemed less hazardous to leave them under-armed and exposed to attack than to arm them adequately and run the
risk that they themselves would be the aggressors.

While most Americans, including many of those in
Congress, had remained unaware of Korea and its problems, the stage had been set there for one of the most
painful episodes in American history. There had been not
the slightest sign of treachery. The fault lay not so much in
what we had done as in what we had left undone.

This is not to say that we made no mistakes. Our
flounderings in the early years of our occupation of South
Korea were bad enough, and still more serious errors were
to follow. In fact, two of our worst blunders in modern
times took place in Korea. One was our obvious and freely
expressed pleasure at being out of Korea and the strong
implication in the statements of some of our leaders that
nothing could induce us to go back there. It seems probable that the Kremlin leaders took these as cynical declarations on our part that South Korea was a pawn in the
game which we had decided to sacrifice to them, and there

may have been considerable surprise and perhaps a little consternation when we reacted quickly and vigorously to Communist aggression there.

After the war had started we committed a second great blunder, this time in the military field, when we continued the movement of uncoordinated columns into North Korea even after we had discovered that new and possibly superior forces had moved into position against us. Although many have attributed the resulting military disaster, one of the worst in American history, to a failure of military intelligence, it appears to have been more the result of misjudgment on the part of the American military command. It may have been assumed that the same audacious forcefulness of purpose that was proving so effective with the demoralized people of a defeated Japan would prove equally effective with the high-spirited Chinese Communists who had just won out in a long civil war at home. If so, this is another sad instance of American inability to understand Asians, for the Chinese were scarcely in the same mood as the Japanese. In any case, these blunders, however costly, were made far along in the story, and much of what happened might well have taken place in one way or another even if these specific errors had not been made. Our big mistake—the great sin of omission—took place primarily before 1949; perhaps it might be fair to say even before the end of the war with Japan.

Korea and China both reveal not simply distressing failures in American foreign policy, but frightening inadequacies in our whole approach. The United States has been less directly involved in Indochina, but the story has been essentially the same there: we have been unwilling to face up to the real problem until it was too late to hope for any truly satisfactory solution. In all these areas we see a powerful but politically naïve and off-guard America

exposing itself to attack and then struggling desperately
for sound footing as it reels from one blow to the next.
This is scarcely a comforting picture. We have already
tasted in these three countries the bitter fruits of ignorance and indifference, but Asia contains other potential
Chinas, Koreas, and Indochinas, for which we are today
no better prepared than we were for these earlier disasters.

Even with the greatest effort to understand and prepare for our problems in Asia we perhaps could hope for
nothing more than a gradual shift of the balance between
failure and success. We do, however, have proof from past
experience that we are capable, when we try, of a vastly
better record than we have shown in China, Korea, or
Indochina. In the Philippines we can discern a mixture
of partial understanding and partial failure to see our
problems. In the early postwar years in Japan we have a
clearer and for the most part even happier story.

It is a strange irony of history that our preoccupation
with the defeat of Japan so blinded us to our other Asian
problems that we prepared on the whole wisely for the
postwar needs of our defeated enemies, but ignored those
of our victorious or liberated friends. We turned our backs
on the problems of colonial Asia; the American public
was left to awaken in disillusionment from the dream of a
"great sister republic" in China to the reality of a chaotic
and war-racked nation; and the soldiers we were sending
to Korea had to discover painfully for themselves that
there was more to liberation than marching under tri-
umphal arches. Meanwhile our government and people
were preparing seriously and realistically for the problems of a defeated Japan. Thousands of men were trained
in the Japanese language, primarily for the purposes of
war but also for the problems of peace. Our occupying
forces entered Japan with a great deal of knowledge about

the land and its people and found the Japanese, with their high level of technical skill and their temporarily deflated national pride, far more co-operative and friendly than had been expected. The result was the development of an amazing degree of goodwill and trust between victor and vanquished, which, though much diminished today by subsequent frictions, is still one of our major assets in the Far East.

A still more important factor was that the dynamic and broad-visioned representative we sent to Japan not only was himself familiar in general outline with the problems he faced but was provided with an excellent over-all blueprint for his guidance. Before the end of the war many able and technically competent persons had given much thought to the problems of reforming and rehabilitating Japan. It must be admitted that the result-ant plans were in part based on erroneous premises and in part were to prove impractical for other reasons, but by and large they were both wise and realistic. It is primarily because of our daring and comprehensive plans and our continuing efforts to understand the basic problems we faced in Japan that the American occupation of Japan proved a great success, at least in comparison with our dismal failures on the nearby continent. Granted that the attitudes and skills of the Japanese made the task easier; granted that our complete control over Japan and its peo-ple made the execution of a positive program relatively simple; still, without the thought and preparation we de-voted to the problems of Japan, these advantages might easily have turned into liabilities, and relative success into catastrophic failure.

The need for thought and preparation may be clear enough, but one question remains: thought and prepara-tion by whom? Is it a question of training a few hundred, perhaps a few thousand experts, or do we need something more? Adequate training of even a limited number of specialists is in itself no mean task, considering the vastness of our ignorance and the subtlety of some of the problems, but unfortunately this would be only a beginning. In other times, even the most basic problems of foreign policy could be left entirely to the informed judgment of a relatively small group of leaders. In eighteenth-century England, for instance, there was little need for the masses to understand the details or even the broad outlines of foreign policy. The same is true and to a far more extreme degree in totalitarian regimes of our own day. But this is in no sense so in the United States or, for that matter, in any real twentieth-century democracy.

We come to our period of world leadership not only at a time when international relations are far more difficult and complex than ever before, but also when action in this field is subject to the judgment and eventual control of the whole public, not merely of an informed elite. In some fields of knowledge, such as the natural sciences, a little expert understanding can be enough. The realities of the atomic age are readily accepted by us all, though few can really understand them. But foreign relations are no exact science; here there is no clear line between verifiable fact and mere opinion, between tenable hypothesis and unfounded speculation. Perhaps in times of total war the public does temporarily relinquish or at least defer its right to judgment on each individual matter in the field of foreign relations. But in peacetime and our intermediary age of limited warfare and unlimited ideological conflict the public cannot give up this right for long and still hope to maintain a democracy. And so long as we are a democracy, specialists, however wise and well informed, are of little value unless there is comprehending congressional support; and congressional support is improbable, if not entirely impossible, without popular understanding and approval. The need for knowledge and understanding exists at every level, from Pennsylvania Avenue down to every Main Street.

Here indeed may lie the nub of our problem in our relations with Asia and perhaps one of the gravest aspects of the challenge of totalitarianism in our day. We have grown up with our domestic problems; all Americans are to some degree experts on them. But in our rapid rise to international power we have had little opportunity as a people to become equally informed on foreign matters.

Because of our basically sound reliance on mass opinion and the cumulative wisdom of the average man, we quite naturally suspect the judgment, if not the knowledge, of the specialist, since his very act of specialization has made him no longer average. But the average American almost by definition does not have adequate knowledge of the physical facts regarding Asia and is even less prepared to understand Asian attitudes. It is a huge jump from the broad wheat fields of Kansas to the narrow rice paddies of the Philippines. What may seem like obvious common sense in Brooklyn or Peoria may be folly in Tokyo or New Delhi. Diplomacy has been called the art of tactful phraseology and judicious silence. What may seem well worth saying in Georgia or California may be best stated otherwise or perhaps left completely unsaid in Burma or Iran.

The advantage of mass wisdom in domestic matters can easily become the liability of mass ignorance in foreign affairs, and the superiority of a democratic system its Achilles' heel in a world in which the problems of foreign relations are paramount. The foreign policy of our totalitarian adversaries, just because it is framed and judged only by an informed elite, can be swift and clear in formulation and deft and deadly in execution. To meet this danger we must develop a far larger and decidedly more expert body of specialists in whom the rightly suspicious average man can put more trust, but at the same time we must also develop a far more understanding general public. This is a stupendous task, but one that we must undertake with vigor and dispatch if we wish to see the United States better able to deal with its problems in Asia.

3. *What Do We Want?*

Before we can have much hope for success in our dealings with Asia, we must first define more clearly for ourselves what are our basic objectives, pay much more attention to discovering the realities in Asia with which we must deal, and finally work out upon the basis of clear objectives and adequate knowledge a more realistic strategy. Our first task is to decide what we want, but actually this is the least of our problems. Whatever variations there may be in the specific definitions of our basic aims in Asia, there should be little dispute over their essence, which is primarily our own peace and security.

Fortunately we have no tradition of imperialistic aggrandizement that would now have to be painfully discarded. Despite the annexation of the Philippines before the close of the last century, we never joined the wild scramble of the European powers for imperial domains and consequently have no embarrassing vestiges of empire to complicate our relations and confuse our thinking. Our guiding star was not empire but mutually profitable trade and cultural relations with Asia. As expressed in the Open-Door Policy in China and implied elsewhere in our diplomacy, this meant opposition to the growth of other empires, not out of fear for our own safety but merely to keep the door open for American traders and missionaries. The war with Japan and its aftermath, however, have demonstrated the complete inadequacy of trade and cultural contacts as our basic aim. Naturally we remain interested in fruitful economic and cultural relations with Asia, but we now realize that there is no prospect of the development of a trade profitable enough to compensate to any appreciable degree for the vast costs of our year-to-year relations with Asia, much less the two major wars we have already fought there and the others that may be forced upon us if our contacts with Asia do not improve.

The one overriding objective in our relations with Asia or any other part of the world today is inevitably the furtherance of our own peace and security. There is certainly nothing that we can obtain from Asia by trade or any other means that is one hundredth or even one thousandth as valuable to us. In the context of the close military balance between us and our avowed enemies, we wish the situation in Asia to be as advantageous to our military safety as possible. In the context of the precarious world order in which we live today, we wish to see Asia in so far as possible strengthening rather than weakening the peace and stability of the world.

A few may object to such a definition of our aims as too self-centered and not sufficiently altruistic. In the past many of our contacts with Asians, however they may have appeared to others, were entirely philanthropic from our point of view. But these were primarily the activities of Americans as individuals and as private groups, not of Americans as a national unit. It is of course to be hoped that private American philanthropic activities in Asia will grow and that our government will continue its sympathetic interest in these undertakings of its citizens. Our national foreign policy, however, cannot be based on philanthropy, and to attempt so to base it would merely be to invite confusion in our own thinking. When Americans or any other people act as a national group on foreign policy, enlightened self-interest is the only possible guide and one for which they need no apologies. Enlightened self-interest has been the key to progress within the national units of our democratic social order, and there is no reason why it cannot prove equally fruitful in the international field.

A much more valid objection could be made on the grounds that the definition of our basic objectives in Asia as our own peace and security is so general that it means nothing definite and so obvious that it is only an empty platitude. Our peace and security may mean one thing in dealing with the strategic Suez area and another in remote Nepal. If only the immediate present were considered, these goals might simply imply non-involvement in Asia or, at the other logical extreme, merely a series of military bases. If on the other hand we are thinking in terms of a longer time-span and a period when fast-growing Asia has a more decisive role in international relations than it has today, then peace and security may involve very much more complicated problems than either non-involvement or military bases.

The present military situation must, of course, be a first consideration. Asia is inescapably part of the world balance of military power, and military commitments and military gains or losses there count in the over-all balance sheet. A close look at this balance sheet, however, will reveal that the Asian entries are on the whole extremely small when compared with those written in for ourselves, Russia, and Europe. Suppose for instance that the hundred million people of Afghanistan and Pakistan with the military power at their command should wholeheartedly join the Communist side—fortunately, an entirely unlikely possibility today but nevertheless a good hypothetical case.

How would this affect the present balance of power in the world? Very little, if at all. The loss of Afghanistan and Pakistan would be a serious blow to the prestige of the free world and might produce serious political repercussions throughout Islam, but it would deprive us of no substantial military or economic assets. It would bring to the Russians no new industrial power, and the addition of these technically backward people to a side that already has far greater human than industrial resources would add relatively little to its military strength. There would be an increase in Communist pressure on India and Iran, but this might also increase resistance to communism in these lands.

But imagine a similar wholehearted shift of one hundred million people or only half as many in Western Germany or any other area along the borderline between the Communist and free worlds in Europe. Because of the industrial power and technological abilities of these people as well as their geographic position, such a shift would so weaken our side and strengthen the other that any defense of continental western Europe would become highly problematic. The balance of military power might then be disastrously weighted against us. Obviously in Asia and Europe we are dealing with strategic considerations so different in degree that they are almost different in kind.

Asia is, of course, a huge area within which there naturally are extreme variations in strategic significance. In fact, in terms of the immediate military situation, Asia might be divided into three distinct zones. First there is one small area so different from all the others in industrial development and skills and therefore in military potential that it is in reality a separate sphere in our foreign relations. This is Japan, which is the only country in Asia that has a high degree of industrialization. Once this made

Japan a major world power, and, while she is at least in relative terms a far less mighty nation now than two decades ago, she still has the industrial base and technical skills that are essential for the production of modern military power. While ranking far below the industrialized areas of North America, the Soviet Union, western Europe, and the British Isles, Japan still ranks after these as the fifth most important industrial area in the world and the only one of present military significance in Asia. In fact its isolation from the other great industrial centers of the world makes it all the more important in world strategy and helps explain how the Japanese a few years ago were able to dominate so much of the world's population from so small an industrial base.

The denial of Japan's industrial capacity to us at a time of crisis, such as the Korean War, would greatly increase the strain on our own resources and diminish the possibilities of our action in Asia. The full use of the Japanese industrial potential to build up military power against us would greatly worsen our military situation, threatening our control of the whole western Pacific and cutting sharply into the military strength we could put into the balance against the Soviet Union in Europe. Japanese industrial capacity, if devoted to a rapid build-up of Chinese military power, could do even more over the years to tip the scales against us. Japan obviously is a part of Asia that counts a great deal in the immediate military balance of power, and this is one of the main reasons why we have entered into strong commitments for its defense.

Another distinct strategic zone in Asia is its western part, which is somewhat confusingly known as both the Near and the Middle East. Although it is an arid region of sparse population and low industrial development, there are two strategic considerations that set it off from the rest of Asia. First is its geographic importance because of its position on the flanks of Europe and because of the great water route between East and West, which passes through this region at Suez; and second there is its great subsurface treasure of oil. Because of these two factors the nations from Egypt and Turkey eastward to Iran undoubtedly constitute a zone of high strategic importance. The military and economic weakness and the political instability of these countries, however, make their defense a most difficult problem. As a consequence, it has not been possible to develop a defense system for this region comparable to those for western Europe and Japan, but our government has established through NATO close defense commitments with Turkey, the one country in this area which both wishes such relations and is capable of contributing to them.

All the rest of Asia forms the third strategic zone, which lies between the other two smaller fringe areas in a great arc from Afghanistan and Pakistan through southeast Asia to China and Korea. This huge central zone is characterized for the most part by staggering populations, low industrial development, and relatively little immediate strategic importance. All areas of the world, of course, have some military significance, and certainly this vast region of tremendous masses of people and close and extended proximity to Soviet borders is no exception, but its strategic importance is for the present slight compared with that of Europe or even the fringe zones of Asia.

Such a statement may sound strange in view of the bitter and costly war we have already fought with Chinese armies in Korea and the continuing threat of war in Indochina and other parts of this region. One might assume that because this is the part of the world where we of the West have been forced to fight Communists openly, it must be the most strategic area rather than the least. But the contrary is actually the case. If there had been fighting in Europe on the scale of that in Korea, it would almost certainly have developed into a global war. Even in the two fringe zones of Asia it seems improbable that general war would not have resulted from a large-scale commitment of American or European troops against soldiers armed at least in part by Russia and under direct or indirect control of Moscow. It is only because this part of the world is of relatively little strategic importance that these limited wars could have occurred at all.

This point of view is borne out by any realistic appraisal of the probable role of this part of Asia in a global war, if one were to break out in the near future. As we have already discovered in the war with Japan, it would only be a minor inconvenience to us if we were denied the economic production of this area in wartime. The addition of these resources to the Soviet Union would mean even less, for the great central mountain barrier of Asia makes significant economic contact with most of this area impossible for those who do not control the seas, and the Russians, short of complete victory, most certainly would not have free access by water to this part of the world.

It seems probable also that the military power of this area would not prove decisive or even very important in any total war in the near future. This is because such military power as exists in this zone of Asia is largely immobile. It is formidable on its own soil or in close land proximity to its homeland, as we and the Japanese before us discovered in fighting the Chinese. It cannot, however, project itself to other areas, and consequently each side in a major war would be careful to avoid commitment of its forces against this immobile Asian military power and would concentrate its striking forces on the more crucial area of Europe and the North Atlantic, to which Asian strength could not reach.

It is easy to see that India and the countries of southeast Asia, even if enthusiastically participating on one side or the other in a global war, would not for the present be able to furnish decisive military power on any critical battlefield, but there may be more question with regard to China. To be sure, the complete and wholehearted shift of the five hundred million people of China from the Communist side to ours would seriously complicate the problem of land defense for the Russians. On the other hand, continued adherence of the Chinese to the Communist side poses only a minor military problem for us in the eventuality of a full-scale war in the near future. China does not at present possess the industrial capacity to equip its own armies adequately for modern war or to move them to distant areas of battle. It adds millions of potential fighting men to the Communist side, but for the Russians the limiting military factor is not men but machines, and as far as machines are concerned, China at present is a drain on Communist power and not an asset.

Chinese strength, however formidable it was in Korea, is of an entirely different and lesser order than that of Japan in its recent war with us. We met tremendous Japanese military power that was entirely the product of Japan itself and had been extended thousands of miles by sea and air from its home base. If Russia comes to produce more machines of war than its own manpower can handle, or if China begins to produce enough machines to arm and move its own vast hordes, then China could become a great military asset to the Communists; at present, however, for all its hundreds of millions, it adds very little to the immediate Communist military potential in a global war. China geographically extends Communist defense commitments without adding appreciably to Communist striking power.

But what about the importance of this part of Asia

as a base for aerial or land attack? Does this consideration not make all of Asia a highly strategic area? There is, of course, some truth to this point of view, but less than is generally supposed. If this area were entirely in Communist hands, Soviet bombers would be closer to Australia, but no nearer to any of the main bases of Western strength. On the other hand, we would have to have airfields in the remote inner Asian regions to be appreciably closer to the main bases of Soviet power than we already are in Europe, Turkey, the Arctic, and Japan.

In any case, to attempt to reach Russia through this part of Asia would be to go the far way around the world and across tremendous geographic barriers. A more direct approach to an enemy, even against stubborn defense, is often more effective and in the long run less costly than a very roundabout approach. For instance, during the war in the Pacific we attempted to get at Japan by way of India and China, but difficulties of distance and terrain robbed this hooked blow of any real punch, while the undiminished power of our direct blows across the Pacific beat down all Japanese resistance. If a full-scale war were to break out in the next few years between the Communists and the free world, it is likely that Asia as a whole would play the same secondary role that China played in the Second World War. It seems probable that Near Eastern oil and the Suez Canal would occasion some skirmishing in that area and that each side would be interested in ensuring that the Japanese military potential would not be utilized by the enemy, but otherwise Asia might figure relatively little in the outcome.

The question then arises why we ever became involved in the war in Korea if the greater part of Asia is of so little immediate strategic importance to us. The truth is that we entered the fighting not because of South Korea's military importance to us but rather despite the

strategic liability of our position there. Offensively Sou
Korea means nothing to us. Air bases there are not s₁
close to Russian soil as far more secure and convenient
bases in Japan and Okinawa, and are only insignificantly
nearer to China. South Korea is on a land route toward
Soviet centers of power which is impractically long and
rough and guarded by huge Communist armies that cannot be used elsewhere.

Defensively South Korea is more of a liability than
an asset. Its manpower and industrial resources are negligible compared with those of surrounding areas, and even
for the defense of Japan it is of little value. If we had
stronger ground forces than the communists in this part
of the world, South Korea might be of some defensive use,
but we enjoy no such superiority today, when Japanese
military strength is largely industrial potential, and we
find sharp limitations to the numbers of men we can di-
vert to this single sector in a long line of defense. With
the limited land and air power at our command and with
our undisputed mastery of the seas, the defense of Japan
is very much easier and less costly on its natural water
frontiers than on any land frontier across the middle or
even at the northern boundary of Korea.

It was because of these strategic considerations as
well as our acute manpower shortage that we withdrew
from Korea in 1949 with such obvious relief; and we returned there in 1950, not at all because of local military
considerations, but purely because of global political
strategy. We sought to check open aggression in Korea
solely because we believed that if aggression had gone
unchallenged in Korea, our whole long-range program for
peace and security would have been undermined.

We have pinned our ultimate hopes on the development of a democratic world order in which international
disputes, like those within a democracy, will be settled

by peaceful democratic procedures. Such an international
system must be world-wide if it is to have any hope of
success, applying as much to remote and nonstrategic areas
as to those with which we are more immediately concerned. Open military aggression in Korea was a direct
challenge to the United Nations and the whole concept
of a democratic world order. This is the political challenge we met, even though to meet it we were forced to
re-enter an unsound military position at great cost to ourselves.

The Korean War thus reveals another dimension to
our Asian problem. Asia is the area in which the whole
attempt to create a democratic world order may meet its
most crucial tests. It would appear to be no mere accident
that the League of Nations, though primarily a European
organization, suffered its mortal wounds not in Europe,
but in Asia and Africa, and that it has been in Asia that
the United Nations has had to meet its most serious tests
to date. While our security at present depends on a balance of power elsewhere in the world, it may well be in
Asia that our plans for peace and security in the future
will be proved either a success or a failure.

We can draw another general conclusion from the
Korean War. In Asia long-range considerations may on
the whole be more important than short-range strategy.
Certainly this was true of the war itself, for we were willing to suffer short-range losses and run the danger of an
immediate global explosion solely to maintain a long-
range ideal, which is as yet more a hope than a reality.
This is not a surprising situation in view of the fact that
Asia, while of relatively little immediate military importance, is growing faster in national power than any other
part of the world. Under such conditions it is perfectly
understandable that the future of Asia some decades

hence may be of greater concern to us than the present situation or even that of the next few years.

If our sole concern were an all-out war with the Communists in the near future, then we could virtually ignore most of Asia, and our present frustrated concern over that part of the world would be quite absurd. But we naturally hope that by continuing to match Soviet power we shall be able to avoid such a war and that there is a future to look forward to and plan for beyond the immediate military crisis. It seems quite possible that the present military stalemate will continue indefinitely, just because of the certainty that both victors and vanquished in an atomic war will suffer grievously if not mortally. In the meantime a resurgent and at least partially industrialized Asia may well become the area of balance, throwing preponderant and decisive weight to one side or the other without a major battle having been fought.

If Asia some decades from now becomes a stable and powerful segment of a democratic world order, it might give such added strength to our side that the military crisis would gradually fade away. On the other hand, it is conceivable that we might continue successfully to match Soviet power, only to wake up one day to the realization that a powerful and at the same time totalitarian Asia had entirely destroyed the balance we had so carefully sought to maintain, and in doing so had also destroyed all hope for a democratic world order. Another possibility is that, even though the issue between us and the Soviet Union were to be settled in our favor by war, a reunited but sorely wounded West might then suddenly find itself facing an even more perilous problem in its relations with a resurgent but hostile non-Western majority of mankind.

We are today only too keenly aware of our recent folly in concentrating so exclusively on the defeat of our immediate enemies, Germany and Japan, that we failed to see the still graver problems looming behind the war in which we were engaged. We dare not continue to let our preoccupation with the present prevent us from making adequate preparations for the future. While Asia is only a minor part of our immediate military problem, it is quite clearly a much greater part of our problems of the future. Our objectives and strategy in Asia must of course be conceived of in terms of the immediate situation, but they must also make sense in terms of the eventual outcome in Asia some decades from now or else they make no real sense at all.

PART TWO:

4. Traditional Asia

There is a great difference between agreeing on our general objectives and deciding on concrete policies. The latter require a much more detailed statement of specific objectives—in other words, a full formulation of strategy. Before this can be undertaken, we first must consider the realities of Asia with which we must deal, for these as much as our basic objectives will determine what our strategy should be.

We can approach the situation in Asia in two different ways. One would be simply to analyze where military

The Situation

power exists at the moment and what are the political and economic facts with which we must cope today. But if we are also concerned about future developments, then the direction in which affairs are moving is even more significant than existing conditions.

It is easy to see, for example, that the status of India twenty years or, perhaps still more, forty years from now is really of vastly more importance to the United States than the precise situation of the moment. India, after all, plays little if any part in the military balance of power in the world today, but her national strength is likely to continue to rise rapidly. In China present realities are of more obvious concern to us, but here, too, one can see that the difference between a Communist and a non-Communist China may be of less importance to us today than it will be thirty years from now, when China will presumably be much more industrialized and therefore far more powerful than she is at present.

It would of course be folly if, in attempting to bridge or dam a swift and mighty river, one assumed that the waters were stagnant and disregarded the strength and direction of the current, the volume of the flow, and its seasonal fluctuations. To attempt to take effective action in Asia, purely on the basis of present conditions, particularly if one has any thought of the future, would be equally absurd, for to do so would be to overlook the tumultuous flow of history.

Naturally the only way to ascertain even roughly the direction of motion in Asia is to take a long historical look at what has been happening there. For our purposes the segment of Asian history from which we can learn the most is undoubtedly the past century of mounting reaction to Western political and economic domination. This period is in fact the beginning of a whole new phase of Asian history and, for that matter, of world history, for in it began the significant mixing of the great traditional civilizations of the past to form the unitary world that we can see taking shape today.

There were contacts and interchanges between the great areas of higher civilization in the world before recent centuries, but such contacts were relatively unimportant in the development of these individual areas. Alexander's conquest of northwestern India no doubt had some lasting influence; the silk trade between China and Rome is said to have had unfortunate repercussions on the

Roman economy; many of the nomadic peoples driven by Chinese military might out of eastern Asia spread a trail of havoc in India, the Near East, and Europe; the long interplay between the Islamic and Christian areas left its mark on both; and the growth since the seventh or eighth centuries of oceanic commerce around the southern shores of Asia stimulated a tremendous economic development in China and perhaps in many other areas as well. The participation of Europeans in this world oceanic commerce after the sixteenth century and their rapid domination of it through superior seamanship and gunnery set the stage for great economic growth in Europe too. But, despite this commerce and many other contacts, East remained essentially East, and West remained West, at least through the eighteenth century.

It is impossible to draw sharp lines between one age and another, but during the nineteenth century the commercial contacts between East and West began to develop into something more. Western political institutions, industrial modes of production, and patterns of thought were beginning to have a tremendous impact on Asia. Subsequently, and by almost imperceptible steps, this one-way flow began to change into a two-way interchange of influences, as the Asian reaction to the West mounted in intensity and began in turn to affect the West. This particular phase of history is still in its early days. Looking back on our era from the vantage point of some future age, men may very possibly see as its main theme this confrontation and merging of East and West, while the present military balance between the Communists and the free world may appear no more than an incidental variation of the story.

In any case, it is the past century of strong influence of the Western world on the East and growing Asian response to this challenge that is the primary historical context of our present relationship with Asia. We must, however, glance back behind this recent turbulent period to the more placid flow of earlier ages, when Asian cultures were still intact and little influenced by the West, despite European overlordship in some lands.

Perhaps the most important fact about this earlier Asia is that it was in no sense a single unit, as we of the West have always tended to assume. With the characteristic self-centeredness of all mankind, we usually have divided the world into ourselves and others, lumping all men and regions that did not obviously belong in our Western, Christian civilization under the vague terms "Oriental" and "Asiatic." Actually in recent times, when Western civilization has expanded to cover many of the once remote and backward parts of the world and the power of the Occident has cast a shadow over all other regions, there is some reason for a division of the world into Western and non-Western halves. In earlier ages, however, this was a gross and typically parochial misconception.

The unity of the Asian or non-Western world is a largely negative unity. It is in fact merely the part of the world that is not the Occident and therefore has reacted to or, one might say, against the dominant position of the West. It is the bulk of the world which, unlike the West, did not in recent centuries develop new scientific concepts and, from these, new and vastly superior means of production and, from these in turn, preponderant military power. In other words, it is the area which, unlike the West, continued in the age-old human tradition of low per capita output and therefore of mass poverty by modern standards. Poverty and weakness in the face of ascendant Western economic and military power have been common to all Asian lands, but they have scarcely forged any positive bonds of unity. Such conditions once were common to all civilizations, and the Western departure from this human norm, while creating a common menace, did not make the other great civilizations any more of a unit than they had been before.

Preponderant Western power has posed a challenge to the ideals as well as the political, economic, and social institutions of all the countries of Asia, and there has naturally been much in common in the various responses they have made to it. This is what is meant when people today speak of the Asian mind or the Asian point of view. An Arab, a Hindu, a Chinese, or a Japanese will react somewhat alike to many of the specific aspects of Western economic or political domination, but this again is a purely negative agreement. It does not mean that they have much in common that is positive. In fact, traditional Asia, before the West's preponderant power forced it into a sort of negative unity against us, showed even greater diversity between its major cultures than existed between Western civilization and some of those of Asia.

The pre-contemporary world fell into four fairly distinct major zones of civilization: the branch of ancient Mediterranean culture which developed through the Greco-Roman and Christian traditions into Western civilization; the branch of this same ancient culture which became the Islamic civilization of western Asia and northern Africa; the civilization of southern Asia centering on the religious and social concepts native to the Indian area; and the civilization of eastern Asia, centering on the writing system and the political and ethical concepts of China. Naturally there were significant cultural variations within these great zones of civilization and many border areas with a mixture of features from two or more of them. These four major types of civilization, however, still constitute large and fairly homogeneous units that are quite distinct from one another.

Of these four major civilizations, the two that seem to have resembled each other most closely, at least until recent times, were the Islamic and our own. Deriving from the same ancient origin, these two quite naturally share many basic traits, such as absolute and exclusive monotheistic forms of religion, a dualistic approach to the problem of good and evil, and perhaps a greater emphasis on the military arts and the leadership of military men than is to be found in the other two civilizations.

This Western pair of civilizations is thought by some to be balanced by an Eastern pair, the Indian and east Asian, but actually these share more that is fundamental with our civilization than they do with each other. Many very interesting and stimulating theories regarding humanity have been based on the assumption that there is some basic unity between Indian and Chinese civilizations which contrasts with that of the West. While no one would deny the validity of some aspects of these theories, a more penetrating analysis might be based on the assumption that either Chinese or Indian civilization was basically similar to that of the West and fundamentally different from the other.

There is no greater contrast among the higher cultures of the world than that between the main streams of Chinese and Indian civilization. The Hindu throughout history has shown himself to be the most inclined of all human beings to an other-worldly emphasis in his thinking and a pessimistic disregard or even a complete denial of the realities of this life; the Chinese, on the other hand, has usually shown himself the least interested in problems of an after life, if such he feels exists, and the most concerned, usually with fundamental optimism, about the problems of political and social organization in this world. Indians have tended to be absorbed in the intricacies of philosophic thought from logic to metaphysics and have often matched this interest with an extremely ascetic mode of life; Chinese, in contrast, have paid relatively little attention to such abstract areas of thought in their tremendous interest in social ethics and political philosophy, arguing about these through apt illustrations rather than by logical deduction or syllogism. They have matched this intellectual bias with an emphasis on an active, acquisitive life and a family-centered social pattern in which celibacy and mortification of the flesh are considered crimes against one's ancestors. In India religious concepts have been woven into all aspects of society, including the fabulously intricate caste system, while in China religion has usually been considered a very minor aspect of life for both the individual and the state, and the best minds have usually been devoted to such problems as family ethics, political philosophy, and the selection of talent for government. In all these very fundamental aspects of human thought and organization it can be seen that Western civilization has tended to stand between the two extremes represented by India and China, perhaps somewhat closer to the Indian in medieval times and nearer the Chinese today, but consistently nearer to these other two than they have been to each other.

With such fundamental contrasts between India and China, it is easy to see that we have no single starting-point in a traditional Asian civilization. We must not let the obvious parallels in Asian reactions against the West blind us to the very important and deep differences between the various countries of Asia which stem from their traditional civilizations and may have even more influence on their future development than does the present chaotic period of transition through which they are passing. For example, the relative speed with which different Asian peoples have responded to the challenge of the West shows us clearly how great the influence of the traditional societies can be, for there were tremendous differences in the speed and type of reaction in different Asian lands, even when there was little difference in the challenge itself. In fact, some countries in which the Western challenge was weak and late responded much more rapidly and vigorously than lands where it was early and strong.

In India the territorial nibbling by European countries went on for centuries, and the colonial conquest of the whole land had been completed long before there was any significant response to the West. In China, on the contrary, vigorous opposition held the European powers at bay until well into the nineteenth century, when Westerners at last began to make significant territorial and economic encroachments upon the Chinese Empire. The response to this situation in China was stubborn, if not at first effective, and after less than a century of trial and error the Chinese were able to develop methods of response which put an end to the days of crude imperialistic domination.

In Japan the speed of reaction was still greater. The fear that foreign contacts might lead to attempted foreign domination had induced the Japanese to drive out virtually all Europeans in the first half of the seventeenth century, and from then until the middle of the nineteenth century they managed to keep the West at arm's length. Then in the course of a few years they became convinced by demonstrations of Western naval superiority that Japan could defend itself only by adopting Western military techniques, and long before Occidentals had penetrated far into Japan, much less established colonial enclaves, the Japanese reacted with such energy and violence that within a few decades they were able to defeat Russia, one of the chief imperialist powers of the West.

The difference in the speed of reaction between the Indians and the Chinese is clearly traceable to the fundamental difference between their two civilizations. To the Indians, who thought of themselves as religion-centered social groupings rather than a national unit, the appearance of new foreign conquerors did not seem to be a serious challenge. Not until the West had thoroughly penetrated the higher levels of Indian society did Indians, now thinking perhaps more in Western than in traditional terms, begin to show much concern over the political domination of their land by outsiders. The Chinese, on the other hand, had always regarded themselves primarily as a political unit—in fact, as the unique civilized nation of the world—and to them the violation of Chinese soil by barbarian conquerors was an immediate and drastic challenge, which they sought to meet at once, though it was not until after several decades of acquiring Western concepts and techniques that they were able to do so with much success.

The still more rapid and complete response of the Japanese to the Western challenge is perhaps a little more puzzling. Some have sought to explain it by the appearance of a dynamic young leadership, but this is merely an attempt to explain the response as a whole by one of its elements. Others, comparing Japan with China, have explained it in terms of the smaller size of Japan and the greater ease with which the West could penetrate all parts of it, forgetting that the Western penetration of India, which was a fact and not a mere possibility, had produced no such rapid response and that an island like Java, which was smaller than Japan and completely dominated by the West at an early date, reacted as slowly as India, probably because of the fundamental substructure of civilization it had derived from India.

The rapidity and effectiveness of the Japanese reaction must be explained primarily by the traditional civilization rather than by accidents of geography or variations in the challenge from the West. Since the Japanese were an offshoot of Chinese civilization, they shared the same emphasis on the political unit, and consequently their reaction to the territorial menace was much greater than that of the Indians. But beyond this there were certain peculiarities in the Japanese cultural pattern which permitted them to react more effectively than did the Chinese. For one thing, unlike the Chinese, who believed that everything outside of China was barbarian, the Japanese had always been aware of the greater age, size, and prestige of China, and fully realized that they had derived much of their higher civilization from their continental neighbors. As a consequence, they more quickly comprehended the nature of the foreign threat to their political and economic institutions and also found it far easier than did the Chinese to realize that there was much that they could profitably learn from the West.

Perhaps because of their long relationship of half-recognized inferiority to China, the Japanese had also developed at an early date a compensatory concept of national identity. In other words, there was a far more generally accepted feeling of nationalism there than anywhere else in Asia. It could be that the same sense of inferiority to the classic Mediterranean regions was a contributing factor to the rise of nationalism in the lands of northern Europe. In any case, Japanese nationalism did parallel that of Europe to some degree, and the Japanese therefore found it possible from the start to react to the challenge of the West as a truly national unit and not simply as a traditional political unit like China or a still vaguer cultural grouping like India.

Another factor was that in the middle of the nineteenth century the Japanese were in the final stages of a long period of feudalism, which is one of the very few close parallels to Western feudal experience outside the bounds of European civilization. From feudalism the Japanese, like us, derived an emphasis on the military arts and the leadership of military men which made it much easier for them than for the Chinese or Indians to grasp and master the military skills of the West. Feudalism, which is a notably unstable form of social organization, was in the process of collapse in Japan when modern Western ways were introduced, and this situation may also have made the rapid adoption of new ways easier for the Japanese than it was for the Chinese, who in the eighteenth century could boast as stable a society as any advanced people have ever enjoyed.

The Japanese success in reacting effectively to the challenge of the West was not limited merely to the political and military fields. They also proved far more immediately successful than the other peoples of Asia in adopting the new techniques of industrialization. In part this may have been the result of the collapsing feudal economy, in which an incipient capitalism was already beginning to appear. Having already made the first step into a capitalistic economy, the next may have been relatively easy for them. Another factor could have been the system of primogeniture in Japanese feudal society, which forced younger sons out into the world where they, more easily than the family-bound younger sons of China, could develop into economic entrepreneurs as well as intellectual and political leaders. Still another factor may have been the Japanese ethics, which developed out of feudalism and Buddhism much the same combination of asceticism and inner drive which is characteristic of early Protestantism in the West and is thought by some to have contributed to the development of capitalism there. Such factors may seem extremely intangible, but one can see how important they can be from the example of the Parsees of India, who, while only an infinitesimal part of the total population, have played an important role in the modern commercial and industrial development of the whole country, presumably because of their distinctive religious and ethical concepts.

The factors listed above are not meant to constitute a full analysis of the reasons why there were such differences in the speed and effectiveness of the reaction to the West in the various parts of Asia, but merely to indicate the type of differences between the various Asian cultures that may have had an important influence on the outcome. It does seem evident that differences of this sort were vital in determining the time and nature of the original reaction to the West in Asia, and it seems safe to assume that such differences will also have a great deal to do with future developments there. The traditional Asian societies cannot be relegated to ancient history; they continue to be a very vital part of the world we live in and the world that will emerge in the future.

5. *The Impact of the West*

The territorial encroachments by European powers in Asia during the past few centuries were nothing new in that part of the world. Conquest by outsiders was part of an age-long pattern in most Asian lands. Throughout Indian history invaders had debouched from the Khyber Pass onto the great northern plains, and Chinese history for long periods has presented an alternating pattern of Chinese conquest of contiguous lands and the overrunning of China by its nomadic neighbors. The political domination of Asia by Europe, however, has proved far different from these earlier conquests. In the past, foreign rulers came and went, but the political and social institutions of Asia continued with little or no change. But conquest by the Europeans, even though very brief and quite incomplete in many places, has left incomparably greater traces.

Today this latest flood of invasion has ebbed from almost all parts of Asia, but the familiar contours of traditional Asian political institutions have not emerged from the receding waters. Except for extremely remote places to which the tide never penetrated with much force, most native Asian political institutions appear to have been washed away. In no important Asian land has the native political system of a century ago survived intact today, and in most countries there remain only minor survivals in local government or purely symbolic vestiges of the older national orders. There are, for example, the native princes of India, who have been transformed into governors in a transitional step to their almost certain ultimate oblivion. Another symbolic survival is the Japanese emperor, who, though still retaining the ancient title, has undergone in the past century at least two complete transformations in his actual relationship to government.

A traveler in time from any major Asian country of a century ago would find little in the political situation of his native land today that he could either recognize or understand. On the other hand, a nineteenth-century Occidental would find much in twentieth-century Asia that was familiar, and those political and economic institutions that were strange to him would be in large part institutions that had appeared in the West since his day. Whether the regime is at least in part democratic as in India, Japan, and Turkey or whether it is more or less dictatorial as in China, Iran, and Egypt, there has been the same sharp break with the past in the course of this one century, and in no Asian land does any wholesale restoration of traditional political forms lie within the realm of possibility.

While the break with the past is perhaps sharpest and most evident in the political field, one can discern a similar though more slowly developing shift in other aspects of life, such as the economic, the social, and the ideological. And the shift in each case is toward what is familiar to us in the West—away from handicraft industries toward machine production, away from aristocratic or strictly class-divided societies toward more egalitarian if not always freer societies, and, if not away from native patterns of thought, at least toward the inclusion within the native philosophical framework of many concepts that hitherto were peculiar to the West.

The extent of the impact of the West and the change it has brought to Asia may be best seen through a few examples. Japan, as the nation that responded first and most fully, is a good case in point. To the Japanese of the middle of the nineteenth century the challenge seemed at first purely military. Fortunately for them, they were able to comprehend the superiority of Western military power more rapidly than did most other Asians. They realized almost at once that until they possessed warships and guns comparable to those of the West, they were virtually helpless before Western military might.

This was essentially a military problem, and the first Japanese efforts were directed to meeting it in strictly military terms. It soon became evident, however, that political changes were also necessary if the requisite military power was to be produced. Japanese feudalism of the early nineteenth century was a much more closely integrated system and possessed vastly greater military power than any of the medieval feudal regimes of Europe, but it was obviously far too disunited and weak to meet the challenge of the unified nation-states of the West. Japan had not only to produce the weapons of the West but also to achieve the unity of a modern European nation before it could hope to meet the West on equal military terms.

The Japanese leaders quickly set about eliminating the semi-autonomous feudal domains into which Japan had been divided for many centuries. They substituted a centrally controlled system of local government based primarily on the pattern of nineteenth-century France. They also scrapped the whole feudal concept of an aristocratic army of the samurai elite and rapidly created a modern army through the conscription system. But before they could transform the peasants and plebeian city dwellers into effective conscripts for the Japanese army, they had to give these potential new soldiers equal legal status with the former feudal aristocrats. The Japanese were thus forced to substitute in rapid succession the military, political, and social organization of the modern West for the whole aristocratic feudal system that for some seven centuries had been the basis for the Japanese political and social pattern. Of course there still are feudal survivals in Japan, just as there are in many parts of Europe, particularly in attitudes and social relations, but for the past six or seven decades Japan, despite violent fluctuations between dictatorial and democratic forms of government, has resembled the modern West far more in its political and military institutions than it has Japan of any earlier period.

The creation of a modern army and navy in Japan also required the creation of modern armament industries, but this was not the only break or even the major one in the traditional economy. New mechanized forms of communication, such as railroads and telegraphs, were needed for political unification, and something had to be done about the cheap machine products of Western industry which had come to Japanese shores with the warships of the West and threatened Japanese independence almost as much as did the naval guns. Because of the superiority of Western military power, the Japanese had been forced to open their doors to foreign goods and to forgo by treaty any but the lowest of tariff barriers against imports from the West. The resultant flood of cheap cotton goods and other manufactures ruined Japanese handicraft industries and resulted in a serious drain on specie. Japan was threatened with a complete financial collapse that would have defeated all efforts at military reform. There was also a pressing need to rehabilitate the now jobless feudal warriors and handicraft workers.

Armament industries alone were obviously not enough to meet the needs of the situation, and the Japanese leaders were forced to embark on a sweeping program of industrialization. Telegraph lines soon were laid the length of the country, and railways were constructed between some of the principal cities. New spinning and weaving industries gradually stemmed the disastrous inflow of foreign goods, and before long the mechanization of the silk-reeling process gave Japan its first important export commodity and a source of much-needed foreign exchange. Thus in light industries and in communications as well as in the arsenals needed for war, Japan was forced to rush precipitately toward industrialization.

But to industrialize successfully and to modernize their military and political techniques, the Japanese also needed new and more widely disseminated knowledge. From the start the leaders recognized that Western scientific education was as necessary to Japanese military strength as battleships, that conscripts had to be able to read orders as well as shoot guns, that factory technicians were as important as steam engines. Japan therefore was forced into a great educational experiment. Within a generation or two universal primary education had produced a public comprised of peasants and factory workers who read newspapers as a matter of course, and a great variety of institutions of higher learning had developed a huge number of highly educated people who had imbibed a great variety of Western ideas along with the scientific facts they originally sought.

All these great changes were already far along by 1890. Japan, which as late as 1853 had been an almost entirely isolated, pre-industrial, feudal land, had been forced in a period of less than four decades to abandon virtually all of its feudal past—political, economic, social, and ideological. The Japanese had started out merely to match Western warships, but to do this they had been forced to attempt to match almost everything else in Western society.

During the next two decades the Japanese proved that they had met the original military menace when they defeated first China and then Russia in two successive wars. But this did not result in a diminution of the rate of change in Japan, much less any significant reversion to previous feudal patterns. On the contrary, once started, the process of change appeared to be self-generative, and decade after decade since 1890 Japan has continued to change, if not at a steadily accelerating pace, certainly with no marked drop in speed. The impact of the West, instead of being one simple blow that required but a single readjustment in Japan, appears to have been a rapid succession of blows, which has knocked Japan completely off its earlier balance and thus set in motion a series of successive readjustments that as yet show no sign of abatement.

The feudal system of Japan may have collapsed so rapidly and completely because it was less able to meet the challenge of the West than were the traditional regimes of some other Asian lands. These other regimes, however, while sometimes giving greater initial promise of adjusting successfully to the challenge, have in the long run shown themselves no more able to do so. The centralized, bureaucratic Chinese Empire, for example, appeared at first to be a political system that, with only minor changes, could meet the West on equal terms; but by slower and more painful steps it, too, has given way completely to a regime attempting to pattern itself entirely on a Western model. At no point was there as abrupt a change as took place in nineteenth-century Japan, and there are still strong elements of continuity between the traditional Confucian bureaucratic elite and the present Communist bureaucracy of China, but the techniques and philosophy of these two ruling groups are almost entirely different. The resemblance between mid-twentieth-century Chinese government and the traditional Chinese political system are for the most part the natural parallels between any two bureaucratic systems, while in guiding concepts and ideals the two are in many ways diametrically opposed to each other.

The Chinese, when they first became aware of the menace of foreign guns and warships, imagined that some minor tactical changes or, at most, the adoption of certain Western military techniques would solve the problem. When this approach proved inadequate, they developed the concept that they would borrow the external tools of Western civilization while retaining intact the spirit and essential inner forms of their own culture. But to operate the new tools, a new education was necessary. Among the first major casualties of the old order were the classical literary and philosophical education and the system of national civil-service examinations which for over a thousand years had ensured that the leaders of China would have a common Confucian ethic and a common political point of view. The young men of China began to stream abroad to Japan, the United States, and Europe to learn the operation of the new machines, and in the process they learned the more basic concepts of the West as well. Sun Yat-sen himself is a good example of the discrepancy between objectives and accomplishments in this phase of Chinese history. A Western-trained doctor, he believed that what China needed from abroad was Occidental science, but in fact his main contribution to China was to aid in the great transition from the native political ideal of a benevolent monarchy to the distinctly Western ideal of a republican form of government.

The Chinese opened their gates and minds more cautiously and unwillingly than did the Japanese, but Western machine goods destroyed the traditional economy just as inevitably as in Japan, even if more slowly. Once Western techniques had started to flow into China, there was no damming the flood of upsetting ideas that accompanied them. Each new decade saw greater and greater changes in China, and each generation witnessed a further shift of the Chinese youth away from the traditional ideals of the past toward the typical ideals of the West. In some ways the present Communist regime appears to have reached the ultimate in the rejection of China's past, condemning as it does the whole family-centered ethical system on which Chinese society has been based since ancient times; but the present phase is certainly not the final stage. For more than a half-century we have seen a steady and rapid acceleration of change in China, and there is no reason to believe that the rate of change will slacken for some time to come.

In India the challenge of the West came in a very different way from what it did in Japan or China. As we have seen, Indians did not at first feel that territorial encroachments by European powers or the gradual absorption of the whole area by the British raj endangered

their way of life. Even the challenge of the machine production of the West, though disastrous to certain sectors
of the native economy, was not conceived by most Indians
to be an object of concern. There was no reason for a
multi-caste society like that of India to fear the addition of
a new set of conquerors and a new caste in a thin layer at
the top of the state.

The British challenge to India came through education rather than conquest. Indian civil servants were
needed to help rule the vast subcontinent, and the British
therefore encouraged the training of young Indians in the
English language and in English techniques of administration. The education of these young men was thought of
as basically practical and technical, but it could not stop
there. There was no dividing line between British techniques and British ideas, and in time there developed a
large group of potential Indian leaders who thought as
much in terms of their Western education as in the traditional concepts of the society from which they came.

A profoundly Indian figure like Gandhi himself perhaps best illustrates the point. Increasingly in his later
career he reverted to age-old Indian attitudes and Indian
modes of life, but he was certainly as much a product of
British education and life in London and South Africa
as he was the product of Indian culture. He advocated the
use of the native spinning-wheel to bar the products of
Lancashire, but his whole concern over this economic
problem was the product of Western thinking. His great
weapon was the native Indian technique of non-violent
resistance, but the fact that he used the technique primarily to resist foreign rule shows that he was thinking
essentially in Western terms. His great appeal to his countrymen was a typically Indian form of saintly asceticism,
but he made his appeal not to the traditional Indian caste
groupings, which he in part rejected, but to all Indians as

a national grouping of the Western type. Gandhi championed native Indian traditions, but he did so in such a way and for such reasons that he, perhaps more than any other man, opened the floodgates to Western ideas. In India, as in China and Japan, the influence of modern Western culture seems to be growing steadily. Nehru is a far more Westernized man than Gandhi, and Nehru's successors in turn are likely to be less traditionally Indian if not more specifically Occidental than he.

The same story repeats itself in one form or another in almost every Asian country. In some areas the impact of the West is far advanced; in a few remote corners it has hardly started. The variations in the ways in which it is felt are as many as there are different native societies and distinctive local situations. The need of the Western world for oil has had a tremendous economic effect on Saudi Arabia and the petty principalities of the Persian Gulf, though Western political concepts have still had no appreciable influence on the life of the Bedouin. At the same time, the economic life of an Indonesian village may be little influenced by the West, while the very existence of an Indonesian Republic is clearly the product not only of Western concepts of nationalism and democracy but also of the long colonial rule of the Dutch over a specific area that otherwise would not probably have developed any identity as a single national unit.

No one would deny the profound influence of the West on Asia at the level of national organization, but some may feel that it is merely the superstructure of society that has been affected and that for the vast masses of Asia there has been little change to date and no reason to expect important changes in the future. There is no denying that the harsh economic realities of peasant life in Asia are not easily changed, and undoubtedly the impact of the West has been greater at the top of society than at the bottom. On the other hand, we often under-estimate how heavy the blow has been at the lower levels, and the inevitability of profound changes throughout society if any great change takes place at the top.

In Japan the agricultural cycle of hard work for the peasant on his tiny plots of rice paddy may be little changed from feudal times and indeed may be unchange-able. But the peasant himself is a greatly changed man. What a difference there is, for better or for worse, be-tween the browbeaten feudal peasant denied all access to the sword and the sturdy peasant conscript of more recent times, who gloried in his days as a member of the arrogant, conquering army of Japan! The tradition-bound wielder of the hoe has become a scientific farmer who, within the limitations of his narrow fields, is as efficient a producer as any in the world. The feudal peasant did not even have the right of verbal protest against misgovern-ment, but his present descendant, whether a unionized worker or still on the ancestral farm, listens to his radio and reads his daily paper and is at least a very conscien-tious if not always a politically aroused voter.

A change of this sort has not as yet come to all of Asia, but it seems predictable. The machine goods and machine techniques of the West have struck not merely at the national economies of countries like China and India but at the economy of each individual village. A consider-able portion of the human energy in the typical village once was devoted to off-season handicraft industries, but sooner or later these are almost certain to be destroyed by machine products, whether foreign or domestic. To offset this loss of income, the village must either increase its agricultural productivity, usually through Western tools and scientific knowledge, or seek new supplementary sources of income. The surplus manpower will almost inevitably be drained off to the cities as rapidly as facto-

ries can be built there, and perhaps, as in Japan, the
factory will come to the countryside. In that case many
peasants will become semi-industrialized workers, devot-
ing their spare time to simple industrial processes that can
be performed in a room in their farmhouses or else com-
muting on a part-time basis to some rural industrial plant.

As the superstructure of the state is reorganized,
other powerful new influences will undoubtedly come
into the peasant's life. Perhaps through conscription he
will be dragged away from his village for a time to national service and in the process will find himself changed
from a villager into a self-conscious citizen of a modern
nation. When the economy will permit it, a school will
be built in his village, and his children and perhaps he
himself will be made literate and in the process will find
that they have been given many new ideas as well as a new
skill. A village in which the children go to school even for
a few years and in which the young men go away to military service or perhaps only to work for a while in city
factories is no longer the traditional Asian village.

Thus the impact of the West penetrates to every
corner of society, and it affects not simply the surface
forms of life but often enough the very bases of the civilization. In the case of Japan, it was clear that feudalism
both as a social system and as an ethical ideal had to go
in the face of the Western menace. When the Japanese
sought to borrow our modern tools and techniques, they
were forced to compress into a few decades many of the
great economic, social, and ideological changes we ourselves had experienced over several centuries, as our originally feudal society slowly evolved into the one we have
today. This of course necessitated tremendous changes at
every level in Japan, but apparently these changes were
not so difficult to make or so fundamental as those forced
on the Chinese when they attempted to borrow Western

machines and techniques. For them it proved necessary to attempt an abrupt reversal of the basic principles of their whole ethical and social system.

Chinese ethics and social organization have since ancient times been family-centered and particularistic. In other words, the determination of right conduct depended upon the particular relationship between two individuals. There was no code of universal love to be applied as best one could, but rather a series of specific social obligations depending upon family or pseudo-family relationships. The first duty of the individual was to his parents and then in descending degrees to surrounding circles of relatives or to those to whom for specific reasons he owed a sense of duty. It was essentially immoral to treat a stranger with the same generosity and love as that reserved for a distant relative, much less a close member of the family.

This is a very different ethical system from our own and one which we, by all our traditions, would be inclined to condemn, even though we must admit that it comes closer to raw human nature than our own system and that it did work well in China for thousands of years. But there is no point in sitting in abstract judgment on the relative merits of the Chinese emphasis on particularistic ethics and our universalistic concepts which have been expressed in such admonitions as "love thy neighbor as thyself." The important thing is that Western machines and techniques have not worked effectively in China so long as the native Chinese ethical attitudes remained unaltered, and the Chinese people have therefore been forced to turn with reluctance and confusion away from the traditional ethical system toward our own.

Whether the problem is the creation of a modern factory or a modern army division, it is quite clear that the particularistic family-centered approach of Confucian

China will not work. A general or a factory manager is laboring under a serious handicap if his first criterion in the choice of his officers or assistants is the individual's family relationship to himself, not the man's ability to perform the duties of his position. The resultant army division or factory will be far less efficient than if organized by a man who is not encumbered with the belief that his nephews and cousins have the first call on any job he has to offer. The problem, of course, has rarely presented itself in such simple terms, but here in a nutshell is the great ethical crisis of modern China. We have heard a great deal about Chinese corruption, but much of this corruption has been in reality the attempt to continue traditional family-centered ethical concepts in Western-type institutions which cannot work efficiently on such a basis.

Each major political change in China in recent decades has been accompanied by a step, either conscious or unconscious, away from the Confucian ethical traditions and toward our own. Each Chinese group that has presumed to speak for the future, whether Kuomintang, Communist, or democratic "third force," has at least in theory championed the Western rather than the native ethics. In fact the Communists, sharing with us, as they do, our universalistic approach to ethical questions, represent the most extreme of the Western challenges to Confucian ethics to date. They have quite deliberately singled out the old family-centered society and ethics as one of their chief targets. However abhorrent we find the Communist insistence that children should denounce their parents, we cannot but recognize in this a horribly extreme form of the Western ethical challenge to China.

No one would claim that most Chinese have already shifted from a family-centered to a universalistic basis of ethics, and it is problematic how far this shift will ever go. We of the West, despite the universalism of Christianity, once lived in a feudal society dominated by personalized ethical relationships, and even today our practical ethics is a compromise between universalistic and particularistic principles. The Chinese as a whole may never go even as far toward the universal extreme as we have, but still it seems highly improbable that they will return completely to the ethical position that once proved adequate for them. The same is true of India. The whole Indian social system based on caste appears irreconcilable with Western machines and techniques. Most Indian leaders seem to recognize this and appear willing to abandon at least part of the native social and ethical system. It seems altogether probable that eventually much of the system will be profoundly modified if not entirely destroyed. Thus we see that the impact of the West most certainly is not confined to the surface of Asian societies; it inevitably penetrates to the very ethical core, where the shock actually may be greater than at the surface.

There can be little doubt about the profundity of the impact of the contemporary Western world on the traditional civilizations of Asia, but there is considerable doubt whether it is really the traditional civilization of the West that has had this influence. The universalistic ethics of the West, despite superior European military power, had no appreciable effect on China or India in early modern times. In fact, if there were any important influences of one civilization on another in the seventeenth and eighteenth centuries, they were perhaps the æsthetic influence of Chinese art forms on European art and the intellectual repercussions of the Chinese civil-service system on aristocratic Western political concepts and of Chinese humanism on the more theological thinking of Europe. Asia itself seemed quite impervious to the political or social institutions of the West, and to our religion and ethics as well.

Only when it became evident that the modern factory, the modern army, and the modern nation-state required a universalistic ethical basis for effective operation did this Western concept have any appreciable influence on Asia. This perhaps is not surprising when we stop to remember that it was not until the rapid development of these and similar phenomena during the past two centuries that our traditional universalistic ethics began to have an overwhelming impact on our own society. The equal treatment of all men only recently developed in the West from a somewhat remote ideal in a thoroughly particularistic, aristocratic society into a practical working ethical system for everyday life.

Look back at the Western world of the middle of the eighteenth century with its hereditary aristocracies, its sharp class lines, its monarchic authoritarianism, and its limited democracy of the privileged classes, and you will realize that something fundamental has happened to us, too, during the past two centuries. This something may be the machine with all the possibilities it has opened up for mass production, mass communication, mass organization, and mass control. Whether we of the West have followed the road leading to the present twentieth-century democracies that are truly of the people, or the other road to the slave-state egalitarianism of the twentieth-century "people's democracies," we have all gone through the same process of moving away from handicraft industries toward machine production, away from hereditary, aristocratic societies toward more egalitarian and mobile social systems, away from fragmented economic and political systems to ever more closely integrated economic and political units.

It is perhaps impossible to sort out in contemporary Western civilization the traditional pre-industrial elements of our culture and those that have been produced as a result of the impact on us of modern scientific thought and machines. The two have become too intermingled in the West during the past few centuries of rapid evolutionary development to be separated from each other. We should always bear in mind, however, that the pre-industrial West proved itself incapable of any significant influence on Asia. Despite the arrogant assumption of Westerners that the innate superiority of their civilization must inevitably be recognized by everyone, it was only a recently acquired technological advance and the military power it engendered that made such an assumption at all plausible. What we have been describing as the influence of the West on Asia might be more accurately defined as the impact of the age of machine production on Asia. In other words, this may not be so uniquely an Asian problem as we have usually thought, but merely the Asian version of a world-wide phenomenon.

The West has been less violently disrupted than has Asia by the coming of the machine. For us it has been for the most part an evolutionary process, coming largely from within our own culture. The very fact that industrialization developed first in Western civilization would suggest that our particular civilization had a better basis for accommodating itself to the change than did other cultures that were not already evolving in this direction of themselves. Even so, modern scientific thought and the machines it has produced have had a tremendous and sometimes profoundly upsetting impact on the West too. It has evinced itself in such spectacular upheavals as the French and Russian Revolutions as well as in the less startling but equally significant evolutionary adaptation of social and political institutions to the new technology in such countries as Great Britain and the United States.

The impact of scientific thought and the machine on most of Asia has naturally been far more abrupt and harsh, coming as it has from the outside and striking cultures that were not already in the process of creating a place for such developments. There has been little possibility for native institutions and the machine to adjust to each other by slow evolutionary steps. When the full-blown factory technique is forcibly inserted into a pre-industrial society, traditional social and political institutions often cannot meet the challenge, crumbling rather than adapting themselves to the new conditions. But in essence the challenge to traditional ways of life, though greater in degree, is not different in kind from the challenge in the West. Because of the longer time-span, we tend to forget how the machine has denuded of farmers an area like New England and studded it instead with industrial towns that have a whole new form of life, how the rural South today is still feeling the rude impact of the machine on its economic, social, and political institutions, and how the process of adaptation to the machine is still quite incomplete in rural France or Hungary.

In the West we have seen during the past century that the machine and the new opportunities for independent economic employment it has provided have profoundly influenced the role of women in family life and in the economy and politics of the nation. The change is perhaps far from complete anywhere, and the lags in certain lands, notably in the less industrialized Latin nations, are pronounced. The direction of change, however, has everywhere been the same—toward greater equality between the sexes in family life, toward greater independence from the family in the choice of mates or of modes of life, and toward greater economic and political equality with men outside of the family. But when the machine begins to produce these same changes for the same basic reasons in Japan or when the Chinese Communists move in this direction because of a determination to adjust to industrialization and "modernization" as they envisage it, we call it the revolutionary impact of the West, rather than the influence of the machine. The challenge to traditional institutions in these cases is more direct and the emotional struggle within the individual more painful than in the West, but the basic reasons for change and the direction it takes appear to be much the same in Japan and China as in Canada and Italy.

The inability to distinguish between the impact of the machine and foreign cultural imperialism exists in the West as well as in Asia. When cheap new machine techniques of preserving and packaging foods begin to influence the economy and eating habits of the French, they tend to decry the baneful influence of American tin-can civilization. When the universal human love of sugar and a cool drink are combined with cheap new machine techniques of bottling liquids and refrigerating them to produce a soft-drinks industry, the French again protest against American coca-colonization, without realizing that the accidental historical priority of the United States in this particular technique has relatively little to do with the development of this phenomenon in France.

It is hardly surprising that in Asia the sequence in which the machine age has come to the world—to the West first and then to Asia—has loomed larger in men's thinking than the actual change itself. But we can perhaps better understand the nature of the age in which we live if we think not so much in terms of the influence of the West on the East as in terms of the successive impacts of the machine, first on the West and then on the East.

We appear to be participating in a great change in human civilization comparable to the development of agriculture and the coming of bronze and iron. It may be very much pleasanter during the period of transition to be in the society where the innovation comes through gradual evolutionary steps rather than in a society where it comes through foreign conquest, but in the long run it may make little difference where the change comes first. What difference does it make today that iron was used near the shores of the eastern Mediterranean long before it was used in England or North America? The significant thing is the technological advance, not the identity of those who first achieved it.

6. *The Asian Response*

Although the impact of the contemporary West on Asia is more the result of a recent technological innovation—mass production by machines—than of traditional, pre-industrial Western civilization, this does not alter the strong Asian consciousness of the fact that the blow has come from the outside. The whole problem of adjustment to the machine age in Asia has been vastly complicated by the almost universal identification of the forces challenging Asia with Western civilization itself.

One result of this situation has been a tendency to confuse the real challenge to the traditional societies of Asia with incidental idiosyncrasies of Western civilization that in fact constitute no challenge at all. For example, Western hats and a variety of elements of Western clothing have often been borrowed in Asia, as if they carried with them some magic potency for modernization. While a hat may well influence the mood of the wearer, it is obvious that an industrial civilization does not depend on the wearing of a military cap or a Homburg. The leaders who modernized Japan in the nineteenth century believed for a while that it would be necessary to create a social court life in Tokyo like that of the royal courts of nineteenth-century Europe, not realizing that this sort of social life was a remnant from the dying, aristocratic past rather than a necessary component of the new machine age. Their ludicrous efforts at grand costume balls were soon found to be unnecessary in the Japanese plans for modernization, and when the Japanese finally did begin to develop social institutions somewhat like those of the modern West, it was as a result of a much more spontaneous response to the industrial age and in a decidedly more modern form than costume balls at court. The natural and therefore probably more lasting social response to the machine age in Japan has been seen in such things as the growing equality of the sexes, the appearance of public dance halls, and boy-girl dates at the movies.

Surface phenomena such as hats and costume balls are, of course, of little importance, but the confusion between what in the modern machine age Asians must adjust to and what can be disregarded as merely an accidental Western variant of the pattern extends into more important areas as well. Much of the sometimes slavish copying of the details of Western political democracy in Asia can be attributed to this confusion. One might also say that the present Chinese Communist response to the challenge of the industrial age, while undoubtedly in part a natural reaction to the machine, includes a tragically large proportion of entirely unnecessary elements borrowed directly from one particular Western pattern, that of Communist Russia.

The fact that the machine age has come to Asia in the guise of Western civilization has also given an unfortunate coloring to the whole Asian response. The machine has come to Asia, not as something appearing naturally within the native culture, but as a foreign menace—as the warships that the Chinese and Japanese sought to repel or the machine goods that both Gandhi and the leaders of Meiji Japan felt were a threat to their respective societies. Throughout Asia people have often been unaware that they were responding to the neutral technological advance of mass production through machines and instead have only thought of themselves as reacting against the specific menace of Western military, economic, and cultural imperialism.

If there are any attitudes common to all Asians, they are a fundamental resentment against Western domination in the recent past, a deep suspicion of Western motives in the present, and a very real fear of Western actions in the future. While physically and institutionally Asians are in the process of adjusting to the machine, psychologically they are reacting against the West. Regardless of what the true challenge to traditional Asian civilizations may be, there undoubtedly is an underlying anti-Western bias in the whole Asian response.

There is, however, a curious ambivalence to the Asian reaction against the West. It is in part anti-Western, but at the same time the only effective response Asians have been able to make has been through the adoption of what has come to Asia as Western machines, Western techniques, and Western attitudes. The isolated Asian who has not yet felt the challenge is not responding nor is he anti-Western. His attitude toward us is the same amused curiosity that we have tended to show toward Asians, until we began to realize how they in turn might challenge us. Some Asians have felt the challenge and have responded in purely native terms, and therefore entirely ineffectively. They are typified by the die-hards of feudal Japan who murdered individual Westerners in the early days and by these acts of violence increased the Western menace to their country. They are the Chinese or other Asian extremists who by popular uprisings or holy wars sought to drive out the Westerners and in doing so opened the doors to further Western encroachments. The effective response has come largely from those who, in order to repel the West, adopted the techniques and machines that had come from the West. They have of necessity been as strongly in favor of Westernization as they have been staunchly opposed to the West, being at the same time, thus, both pro and con.

One could almost lay down the rule that Asians are anti-Western to the degree that they have become Westernized. This is more characteristic of nations as a whole than of individuals, but even among individuals it sometimes holds true. Sun Yat-sen, Gandhi, the builders of the modern Japanese army and navy, all shared in one form or another this ambivalent attitude toward the West, and it is probably more typical of leaders like Nehru and Mao Tse-tung today than is sometimes realized.

In postwar Japan perhaps we see an Asian people who have now become so accustomed to the machine age and so used to thinking of many aspects of it as typically Japanese that they are beginning to distinguish between modernization and Westernization. This may be the reason why the Japanese appear to have at last passed the peak in the violence of their reaction against the West and why during the American occupation they seemed better able than most of their American mentors to distinguish between what was essential in a democratic political system and what was just the peculiarly American variant of the pattern. But nowhere else in Asia, with the possible exception of Turkey, can one assume that the peak in the reaction against the West has been passed: it is more likely that it has not yet been reached. For some time to come we can expect that the greater the influence of the industrial civilization of the contemporary West on an Asian people, the stronger will be their anti-Western bias.

The ambivalence of the Asian attitude toward the West may have accentuated the natural swing of the pendulum that is discernible in most periods of significant human change. The adjustment to the machine age has usually come by fits and starts. There have been alternating periods of rapid change and then reversion to older forms and attitudes, but each new spurt of conscious change has tended to carry the country well past the last one. This pattern has been quite distinct during the past century in Japan and has, if anything, become more marked in recent decades. The great swing of the pendulum toward wholehearted Westernization after the First World War was followed by a violent swing away from the West in the next decade and a half. Then came a still sharper swing toward the West when Japan was defeated in the Second World War and occupied by American forces, and in the last few years there has been another but more gentle swing back from this latest high-water mark.

The periods when the swing has been back toward older attitudes do not appear to have been times when ground was actually lost in the over-all process of change. It has usually been during these times that false starts toward modernization have been sloughed off, as when the Japanese recognized the absurdity of costume balls at court and the impracticality of some items of late-nineteenth-century European dress. Moreover, during these periods of retrenchment the fundamental evolutionary process of adjustment to the machine appears to have gone on undisturbed. For instance, the swings away from Westernization never slowed down the steady progress of industrialization in Japan. In fact, it was in the period of mounting antipathy to Western ideals and Western social forms during the 1930's and the war years that one of the greatest steps forward in Japanese industrialization took place. This was the shift from light industry to heavy industry as the basis of the economy.

It was also during this period that the groundwork was unwittingly laid for one of the greatest of the social changes in modern Japanese history. The development of a war economy gave women many new possibilities for employment, enabling them to achieve greater economic independence than ever before. This development in economic status unquestionably helped the women of Japan to take advantage of political equality when given the vote and equal legal status after the Japanese defeat. It also prepared them for the stronger bid for social equality in the family which they have made since the war.

Recent Chinese history shows this same pattern of alternating periods of conscious adaptation to the external challenge and then periods of reversion to earlier forms while the groundwork was being laid for a new surge forward. The pattern was already beginning to emerge at the end of the nineteenth century in the brief reform movement, which was quickly but only temporarily swamped in a tumultuous reversion to tradition. Then followed the upsurge of the Republican Revolution of 1911, ending the old imperial form of government, but again came reversion to the traditional war-lordism of earlier imperial interregna.

The next surge forward was the Nationalist movement of the 1920's, which carried China almost all the way to unification as a modern nation-state, but this, too, receded into so-called corruption, as the traditional ethical concepts of the Chinese refused to give way entirely, and into disruption as the Japanese plunged China into war. And from this last period of confused retreat has come the new and far more drastic push of the Chinese Communists toward a certain type of modernization—a new surge forward which finally has achieved the unification of the whole of continental China as a modern nation-state and has posed a much more direct and crucial challenge to the native ethics than has ever been made before. Predicting the future is a hazardous undertaking, but we can perhaps safely surmise that the latest push toward Westernization will someday recede a little and that other and conceivably far different drives toward modernization may in time supersede it, for the process of adjustment to the machine is far from complete and many profound changes undoubtedly still lie in store for China.

The pattern of alternating periods of conscious approach toward and temporary withdrawal from the machine age is not so clear-cut in most other Asian lands as in Japan and China but there are certainly traces of it elsewhere as in Iran and Egypt, and there is good reason to believe that it may develop almost anywhere in Asia. In countries such as Indonesia and Burma the sudden achievement of independence has brought to the fore a group of very young leaders who are pushing changes as rapidly and as far as they can in their respective countries. But in view of the tremendous economic and political problems they face, it seems probable that either their efforts will fall into alternating periods of advance and consolidation, as in Japan, or else, as in China, the forward-moving wave of change they now represent will someday subside into a temporary *status quo* or even recede, and a new group of young men will take over from them and have their day as the new wave of progress.

In India the situation is obviously different, for the group of revolutionaries there did not win their chance at leadership until they were relatively old. Nehru and his colleagues will soon have to pass on their leadership to younger men, and this group probably will either represent a new wave of perhaps more impetuous advance or else, if they prove merely the *status quo* followers of their great predecessors, will be no more than the lull before a new storm of change. In South Korea we find another revolutionary leader achieving power only late in life. He too will be supplanted soon by younger men, and whether they are American-trained generals of the Republic of Korea or Russian-trained Communist zealots, they are likely to have made a far greater adjustment to the machine age than has Syngman Rhee and therefore will represent a new and more drastic wave of change.

The general pattern may be the swing of the pendulum, as in Japan, or it may be the successive waves of youth, as in China. The important point is that all parts of Asia, almost to the degree that they have responded to the external challenge, have become extremely unstable politically. This should hardly surprise us when we stop to consider the extraordinary political instability of most of the West during the past two centuries, as it attempted to adjust to the machine age—the succession of French republics and German Reichs, to say nothing of the kaleidoscopic political shifts of southern Europe and Latin America. In Asia, where the adjustment is probably even harder to make than in the West, an even greater degree of political instability is only to be expected.

Political instability in Asia is seen not only in the many political revolutions that Asia has experienced in the past half-century but in the fundamental shifts of national policy which have come without any political revolution, as in Japan during the past four decades. It is to be seen in the extraordinarily high percentage of top Japanese political leaders who have been assassinated since Japan started to modernize itself, a phenomenon paralleled by the rash of political murders in Korea since 1945 and the assassination during the last few years of Gandhi in India and of Liaquat Ali Khan, the first Prime Minister of Pakistan.

Instability shows itself even more significantly in the abrupt shifts of attitudes and allegiances that individual Asians have all too frequently made. The classic case is that of the young nineteenth-century leaders of Japan. Most of them started out as violent advocates of the forcible expulsion of Westerners, but after a few clear military lessons they became instead the prodigiously successful modernizers of Japan. The same thing has happened repeatedly in other parts of Asia among individuals and also among masses of people. This is the meaning of the impetuous rush of China's youth into the Kuomintang and then the equally impetuous stampede of these same young people or their successors a few years later from the Kuomintang to the Communist side.

In no part of Asia are attitudes and ideals as stable as in countries like the United States and Britain, and in most parts of Asia they are probably more susceptible to violent and sudden change than in even the most unstable countries of the West. Our sympathetic friends of today, as we have seen in China, can easily become our most doctrinaire enemies of tomorrow. And in the personnel of leadership there is the same instability as in attitudes. It would be reasonable to assume that the next generation of British political leaders is earning its spurs as junior members of the Conservative and Labour parties and that our own future leaders, if not necessarily young politicians of the two major parties, are at least distinguishing themselves in other traditional forms of leadership. A similar assumption for Indonesia, Iran, or even India is less warranted. The great national leaders of a decade or two from now are perhaps as likely to be skulking down an alleyway in furtive flight or confounding their university classmates with subversive arguments as working their way up toward leadership through loyal service to the existing political regimes.

A fundamental reason for the political instability of Asia is that once change starts there, concepts of change usually rush far ahead of realities. In the more advanced countries of the West, ideological changes have come for the most part as natural readjustments to changes that have already been brought about by the impact of the machine. But in Asia, where the challenge has come suddenly and from the outside, the realization of the necessity for change may far precede the ability to effect it. Thus, the Japanese leaders decided that they would have to industrialize their economy, educate their people, and transform the feudal peasantry into the material for a conscript army long before any appreciable developments in these directions had taken place. The abandoning of feudal ideals and concepts came before the abandonment of feudalism itself.

In China the time lag between idea and accomplishment has been even greater. The Chinese declared themselves a republic four decades ago, but today they still do not have an adequate substructure of education and experience to conduct their affairs successfully in a democratic manner. They still have a pre-industrial economy for the most part, but for some decades all Chinese leaders, regardless of their political stripe, have assumed that China should and would undergo a rapid process of industrialization and have been making plans accordingly. China has actually been living in a time of industrial blueprints rather than a period of significant industrialization.

Much the same situation exists in almost all Asian countries. The number of nominal Asian republics and democracies is greater now than in 1912, but few are very much closer to being working republics and democracies than were the Chinese when they adopted the name. Asia is, in fact, more under the influence of plans for change than of actual physical changes already accomplished. And it is much easier, of course, to shift radically from one blueprint to another than from one working social and political system to another.

In countries like the United States and Britain the area for doubt and debate in national affairs, though constantly shifting as some problems are settled and new ones arise, always remains very narrow compared to the society as a whole. The area of actual dispute between the defenders of so-called "free enterprise" and the advocates of the so-called "welfare state" or even of "socialism" always shrinks to an extremely restricted area of practical experiment. The divergencies on political matters are even less extensive. But in China or India the dispute can extend all the way from one theoretical extreme to the other, for most of it is theory and little of it is solid practice. It seems probable that until the societies of Asia have undergone a great deal more actual industrialization and modernization than they have today, there will not be much more stability of attitudes and ideals than there is at present.

It is not surprising that most of contemporary Asia is in a blueprint phase, for Asians often are responding not so much to the actual coming of the machine to their societies as to their awareness of more industrialized national patterns elsewhere in the world. Japan may have been the first of the modern semi-planned societies, but the Japanese were fortunate enough to go through the most crucial stages of change by plan in the nineteenth century when laissez-faire economics and traditional British liberalism like the British Empire itself, were still supreme. As a consequence, they were content to restrict their plans to what they felt were essentials and left considerable room for healthy spontaneous developments. The next great blueprint nation was Russia itself, which, in its attempt to catch up and surpass the more advanced countries of the West, adopted a far more rigid and comprehensive blueprint. And since the Russian Revolution has come the flood of other schemes for change, for the most part in Asia. Perhaps it has been inevitable that these have tended more to the comprehensive and rigid model of twentieth-century Russia than to the restricted and more flexible model of nineteenth-century Japan. Whatever form the blueprint may take, however, the important point is that there are plans for change throughout Asia, whether they be elaborately detailed five-year plans, the dreams of an enlightened native prince, or the gleam in the eye of a would-be revolutionary.

Change according to plan implies change imposed by the few on the many. And this is unquestionably the situation throughout Asia. The early response has in every case been the response of an elite leadership which, largely in anticipation of the impact of the machine age, has forced such changes as it could on the more or less unwilling or at least apathetic mass of people below it. Sometimes this elite leadership has been composed of men who already were in power, but usually it has been a new group of men who have risen to the top just because they had discerned the external challenge and had shown promise of meeting it effectively by adopting Western techniques.

The dominant role of the elite of leadership in Asia is by no means a surprising phenomenon. For one thing, the external impact of the West has always been felt first at the top of society rather than at the bottom—by the Chinese and Japanese leaders who thought in terms of national defense against foreign warships or by those Indians who had received the new higher education. An even more important reason has been the fact that all Asian societies when they first felt the impact were still pre-industrial and therefore tended to be class societies with an elite of leadership of one type or another and a more or less inert mass of peasants and common people below. In such societies the only possible response of the common man was a somewhat aimless type of popular revolution born of desperation, and an effective response to the West could only be expected from the elite.

In Japan all traditions of leadership had been reserved for the feudal lords and the samurai, who were their hereditary administrators and feudal fighting men. It was from the lower ranks of the latter group that the new leaders largely emerged, and they forced changes on their more apathetic compatriots in the arbitrary and dictatorial manner that was traditional in Japan.

In China leadership had for long been one of education rather than of birth, but in a society in which education was distinctly a luxury, such leadership was also inevitably one of wealth. The successive waves of new Chinese leaders have for the most part been drawn from the same privileged educated classes. While they have increasingly tended to stress egalitarian ideals, they have apparently not lost their traditional feeling of being an educated elite or their assumption that they have the right to force their own will on their less privileged and therefore less enlightened countrymen.

We find other examples of the leadership of an educated elite in India and many other countries of Asia where the new leaders have come almost exclusively from among those with the new education. Whatever the attitudes of individual leaders in these lands may be toward the use of force in fostering change, there can be no doubt that all of them must cajole, if not drive, their less comprehending compatriots through many great changes. Otherwise they can have little hope of meeting the external challenge to their lands or meeting the internal challenge to themselves of other potential leaders who may prove more dynamic and less scrupulous.

The division of the traditional societies of Asia into the few who lead and the many who are supposed to follow has meant that sharp differences have always existed between different strata of these societies. It has not always been realized, however, that these traditional differences have usually been accentuated rather than lessened by the first impact of the West. The leadership during the early days of response to the West has often been converted, at least in part, to a new set of ideals, either by study abroad or by some other influence, while the masses, still little affected by the machine or the West, have continued in a way of life based on an entirely different and more traditional set of assumptions. In a large country like our own the differences in attitudes and ways of life between a New York lawyer and a Mississippi sharecropper are certainly great, but the gulf in understanding between even these extremes in our society is very much less than that between the American-educated former Japanese samurai and the still feudal-minded Japanese peasant of eighty years ago, between the Moscow-trained Chinese Communist zealot of today and the politically apathetic Chinese villager, or between the Oxford-educated Indian intellectual and his caste-bound rural neighbor.

The impact of the new age inevitably splits the stratified societies of traditional Asia far apart, further increasing the instability of a society in transition and further emphasizing the native tendency toward a division into a small elite of leadership and a confused and reluctant mass of followers. This was true of the oligarchy of Meiji Japan, and the same cleavage between rulers and ruled can be seen in the Communist dictatorship and party elite of China, the relatively narrow strata of Westernized leadership in India, and the even thinner film of Western-educated leaders in countries like Indonesia and Burma. All of these are elite groups, and all are attempting to activate and transform the vast reservoirs of peasant inertia that lie below them.

This unfortunate re-emphasis of the native tendency toward an elite leadership and the widening of the gap between the reformist leaders and the unresponsive masses, however, may be characteristic only of the earlier stages of the Asian response to the Western challenge. In Japan, where actual industrialization followed this first stage and universal education and many other features of the machine age became firmly entrenched, the leadership has in recent decades steadily lost its elite character. This has been as true in the army as in politics, the civil bureaucracy, business, and the intellectual life of the nation. In all aspects of life the gap in ideals and experience between the more Westernized few and the many has steadily narrowed until it has now reached proportions not unlike those of the contemporary West.

The narrowing of the gap is seen in the fact that, while all segments of Japanese society today are far more influenced by the machine age than corresponding groups in most other countries of Asia, no Japanese group appears as thoroughly Western as, say, the Western-educated leadership of India. While the product of Japanese higher education may know as much about Western science or history as the Western-educated Indian, he has learned it through the medium of the Japanese language, not English, and he therefore thinks and writes in the same language as his less educated compatriots. And the latter, unlike the Japanese peasants of eighty years ago and unlike the Indian peasants of today, have received at least a primary education and know perhaps as much about Western science and world history as the products of primary education in the West. The gap between the professor at Tokyo University and the man in the provincial paddy field has shrunk and now is perhaps no greater than the gap between the Oxford don and the Scottish crofter, which is a big gap indeed, but nothing like the chasm between the traditional Asian peasant and his Western-educated leaders.

The above are some of the characteristics of the Asian response to the challenge of the modern West, but they omit one crucial consideration: what is it that Asians are seeking to achieve by responding in this way? Perhaps the best answer is that, since the challenge has posed itself as the impact of technologically superior Western states, Asians have usually thought of themselves as striving to achieve equality with the nations of the West. The Japanese sought to achieve military equality so that they would no longer be at the mercy of foreign warships; the Chinese sought political equality so that they would no longer be the victims of unequal treaties; the Indians desired national equality so that they could manage their own affairs and not be ruled by aliens.

The very concept of achieving equality with Western nations was a large departure from traditional ideas in some parts of Asia, because it involved the recognition of inferiority by societies that had always assumed the opposite and also the adoption of the thoroughly Western concept of progress—conscious progress from an undesirable national situation to one that would be more satisfactory. The Japanese, who recognized their own inferiority to China in the past, quickly realized their inequality with the West. They were also conscious of the rapid historical evolution that had characterized their history and consequently found no difficulty in deciding to improve their current situation by conscious efforts at change.

On the other hand, the Chinese, who had always assumed their own unique superiority, were slower to realize the inequality of their status and, encumbered with a firm historical concept of cyclic repetition rather than progress, found it more difficult to embark upon conscious changes with the hope of improving their position.

For Indians, this shift in thinking was even more difficult, for among the basic tenets of Indian thought were the assumption that life in this world was inevitably unsatisfactory and the passive acceptance of existing inequalities of human fate as the result of an unending chain of causality, or karma, in which sins of an earlier life explained one's misfortunes in this. But whatever the original philosophic attitudes may have been, the Western concept of progress has won out everywhere in Asia and has given to the leaders, if not the masses, of all Asian lands the hope that the inequality of the nineteenth-century relationship between East and West can be redressed and the nations of Asia can achieve full equality with those of the Occident.

It will be seen that the search for equality is always put at first in terms of the nation, not the individual. There is to be progress in the status of the country as a whole, but not necessarily for the individual citizen. The leaders of Meiji Japan were seeking the advancement of Japan, not personal advancement for themselves, much less for the peasants and factory workers under their rule. The same has been true to a great degree of all the other elite leaders of Asia. But, despite this fact, there can be no doubt that the concept of individual progress has also crept into Asian minds and has become more and more important with each passing decade, as ever larger groups of peasants and city dwellers became conscious in one way or another of the possibility of improving their personal lot through the right sort of purposeful action.

In part this application of the concept of progress to the individual may have been the result of new experiences. In Japan, as it was industrialized, society became more mobile, and opportunities increased for men of ability to achieve spectacular improvement in their economic and even their social status. In the freer societies and rapidly growing economies of the colonial lands of southeast Asia, former indentured laborers drawn from the lowest and most hopeless economic strata of China and India became men of wealth and prestige. Wherever the influence of the machine was felt, however indirectly, new careers opened up for men of talent.

Perhaps a more influential factor has been the obvious attractiveness of the concept of progress, once it has forced its way into a society. If the leaders of a country are firmly convinced that national progress is possible and have started to upset the traditional society in order to achieve this progress, it seems inevitable that individuals within the disturbed society will begin to apply the same concepts to themselves. In a country like India, where the leadership is thoroughly committed to democratic ideals and therefore thinks of national progress as the sum of the progress of the individual citizens, the transference of the concept of progress from the nation to the individual is entirely natural. But even in a country like Communist China, where the leaders have chosen as their working model the Soviet system, which has so consistently and brutally sacrificed the welfare of the individual to national power, the same hope for individual progress appears to be strong.

The Chinese Communists in their rise to power always based their claims on the supposed superiority of their system as a way to achieve power for China as a whole. But it is worth noting that they also based their immediate appeal to the Chinese masses on a promise of betterment of the individual peasant's position—in other words, on land reform. Whether land reform has led to any but a psychological improvement of the peasant's lot is another matter. The important point is that the concept of individual economic betterment is so much part of the Chinese scene today that the Communists, who usually are entirely callous to the individual's well-being, found it expedient to appeal to the peasant's natural desire to own his own land.

It remains true, however, that throughout Asia the chief emphasis in the response to the modern West has been on the national unit rather than the individual. The nations of Asia are seeking equality with the nations of the West, rather than the individual Asian with his counterpart in the Occident. And this may be inevitable, for the peoples of Asia have correctly analyzed one of the chief characteristics of the modern age. In this time of mass production, mass communications, and mass controls over men, the most important unit of organization for mass activity has proved to be the modern nation-state. This is why the Japanese, though already a nationally conscious people, were forced to scrap their feudal divisions and draw together as a truly modern national unit. This is why the Chinese leaders, however deeply they imbibed Western concepts and Western techniques, found no effective response to the Western challenge until the masses of China began to feel a national stirring and joined them in facing the outside world—until the city crowds made boycotts of foreign goods an effective economic weapon and until the Chinese peasant became an enthusiastic, nationalistic fighter for his country. The real explanation of the rapid Chinese rise to military power in recent decades is that larger and larger groups of Chinese have become nationally conscious and therefore have joined in an increasingly effective national response to the foreign challenge.

Much the same situation is to be found in every part of Asia. National units everywhere have proved the most effective units of response to the outside challenge, while tribal, class, caste, family, or even religious groupings have proved more or less ineffective. There are, of course, many variations in the response in different parts of the non-Western world. In primitive areas like Borneo and some parts of Africa the response has scarcely started or has manifested itself in violent but still largely unfocused upheavals, such as that of the semi-tribal, semi-national Mau Mau of Kenya. In the Near East the national response is complicated by the larger and to some extent effective unit of the Arab-speaking world and the still larger unit of Islam. In India it is complicated by the existence of several different major languages within the national unit—a situation that finds no successful parallels in the West, where, except for three or four relatively small countries, the multilingual states have proved incapable of adjusting to the modern age. In southeast Asia it is complicated by the multiplicity of cultures, racial types, and languages within a single national unit. Malaya, with its three fairly evenly balanced ethnic groups—the Malays, Chinese, and Indians—presents an extreme case, but even in the other countries of this area there is usually a wealthy, commercial class of Chinese that contrasts sharply with the mass of impoverished native peasants.

Despite these great variations in the local situation, nationalism is a great and still rising force throughout most of Asia. Often it is hard to distinguish it from anti-Westernism, because so much Asian nationalism is expressed in anti-Western terms. The two, however, are fundamentally distinct. Anti-Westernism may be only a passing phase of the Asian scene, while nationalism, judging from the strong and usually violent national sentiment of even the more thoroughly industrialized nations of the West, has come to stay. Nationalism is the reason for most of the success Asians have had to date in ending the domination by Western nations and attempting to match their power, and it is likely to remain one of the most important and least alterable factors in our relationship with Asia in the foreseeable future.

The other great feature of the Asian response to the modern West has been the determination to industrialize. Most Asian leaders appear to see in industrialization the panacea for the economic difficulties and ultimately the political and social problems of their respective lands. Here, too, Asians have analyzed the nature of the modern age correctly, for if the national state has been the effective unit of organization, it is equally true that the vast increase in human productivity and power made possible by the mechanization of production and communications has been the basis of the tremendous physical superiority the modern industrialized nation has shown over earlier societies.

Often enough the concept of industrialization in the minds of Asian leaders is naïvely faithful to the full industrialized pattern of a huge and rich national unit, such as the United States or the Soviet Union. Because of inexorable economic laws there is not likely to be any healthy development of heavy or even much light industry in certain Asian areas, just as there are large parts of the industrialized West lacking such industries. But the Asians are no doubt correct in expecting the eventual application of modern scientific knowledge and machine techniques to all parts of Asia, even though factory complexes will develop only in certain areas.

The application of the machine to agriculture on the great plains of the American Middle West, which has enabled one man to produce as much food as a host of peasant farmers, is as significant an aspect of American industrialization as the tractor factories of Detroit, built to support mechanized agriculture. A similar development of fabulously successful mechanized farming is improbable in most of Asia, particularly in the overpopulated lands. We do, however, see the start of the inevitable industrialization of all Asia not merely in the sprawling factory cities of Japan, the great Tata ironworks of India, or the Abadan refinery in Iran; we see it as much in the huge irrigation projects of Pakistan and India, made possible by modern science and construction tools, the gradual replacement of pointed sticks by steel plows in parts of southern Asia, the growing use of chemical fertilizers, and the spreading networks of railways and roads in almost every Asian land. All the peoples of Asia in responding to the challenge of the modern West have singled out the establishment of national states and the development of industrialized economies as their first two objectives, and in doing this they have unquestionably grasped two essentials—perhaps the two essentials—in their fight for equality.

7. *Nationalism and Industrialization*

The leaders of the various lands of Asia are, no doubt, correct in the emphasis they have placed on nationalism and industrialization in their attempt to catch up with the technologically more advanced nations of the West. They may also be right in trying to accomplish the necessary changes by a stiff schedule of forced marches, instead of leaving them to slow, evolutionary development.

But there is a vast gap between the determination to develop strong, prosperous nation-states and the actual accomplishment of these objectives. Even a detailed blueprint for change is a very different thing from the change itself. Certain steps cannot be taken until others have already been successfully completed, and many of the most important changes require resources that are not easily found in most of the countries of Asia.

While nationalism and industrialization are in a sense parallel and complementary techniques, they are by no means equally difficult to achieve. The development of a cohesive nation-state based on a nationally conscious citizenry is no simple task, but it is much easier to attain than an advanced economy based on the full use of modern scientific knowledge and techniques of machine production. Only a small part of the total population of Asia has made any great adjustment to modern science and industrial techniques, but it is hard to find any area where the people have not been considerably influenced by nationalism. In fact, with the single exception of Japan, the great resurgence of the peoples of Asia in the past few decades has been the result almost exclusively of their national awakening rather than their much slower progress toward industrialization.

This is not a surprising situation, for nationalism is a state of mind, while industrialization is a physical change. Consequently nationalism, like the concept of industrialization, has been able to race far ahead of the physical realities of industrial progress. It has normally spread from the leaders outward in ever widening circles, starting with the politically conscious and educated classes, then influencing the city populaces before the peasants, and coming most slowly, if at all, to the more primitive peoples still living in tribal groupings. It has spread perhaps more rapidly and uniformly in countries like Japan, where a national school system could indoctrinate children in the faith of nationalism at an early age. But even where universal education is still a hope rather than a reality, nationalism has been able to seep downward through society and outward to almost every corner of the land.

This is not to say that nationalism has been unopposed in Asia. In Japan there seems to have been little to bar it; in fact, the Japanese, as we have seen, started their period of great change as an already nationally conscious people. But elsewhere in Asia tremendous obstacles often stood in the way of nationalism. There have been the strong family loyalties of China, the caste divisions of India, the supranational ideals of the Pan-Arab world and Islam, or the multi-ethnic divisions of some southeast Asian states. These barriers, though usually surmounted, have been by no means leveled, and new ones are rising in some places, such as the linguistic divisions within India, which become increasingly important as the Indians seek to shift for purposes of government and education from English, the language of their Western conquerors, to a native, national language. But, despite all these difficulties, it has been primarily the rising tide of nationalism that has suddenly restored most of the peoples of Asia to independence, and there can be little doubt that in nationalism the peoples of Asia will continue for some time to find their most effective means of meeting the challenge of the outside world.

We must recognize, however, that there has often been a lag between the spread of national consciousness and the development of an effective national response in the individual countries of Asia. Something more than mere national enthusiasm is needed—certain techniques of organization and certain ways of capitalizing on the spirit of unity and the willingness to make personal sacrifices that nationalism breeds. This lag is the reason for the relatively slow and sometimes faltering progress of the Chinese as they strove to draw together effectively as a national unit. This is the reason why the peoples of India and southeast Asia, despite a rising national consciousness, were unable to win their independence until the armies of Japan had shattered the Western colonial regimes, and the military and economic difficulties of the imperial powers in Europe forced them to relax their grip in Asia.

We should also realize that there are definite limitations to the strength and security Asian countries can win merely through the national consciousness of their citizens. Nationalism has sufficed to win independence for most of them and has helped build China up from a military cipher to a formidable power on its own terrain, but it has not won for the nations of Asia a position of real equality with those of the West. The only Asian country that in recent times has enjoyed full equality with the West is Japan, which, because she was industrialized as well as nationally conscious, was able to play the role of a true world power for some decades. But today even Japan, still suffering from the physical and psychological wounds of defeat, is by no means a fully equal nation, and no other Asian land has achieved anything but a somewhat theoretical legal equality with the nations of the West.

The Chinese Communists, for all their military successes against the Japanese invaders and American troops in Korea, have submitted or else are perilously close to submitting to the twentieth-century brand of ideological imperialism of Soviet Russia. With a country of more than twice the population of the Soviet Union, they are at best only the younger brothers of their Russian mentors and are pathetically dependent on Soviet industrial power and know-how for any substantial progress toward their dreams of industrialization. The citizens of most other Asian lands, while perhaps not so immediately threatened by Russian imperialism, are no closer to achieving equality with Western nations of comparable size. While possessing enough nationally aroused citizens to make old-fashioned imperialistic exploitation no longer profitable, they are barely able to preserve internal peace, much less defend themselves against any strong external foe.

The large countries of Asia obviously will not be world powers in any way comparable to those of the West until they too have strong industrial foundations. The small countries of Asia will not equal or even begin to approach the small countries of the West in internal well-being or external influence until they too have applied modern scientific knowledge and machine techniques to their economic problems. In fact, the countries of Asia cannot even exploit the full potentialities of national unity until a considerable degree of industrialization in the broad sense has been achieved. A thorough network of effective communications—roads, railways, airlines, telegraphs, and radio—is a first requisite. A nation-wide system of education is another. Without such things it is impossible to muster the real strength of the masses that make up the nation or to co-ordinate and focus their efforts effectively.

It has been inevitable that as the peoples of Asia have achieved their independence, they have shifted their attention increasingly to the problem of industrialization. But it is a vastly more difficult task to modernize the technology of a country than to arouse its people to national consciousness, for the former requires huge investments of funds, goods, and skills that are not easily acquired in Asia. A communication network or a factory system cannot be built by an Asian country unless it can find men who know how to do it, the proper materials for construction, and adequate financial resources to pay for the necessary men and goods. Even the development of a national system of primary schools requires a capital investment of a size that most Asian countries cannot provide today. The enthusiasm that most Asian leaders have for industrial development is very important, but industrialization cannot be achieved merely by pulling on one's own bootstraps.

Each Asian country must find surplus wealth either at home or abroad or it cannot make the necessary capital investments to lift it from its present status of inequality with the nations of the West. In fact, with the more industrialized countries of the world rapidly increasing their own productivity by constantly renewed capital investments, the lands of Asia must industrialize their economies at a fairly rapid rate even to maintain their present level of relative inferiority. However philosophical we of the Occident can be about this situation, it is not one that many Asians are likely to find tolerable.

One obvious source of surplus wealth for capital investment in Asia is the technologically advanced and therefore more prosperous countries of the West, where the growing availability of investment capital is clearly indicated by the steady decline of interest rates that has been in progress for many decades. Logically it can be argued that Asia can be most quickly industrialized by the investment of surplus capital from the West; practically, however, this can be only a small part of the answer.

During the days of colonial domination it was less of a problem than it is today to find Western capital to invest in Asia. Obviously, to compensate for the greater difficulties and risks involved, the returns had to be higher for such investments than for those made at home. The skilled Western technician would not go to the Orient unless given a much higher salary than if he were employed at home; the investor would not risk his money there unless he felt that the profits would be sufficiently greater to compensate for the increased dangers. But a considerable investment was made on these terms, with very important results. The rail network of India, what railways China has, and a host of other important starts toward industrialization were made in this way.

In recent years it has been customary in Asia to condemn such investments of skills and goods by colonial or semi-colonial powers as examples of "economic imperialism," and it has been popular to blame "economic imperialism" for whatever ills of Asia could not be attributed to political imperialism. Obviously the political domination of one people by another is not desirable, and the arrogant snobbery of some Western businessmen in Asia fully earned the bitter resentment that it brought upon itself. But this does not mean that the investment of Western capital in the colonial and semi-colonial lands of Asia was necessarily a bad thing. For the Western nations it was a satisfactory but often quite minor economic operation. For the Asian countries it usually represented the crucial first steps in industrialization. It is hard to imagine an independent India today without the investment of skills and capital that the British made in India. It is equally hard to imagine as strong and independent a China as we find today without the foreign investment of skills and money in railways, telegraphs, steamship lines, mines, and factories made over the past half-century.

Naturally, the economic impact of the Western world on Asian lands, however it came, always entailed great individual hardships for many people. Furthermore, some colonial regimes hindered rather than facilitated the process of industrialization in their Asian holdings, and there appear to have been all too many cases in which European powers warped the economy of their colonial possessions to fit their own needs. Indonesia and Indochina are examples of this, but even here it seems improbable that we should be witnessing the national awakening of these lands if the Netherlands and France had not invested in them skills and money to the extent they did.

Perhaps the best examples of the healthy development of Asian economies through outside capital are afforded by Korea, Manchuria, and Formosa, the former colonial lands of Japan. Just because the Japanese had fewer territorial possessions than the colonial powers of Europe, they could pour a relatively larger investment into their foreign holdings, once they had developed through industrialization at home a surplus for investment abroad. The Japanese purpose, of course, was to make themselves richer and stronger, but what was the result of these extreme cases of "economic imperialism"? Manchuria became the industrial heart of the whole Chinese area; the communications network and the factory system built by the Japanese were the chief assets the Koreans had at the time of their liberation; and the Formosans came to enjoy a far higher standard of living and level of literacy and technical knowledge than any other large group of Chinese.

This is not to say that the evils of Japanese political domination did not outweigh the value of their economic investment in Korea, or that Japanese rule in Formosa and Manchuria was justified. Nor can one attribute all the economic and technological advantages of Manchuria and Formosa over China proper to the Japanese investment of skills and goods, for Manchuria had great mineral resources, and both areas had relatively large agricultural surpluses. But even after these qualifications are made, it remains true that the Japanese economic investment proved in the long run to be a tremendous asset to the peoples of these areas. The economic tragedy of the rest of the once colonial and semi-colonial lands of Asia is not so much that they formerly suffered from "economic imperialism" as that they did not have enough of it in the form of solid investments by the West.

But this is merely a look back into the past. Asia is not a colonial or semi-colonial area today, and the independent and nationalistic peoples of Asia are in no mood to accept foreign investments on a large scale. With their horror of nineteenth-century colonialism and their rather rigid concepts of economic imperialism, they fear that foreign capital in almost any form might be the opening wedge for foreign exploitation and possible political domination. Whatever the political and economic truths may be today, they have a cogent argument in history, for there can be no doubt that in the past Western merchants and missionaries were the forerunners of Western warships and soldiers. Right or wrong, the Asian distrust of foreign capital is a solid fact, which seriously limits the possibility for the flow of Western capital to Asia.

Actually there is little inducement for Western technicians or capital to go to Asia under present conditions. Today there is bitter resentment of the huge salaries, according to Asian standards, that must be paid even the lowliest of Western technicians to lure them to Asia. As a consequence it seems improbable that many Westerners will be employed by Asians to help solve their domestic problems or that those who do go to Asia will find a favorable environment for their best efforts. Private Western capital certainly will not be invested in Asia unless assured of very high returns, for the risks in the nationalistically aroused and politically unstable Asia of today are much greater than during the colonial period. The expropriation of foreign investments in China and the seizure of the Abadan oil refineries in Iran are all too typical examples of the dangers to foreign capital in contemporary Asia. Even if the peoples of Asia were to welcome foreign capital

instead of fearing it and legislating against it, not r
Western businessmen would be foolhardy enough to risk
much of their wealth in Asia under existing conditions.

Loans by Western governments or international agencies may prove a more practical way of bringing investment capital to Asia, but these, too, have their severe limitations. While many Asians would have little or no objection to loans or gifts from international agencies, the
limiting factors in this case are the agencies themselves, for
under present international conditions they are able to do
relatively little along these lines. In the case of loans from
individual Western nations, the problem is that Asians
often fear these even more than private investments. Even
when the American government has sought to give money
outright to Asian lands, it has frequently met with great
wariness and suspicion and sometimes with flat refusals to
accept the money at all. And there are definite limits to the
amount of money the peoples of the Western democracies
will be willing to give to Asia under any circumstances.
Just as it is elementary human nature for the peoples of
Asia, in view of their recent history, to be extremely suspicious of investments of any sort from the West, it is also
simple human nature for the peoples of the West to be reluctant to give unstintingly to the lands of Asia.

In China we apparently have an extreme case of the
isolation of Asia from Western investment capital. The
Chinese Communists have done their best to liquidate all
foreign investments, and they have willfully cut themselves off from almost all sources of foreign capital of any
sort, obviously fearing the "imperialistic" contamination
of each dollar from the free world much more than the
lack of skills and goods such a policy entails. On the other
hand, they seem to have shown greater willingness to accept economic aid from their Russian colleagues than have
most other Asians from any Western source. But to date

Soviet economic aid has been on a very modest scale. Russia has no great surplus of capital goods, and in addition the Russian leaders may have little desire to see China develop into a powerful competitor. Thus arrangements through Communist governments have so far proved no more successful in opening the flow of Western investment capital to Asia than have arrangements between democratic governments or private individuals.

Under present conditions it seems altogether improbable that an adequate investment will be made in the parts of Asia that need it by the parts of the Western world that are capable of supplying it. Most Asian leaders appear to have reached this same conclusion, though their reasoning may have been quite different. In any case, no one can disagree with their determination to look to their own countries for the bulk of the necessary capital for industrialization and modernization.

It is worth noting that the Japanese made much the same decision under the very different circumstances of the nineteenth century relationship between East and West. The Japanese leaders of almost a century ago were as fearful of Western capital as their contemporary counterparts throughout Asia. They were forced to send students abroad and bring experts to Japan at very great cost, but they reduced or eliminated these practices just as soon as they could. The treaties imposed on them by Western warships had made it impossible to exclude foreign capital, but few Western businessmen cared to invest heavily in an unstable Japan just emerging from feudalism, and the Japanese made few efforts to attract outside capital, especially into what were considered to be the key areas of the economy. Some loans were floated in London, but by and large the industrialization and modernization of Japan was accomplished through capital squeezed out of Japan itself.

The chief means of capital accumulation in nine-teenth-century Japan was taxation. The new centralized government, while paying heavily for the liquidation of the old feudal system, had brought all the agricultural lands of Japan under its direct control and therefore was able, through heavy taxation of the peasants, to drain off virtually all their surplus produce for investment in the industrialization of the economy and the modernization of the government. Some of the funds so obtained were given in the form of government bonds to the former feudal classes as compensation for their lost powers and incomes, but the aristocratic military men of Japan, with their Spartan ideals, proved capable of limiting their consumption and investing much of the new capital in business. Consequently, agricultural taxes either through direct government investment or through reinvestment by the former feudal classes became the chief source of Japanese capital for industrialization and modernization.

This, however, was not the whole story. It should be noted that in Japan, unlike most of the other lands of Asia, a class of small entrepreneurs had been growing up through the cracks of the disintegrating feudal economy even before the big change began. These men, too, proved capable of a rapid rate of capital reinvestment and played an important though entirely unofficial role in Japanese industrialization. And then, Japan had the advantage of being the first Asian land to be industrialized. By mechanizing the cheap and simple process of silk-reeling, the Japanese soon produced an article superior to the hand-reeled silk of China and thus won the lucrative Western silk market from the Chinese. And as soon as they had adopted Western spinning and weaving machines, they found the great cotton-goods markets of Asia almost as defenseless before the factories of Osaka as before the mills of Lancashire.

The more Japan became industrialized, the greater became her advantages over the rest of Asia and the greater her capacities for further industrialization. Perhaps more by accident than design, much of the new industrial and commercial wealth of Japan fell under the control of a few so-called zaibatsu families. However unfortunate the zaibatsu system may have been for Japan politically and socially, it may have contributed significantly to the rapid industrialization of the country. The zaibatsu owned such vast wealth that they probably could not have consumed all the profits of their economic empires even if they had desired to do so. But, in any case, they shared the Japanese tendency toward modest consumption and heavy saving and consequently reinvested most of their profits in their many commercial and industrial enterprises, thus continuing under private auspices the original government policy of a rapid reinvestment of surplus production in industrial expansion.

The other countries of Asia, in seeking to expand at a rapid rate the small starts they have already made toward industrialization, are today confronted with problems in some ways like those of nineteenth-century Japan and in some ways quite different. They will not have the advantage the Japanese had of being the first to combine cheap Asian labor with Western machines. They must instead compete not only with the machines of the West but also with those of Japan and the other rising centers of factory production in Asia. And in most Asian lands there is not much of the entrepreneurial spirit and the natural tendency to save that the individual Japanese showed in the nineteenth century. On the other hand, there is a close parallel with nineteenth-century Japan in their unwillingness to rely primarily on outside capital and the consequent necessity of scraping together a surplus for capital investments from their own relatively weak economies. In many cases the parallel may go even further, for it is difficult to see how most Asian countries will produce the capital investment they need unless the government provides it through crushing taxation that falls for the most part on agriculture.

Asians themselves usually draw the parallel between their lands in the middle of the twentieth century and Russia of three decades ago. Obviously there is a parallel of sorts here, but also two very great differences. Russia at the time of the Communist Revolution was proportionately a far more industrialized land than are most Asian countries today, and the ratio between natural resources and population was vastly more favorable in Russia than in all but a few small and untypical Asian areas. The contrasts are far greater than the similarities between Russia and Asia and make the Soviet Union a very misleading example of the economic problems that most of Asia faces. In these respects the industrialization and modernization of heavily populated and naturally poor Japan in the nineteenth century, despite the very significant time differential, appear to be a closer and more instructive example.

The problem of accumulating capital takes various forms in different parts of Asia. There are a few fortunate countries in the Near East which, because of the vagaries of nature, have relatively light populations on their barren, desert soils, but vast subsurface riches of oil. For these lands it is conceivable that much of the process of modernization and such industrialization as fits their needs could be paid for by their liquid treasures. This is clearly true of the petty principalities of the Persian Gulf and may prove true to some extent in Saudi Arabia and possibly Iran and Iraq, though heretofore very little of the profits from oil have been used for capital investment in these countries. In each case such capital accumulation as occurs will be made by the government rather than by private individuals. This is true whether the government is a semi-nationalized administration like that of Iran or a personal kingdom like that of Saudi Arabia and whether the capital is accumulated through profit-sharing agreements with foreign companies, as in Arabia, or through the type of nationalization of oil resources which the Iranians desire.

In a few other Asian areas, particularly in southeast Asia, there may be adequate mineral resources to carry a significant part of the load of capital investment, if properly exploited. Moreover, countries like Burma, Indochina, and Siam, because of relatively low population densities, can produce large agricultural surpluses that could easily be used to pay the bill of industrialization and modernization. In these countries too it seems probable that the government rather than private individuals will be the agency for converting agricultural surpluses into capital investments.

In contrast to these more favored areas, most of the other countries of Asia, including all the larger ones, have no great mineral resources or agricultural surpluses that can be converted easily into investment capital. There are various exportable minerals in many of them and some exportable agricultural crops, such as the soybeans of Manchuria, the rubber of Indonesia, the jute of Pakistan, the tea of Ceylon, and the cotton of Egypt. These, however, for the most part must be exchanged for foodstuffs and other urgently needed consumer goods, and at best these exportable minerals and crops represent only a very small economic leverage when compared with the heavy population of most of these lands. In the greater part of Asia the governments will find no easily exploitable sources of surplus capital, but will have to accumulate it as best they can from whatever sources can be found.

Although some of the capital needed in Asia may be

accumulated by individuals with unusual economic opportunities or unusual cultural backgrounds, such as the Chinese merchants and entrepreneurs of southeast Asia and the Parsees of India, it seems most improbable that private saving or entrepreneurial activity will play the role it had in nineteenth-century Japan, much less that of private enterprise in most of the West. In most of Asia private accumulation of wealth is simply too slow and uncertain a process to meet the needs. Moreover, where there has been any significant accumulation of private wealth in most Asian countries in the past, it has tended to go into the purchase of land, into trade ventures requiring few long-term risks, or into hiding, but not into capital investments in industry or the improvement of agriculture. If there is to be even a partial achievement of the industrialization that most Asian leaders expect, the various governments of Asia will undoubtedly have to play a large part in the process of accumulating the capital.

While this point is worth emphasizing for Westerners, who are accustomed to the primary role of individual citizens in saving and investment, it is usually taken for granted in Asia. Almost all Asian leaders assume that the government must take the lead in industrialization and modernization, and most also seem to realize that to do this the government must impose rigid controls over consumption, primarily through the imposition of heavy taxes that will absorb almost all surplus production beyond the barest needs of the individual citizens. Since most Asian countries are primarily agricultural, this will inevitably mean, as it did in Japan, discriminatory taxation against the peasant for the sake of industrial expansion.

Even if Asian countries prove capable of accumulating adequate capital through taxation or other means, the problems of industrialization which most of them face will remain extremely complex and difficult. Conceivably a country like Saudi Arabia might find an oil-smoothed highway leading from its pre-industrial poverty and weakness to prosperity and strength, but for most Asian countries progress is likely to be a creeping process of inching forward on many interrelated fronts at the same time.

The fields demanding investments are many and the resources sadly limited. Some areas of the economy will have to be stressed at the sacrifice of others. But what should come first? The factories to produce nitrogen fertilizers and improved agricultural tools in order to increase agricultural production per acre, the dams to increase the over-all acreage, the roads, railroads, and ports to improve communications, the factories for consumer goods to lessen the national dependence on imports, the schools to improve the skills of the citizens so that all these other tasks may be accomplished more successfully? If one major field of industrial advance or technological improvement goes too far ahead of the others, it may create uneconomic imbalances and socially dangerous strains and stresses. Most Asian nations might be compared to a precariously balanced Alpinist. Each must edge one economic foot forward a few inches to a better toe hold in order to enable it to take a slightly higher handhold in another field, for only through such carefully co-ordinated small movements will it be able to raise its general economic level slowly past the first and most crucial stages in the climb toward industrialization.

Even after these early stages are passed, there is little hope that the going will become much easier. The experience of nineteenth-century Japan is not likely to be repeated. With the West making such steady technological advances that it no longer requires even Japan's wonder export of silk, it seems improbable that any of the larger Asian countries will stumble on some new wonder export that will do for it what silk did for Japan. The struggle to industrialize will continue to be a very hard one for the lands of Asia as far ahead as one can discern the hazy contours of the future.

Many people hope that the countries of Asia, without waiting for the slower and more difficult process of industrialization, will be able to achieve through social reforms a second great surge forward toward power and prosperity, comparable to that made possible by nationalism. There may be something to this view. Certainly great new potentialities of energy would be released in any Asian land if social reforms could be carried out which would permit and induce each individual to work for the common good to the full extent of his abilities. This ideal is implicit in Communist theory and is probably shared by most democratic Asian leaders as well. It is difficult, however, to envisage social reforms of this sort which are not so dependent on the upsurge of nationalism or some technological advance as to be little more than phases of these two other phenomena.

Some people would dispute this position, arguing that land reform in the sense of giving tenant farmers the ownership of the fields they cultivate is a good example of a social reform that has vast potentialities in Asia for increased national power and well-being. But land reform is not likely of itself to bring a higher standard of living to any Asian country or more national power. Giving to the tenant farmer the land he cultivates is a great social advance according to contemporary egalitarian concepts, but it increases the productive power of the land little if at all. In fact, there are cases in which the breaking up of large agricultural units into smaller ones has reduced efficiency, and the small peasant owner has proved less capable of making desirable improvements in agriculture than the former large-scale landowner.

The owning of his own land may induce the former

tenant to work harder, though this is usually not so in Asia, simply because most tenants in Asia are forced to work as hard as they can simply to keep alive. The consolidation of the holdings of the individual peasant, which is sometimes associated with land reform, would of course save the farmer countless steps. But in over-populated, pre-industrial Asia the problem is not to induce peasants to work harder or even to save them effort. The real need is to increase the amount of land under cultivation where possible and to increase production per acre everywhere.

The extension of cultivated lands and the increasing of yield per acre depend almost entirely on improved technology. In the overpopulated countries of Asia, where there is little or no new land to bring under the plow, this means primarily more scientific knowledge, better seeds, better and more ample fertilizers, better agricultural tools, and such machines as fit the scale and intensity of the local agricultural pattern. In the arid and sparsely inhabited lands of western Asia the same needs also exist, but perhaps the chief technological problem there is the extension of cultivated land through irrigation projects and mechanized farming. In both cases technological advances depend on new investments of skills and goods in agriculture, not on saving labor, which means little in these lands until industrialization has gone far enough to create new employment possibilities for the labor saved from agriculture. Land reform, however desirable it may be for political or ethical reasons, has little if anything to do with technological advances of this sort.

This is not to say that land reform does not have certain effects that are of tremendous importance internally in Asian countries. It has usually come as a result of the growing consciousness of the peasants that personal economic progress is possible, and it tends in turn to stimulate their political and national consciousness. In other words, it is often associated with and contributes to the whole process of national awakening.

Land reform also has proved a technique whereby leaders have won a popular following and have come to power in some parts of Asia. The most notable instance of this was in China, where it played a large part in the Communist triumph. The peasant's desire for his land has also been a factor in the protracted Huk rebellion in the Philippines, and Magsaysay's rise to power there has in part been a reflection of the popular hope that he will be able to solve the land problem. In India and the Near East land reform has in it tremendous though as yet little exploited possibilities in the domestic struggle for power. In most of Asia land reform is, in fact, potential dynamite in internal politics.

Land reform also can contribute considerably to strengthening the central government by enabling it to impose heavier taxes on agriculture. The elimination of a landowning group standing between the peasant and the national government does away with a type of middleman and permits the peasant and the tax-collector to share between them all the fruits of the soil. In Communist China it seems inevitable that the share of the former landowners will go almost entirely to the government rather than to the peasant. Not only would this be entirely consistent with all known Communist practice; it would also be entirely consistent with the practice of every strong dynasty throughout Chinese history.

In the other countries of Asia, too, the appropriation of the former landowner's share by the government seems an all too probable second step after land reform. In each country the governing elite is in desperate need of new financial resources for industrialization and modernization. Under these circumstances, if peasants do obtain through land reform any agricultural surplus beyond their simplest needs for living, it seems unlikely that even the most democratic and enlightened Asian leaders will leave much of the surplus to be consumed by peasants through a rise in their standard of living.

Land reform, thus, may have a role in the national awakening of the peasants of an Asian country; it may be even more important in the winning of power by certain political groups and in enabling the government to get hold of agricultural surpluses for the purpose of investing them in industrialization. But land reform itself does not produce new national wealth and power. Nor does it seem probable that there are other social reforms that, without requiring great investments in technological improvements, will do much to increase the economic or military power of an Asian nation.

We must conclude that any great or continued advance in power and wealth in an already nationally awakened Asian land will require a capital investment of such magnitude that it can only be accumulated and exploited over a considerable period of time. It would be a mistake, however, to overemphasize the difficulties that lie in the path of Asian countries in their efforts to industrialize and modernize. The Japanese have shown that it can be done with very modest resources by people with sufficient determination, and certainly the leaders of most Asian lands are not lacking in determination. We of the West sometimes tend to be too pessimistic about the problems of Asia. Seeing them from the outside, we look at them, we hope, dispassionately, but this perhaps is to view them inaccurately, for the passion and enthusiasm of the people of Asia are very much a part of the whole situation. If the leaders of Asia were as objectively detached as we sometimes are, then our pessimism might be fully justified, but they are not detached, of course, nor objective, nor dispassionate, and in their emotion-charged zeal and sometimes unjustified optimism lies the chief hope of accomplishing what they have set out to do. The question really is not: "Will Asia be modernized and industrialized?" but "How soon will it happen and what will be the results?"

No one can answer this question with certainty, but it is safe to say that industrialization and modernization may come to many parts of Asia far more quickly than now seems possible. It also seems evident that the chief result will be a great rise in national power. On the other hand, it seems improbable that there will be a great rise in living standards, such as the West experienced when it started to industrialize. A tremendous growth in population has always accompanied industrialization wherever it has occurred in the world. In the West this growth in population was more than compensated for by a still more rapid rise in economic productivity, but it is not at all certain that in most of Asia the growth of production can outstrip the further growth of the already huge populations.

There seem to be two basic reasons for this very significant difference between the possible results of industrialization in East and West. One is that many parts of Asia, for climatic and other reasons, long ago developed as a primary agricultural pattern the intensive cultivation of rice and the concomitant dense rural populations of rice-growing areas. In the West, on the other hand, agriculture remained less intensive and rural populations lighter. This gave a far lower ratio of population to natural resources in pre-modern Europe than existed in much of pre-modern Asia—a discrepancy that in recent centuries has been greatly magnified by the spreading out of the European peoples to cover virtually all the newly discovered lands of the world.

Another important reason may be that the elements of modern science and industry have come to most of Asia in a somewhat different sequence than in Europe. Actually the explosive expansion of population that has gone along with industrialization may be more the result of certain accidental accompaniments of industrialization than of machine production itself. One of the main factors, for example, is the improvement of transportation, which has usually done away with the local famines that once helped to limit population growth. Another major factor is the improvement of hygiene and medicine, which sharply reduces death rates, particularly in the younger, childbearing age brackets. These important developments appeared only slowly in the West and in conjunction with the rapid rise of economic productivity through industrialization and the exploitation of virgin territories in the Americas, Australia, and other formerly primitive and lightly populated areas.

In Japan these developments came rather suddenly in the nineteenth century, also in conjunction with an equally sudden rise in productive power. In most of the rest of Asia, however, transportation adequate to wipe out local famines and enough hygiene and modern medicine to affect death rates have come without a corresponding increase in productive power. Sometimes a pure water supply is the first important impact of the machine age on an Asian village. In such a case the first visible sign of the new age is a greatly increased crop of children and, in time, of young mothers. In other words, population growth has commonly got off to a decided head start over growth in economic productivity.

The result of this situation is the always serious and often calamitous population problem that most of the lands of Asia face. A considerable rate of technological improvement and industrialization is necessary in most of Asia to maintain the growing population at even the present levels of undernourishment. While in most of the West standards of living are still rising despite the terrible destruction of the recent war and the vast sums spent for military preparedness, the same cannot be said for Asia. It seems probable that there are more Asians whose living standard has fallen over the past twenty-five years than Asians whose standard of living has improved. Most Asian countries are struggling desperately with the problem of increasing economic production sufficiently to take care of the annual increase in population. To keep doing even this for long will not be easy; to go beyond this to produce more per capita for a constantly expanding population will be a stupendous undertaking.

Many Asian leaders have come to realize that an unchecked increase of population in their lands may spell ultimate disaster. In Japan the continuation for another two or three decades of the present rate of increase of more than a million a year could rule out any desirable solution of its economic problems. In India, where modern hygiene and medicine are still far from exerting their full effect, the rate of increase is already about five million a year, and responsible government authorities there have estimated that if even this rate continues for another few decades, India will have to acknowledge failure in its efforts to feed itself. Most Asian governments are engaged in a desperate Alice-in-Wonderland race with their own populations, having to run with all their might to stay economically where they are.

In India and Japan government authorities hope to influence population growth by education and exhortation. There is no evidence that such methods have ever produced any tangible results. It seems probable that the social and sometimes even economic pressures inducing peasant families to have many children will prove stronger than any words government officials can say. But at least the population problem is being faced honestly and squarely in these countries. In most other Asian lands with comparable population pressures, the leaders either are unable to see the problem or else have chosen to ignore it. In China, for example, Communist dogma specifically denies that any problem exists, and the Communists, anyway, have chosen to place more emphasis on a large working force and potential cannon fodder than on living standards.

The only factors that reduce appreciably the rate of population growth seem to be much less manageable than words. One factor appears to be a generally high standard of living, which is obviously impossible in Asia now. Another appears to be a high ratio of urban to rural population, for city dwellers commonly do not fully reproduce their numbers, while rural populations tend to oversubscribe their quota. If Asia can look only to such possibilities for slowing the rate of population growth, the future is indeed gloomy. One of these factors is obviously inoperative, and the other could come to most of Asia only after a long period of continued population growth and industrialization has built up huge urban populations to parallel the vast masses of people already on the land. Only in Japan does one find an already industrialized and almost half-urbanized Asian country, and here the total population already exceeds the available food and other resources by such a margin that a speedy stabilization of the still rapidly rising population is even more imperative than elsewhere in Asia. Stabilization is likely to come much sooner to Japan than to any other major Asian country, but there is a strong possibility that even then it will come too late.

The economic prospects of all Asia are certainly perturbing. It could be argued with considerable plausibility that the only possible outcome of present population trends is economic disaster. At best there is little hope that most of Asia will experience as rapid a rise in living standards as occurred in the West during the past two centuries. Asian populations undoubtedly will continue their phenomenal growth for at least a while longer, and very probably most Asian lands will build up far greater industrial power than they now have. But what will be the ratio between these two different types of growth? On the whole it would seem improbable that economic development will far outstrip population growth, unless tremendous new sources of food and energy are made available by some spectacular technological advance. It therefore would be safest to assume a developing Asia in which nations through industrialization increase rapidly in power, but the individual citizens remain extremely poor.

8. *The Political Choice*

The difficulty of accumulating adequate capital for industrialization and the prospect of continued low standards of living are major problems for the peoples of Asia, but it could be argued that these are not in themselves of vital concern to the United States or the rest of the Western world. For us the primary question is what role Asia will play in the mortal struggle between democracy, based on the great ideal of individual human freedom, and totalitarianism, based on the working principle of the bondage of the individual to the state. Some would narrow the problem still further to the question of how the peoples of Asia will line up in the continuing military skirmishes of the cold war and in a possible global showdown in the near future between ourselves and the Soviet Union.

These great questions of domestic and international politics are naturally of deep concern to Asians as well as ourselves. They may not be as clear-cut as the economic problems, but they are certainly of equal importance and could determine the whole future of Asia, economically as well as politically. The Soviet Union is a clear example of a regime which, because of the political techniques it adopted, lost sight of its stated economic aims as well as its political objectives. The use of cynical and brutal coercion as the evil means of achieving supposedly good ends turned the original communist ideal of the equal betterment of all mankind into the actual enslavement of everyone. The government, which in time was supposed to wither away, was transformed into a political monster that devours its own people to keep itself alive. The same tragic transformation could, of course, take place within the nations of Asia. And in international relations the nature of the political system may prove even more important. It appears quite obvious to us that there would be no room in a Communist world for free and equal Asian nations and that this fundamental ambition of Asians can only be achieved through a successful application of democratic principles to the international scene. It also seems possible that if all of Asia were to go Communist, there eventually would be small room for democratic freedoms anywhere in the world.

For these various reasons it is quite natural for us to start with political institutions and foreign alliances when considering the situation in Asia. But in Asian eyes these political questions often appear entirely secondary. The definite choice between democracy and totalitarianism or between one international alignment and another seems to many Asians either unnecessary or at most a matter of tactics rather than a decision on ultimate objectives. They simply do not understand what we mean when we insist that they make such a choice, for their primary aim is not to achieve either a democratic or a Communist system but to win full equality with the West. To do this they have decided to make tremendous and emotionally agonizing alterations in their traditional societies and to devote their full energies to the modernization of their economies and institutions. For them this is the big decision and one that they have already made. Democracy and communism or conflicting choices in international alignments, on the other hand, appear to them to be merely alternate means to this single end, and if a choice must be made between them, the decision should go to the one that gives the greatest promise of achieving this objective most quickly and most effectively.

Of course, men like Nehru are themselves completely committed to democracy, just as those like Mao are completely committed to communism. But this is by no means true of the potential leadership of lands like India and China as a whole, to say nothing of the vast peasant masses. Asians are not committed to one system or the other in the same way that the people of Britain and the United States are devoted to democracy or the leadership of Russia has irrevocably espoused communism. All the major problems we face appear to be summed up in the choice between democracy and totalitarianism, and therefore this choice itself signifies our ultimate goals. For most Asians the greatest problems appear to be quite distinct from this choice, and they would be willing to embrace either democracy or communism or, for that matter, any other political system if convinced that it was the best means of achieving their fundamental aims.

The subordination in Asian minds of political institutions and international alignments to the achievement of national equality through economic and technological modernization is not simply a curious misconception on their part. There are valid grounds for their order of emphasis. In fact, the national aspirations and economic aims of the peoples of Asia can be understood without any reference to their political institutions and ideals, but the choices Asians have been making and will continue to make in the political field cannot be understood unless one first takes these other factors into consideration.

In the case of China we can perhaps see with particular clarity the way in which Asians tend to regard political institutions as merely means to an end. The basic Chinese objective of building up national strength and achieving equality with the West has remained constant during the past half-century of kaleidoscopic political change. No one can look closely at the recent history of China without being struck by two perplexing and for us very embarrassing problems: why did political institutions and foreign alignments shift so rapidly in China when this basic aim remained unchanged? And, more specifically, why did the Chinese abandon their apparent devotion to democracy and their friendship for us in favor of a Communist pattern of political organization and a wholly Soviet orientation of their foreign policy?

Communists themselves would probably argue that the Chinese eventually adopted the Leninist-Stalinist creed because it correctly explained the historical problems of their land and indicated the one and only road that would lead them to their objectives, but such an interpretation is of course absurd to anyone who has not put on the blinders of Communist dogma. It would be hard to devise a theory of history that applied as poorly as communism does to the experience of the Chinese people and, for that matter, most other Asians as well. The Chinese leadership has become Communist not because of basic Communist theory but despite it.

Marx, living in the heart of Europe at the height of the nineteenth century, when Europe completely dominated the world, devised a peculiarly European interpretation of history. His sequence of supposedly inevitable historical stages from feudalism through capitalism to socialism was not an entirely unreasonable theory for Europe itself in his day, but it meant nothing for Asian lands like China which had never had a truly feudal period, showed few signs of capitalism, and were far from being socialist. Unfortunately for Marxist dogma, what approximations to feudalism had ever appeared in Chinese history had proved abortive and anyway had been experienced far back in China's past.

This embarrassing state of affairs was recognized to some extent in early Marxist theories by the creation of a category of historical development known as Oriental Society, through which conditions in all non-Western countries were to be explained. The nations of Asia were then brought back onto the main tracks of Communist dogma by the concept that Western imperialism had brought capitalism to Asia from the outside and had thus started Asia too on the inevitable road to socialism. This perhaps made sense of a sort to the uncritical mind looking for some simple and supposedly authoritative explanation of what was happening in Asia. Subsequently, however, Stalinist theorizers seem to have rejected or at least minimized the slight accommodation to Asiatic realities represented by the theory of Oriental Society and insisted instead that the traditional Chinese Empire must be accepted in a wholly irrational act of blind faith as the feudal phase of Chinese history.

Another strange Communist dogma that flew in the face of all reality in Asia was that communism would be achieved by means of the dictatorship of the city proletariat. This concept has been absurd enough in the West, where the resistance to communism has commonly been strongest in countries where the industrial workers were strong, and communism has won out for the most part only in lands where the city workers were few and very weak. But in most of Asia this theory meant the even more absurd belief that communism would be achieved through the activity of a virtually nonexistent class. Based as it is on such patently ridiculous concepts, communism obviously did not win out in China simply because of its logic, and the explanation of its victory must be sought not so much in communism itself as in Chinese attitudes and recent Chinese history as a whole.

As we have seen, the Chinese, when they first realized that they must make some changes in their ways of doing things, assumed that some minor alterations of their traditional monarchic government would be enough. However, after various attempts at reform of the existing regime had done nothing to redress the balance between China and the Western powers, some of the younger Chinese intellectuals, and particularly those like Sun Yat-sen who for one reason or another had come to know more than their compatriots about the West, began to think in terms of revolution. The rise of a revolutionary movement itself was in no way a surprising development. Dynastic changes by revolution had been common throughout Chinese history, and the Manchu emperors, being themselves of foreign origin, were particularly vulnerable to the rising spirit of nationalism that Western encroachments had inspired among the Chinese. A more remarkable fact was that the chief revolutionaries aspired, not to the founding of a new Chinese dynasty, but to the creation of a Western form of government. It is not at all strange, however, once they had decided to break with native political tradition, that they selected a republican democracy as the specific Western pattern of government they hoped to follow. In the early years of the twentieth century, when Great Britain and the United States were the Western powers that enjoyed the greatest prestige in the Far East, such a choice was entirely natural.

The revolutionary movement centering in Sun Yatsen sufficed to destroy the Manchu dynasty, and with its demise in 1912 traditional Chinese monarchy became the first major casualty of the Western impact on China. The revolutionaries, however, had much less success in substituting Western democracy for imperial bureaucratic rule. They appear to have assumed naïvely that a democratic republic could be created simply by public declaration and the adoption of a constitution. But this was scarcely the case. Only a handful of intellectuals in China were at all familiar with the basic concepts of democracy, while the vast bulk of the people had not the faintest idea what democracy was in theory or in practice. What was worse, most of them were illiterate and lacked the other means of access to information which we take for granted and without which a modern democratic system could scarcely operate. Even the simplest mechanical procedures of democracy, such as the holding of elections, could not have been put into effect under such conditions, and the fundamental purpose of a democratic system, which is the control of the government by the people as a whole, was altogether visionary.

It is not surprising that the so-called republican government of China soon became a farce. The dwindling authority of the central government was exercised by men who controlled military power in or near the national capital. Meanwhile most of the rest of China broke up into a number of personal domains ruled over by sometimes ignorant and usually unprincipled war lords. Some of these military rulers of republican China had been generals under the Manchu regime, and others were simply bandits in origin, but whatever their background, they showed not the slightest interest in democracy, much less any understanding of it.

The Republican Revolution, which was supposed to help modernize China and thus strengthen its defenses against Western encroachments, had instead resulted in the dismemberment of the empire and consequently had increased Chinese vulnerability to Western inroads. And China, instead of modernizing its political institutions, had in reality reverted to the age-old pattern of military division that traditionally followed the collapse of a dynasty. This was hardly a situation that could satisfy Sun Yat-sen or the increasing number of nationalistically aroused young Chinese. In their disillusionment they began to cast about for some more practical means of achieving a unified, modernized China capable of meeting the West on equal terms. Obviously something more than public declarations and constitutions was necessary.

Sun and his associates were quite naturally attracted by the success of the Communist revolutionaries in Russia who had been able not only to destroy the tsarist regime but also to create one of their own to take its place. Comintern agents sought out Sun in Canton, where he was attempting to regroup his revolutionary forces, and he asked them to help reorganize the Kuomintang, as his movement was now called. An alliance was made with the Chinese Communist Party, and Chinese Communists were permitted to join the Kuomintang while still retaining their original party affiliations. In the reorganized Kuomintang the organization of party cells and the whole hierarchic pattern of ascending levels of control were borrowed from the Communists. Major emphasis was put on creating a military arm of the movement, and Chiang Kai-shek, a young officer who had learned the principles of modern warfare in a Japanese military academy, soon rose to prominence as a leading Kuomintang general.

Sun long before had worked out a program that could now serve as the ideological basis for this new and decidedly more practical approach to Chinese problems. He felt that, as China was not yet ready for full democracy, there would have to be two preparatory phases before it could be achieved. First would come the military unification of China, and then would follow a tutelary stage in which an elite Kuomintang leadership would, by firm guidance, prepare the country for democracy. No one can miss the parallel between Sun's theory and the Communist concept of a supposedly temporary dictatorship of the proletariat which eventually would lead to complete democracy and the withering away of the state. It is equally clear as we look back at history that the new techniques of organization borrowed from communism made the Kuomintang of the 1920's a much more effective force than the naïve revolutionary movement of a decade earlier.

The first or military phase of Sun's program proved largely successful. The Kuomintang armies started northward in 1926, moving behind a spearhead of propaganda and infiltration, and soon took over the Yangtze Valley, the heart of the nation. While the extreme north and some other peripheral areas were never brought fully under Kuomintang rule, China had come closer to complete unity and effective central government than at any time since the collapse of the Manchu dynasty. But as the revolutionaries approached the completion of the first phase of conquest, the problems of the second stage of tutelary preparation for democracy began to arise.

Sun Yat-sen's death in 1925 removed the central figure from the Kuomintang. Furthermore, the revolutionary movement was not really unified but was simply a coalition between the Kuomintang and its Communist allies. Military campaigns can be fought successfully by coalition forces, but tutelage requires a unitary direction and a single set of guiding principles. It was probably inevitable that Chiang Kai-shek, representing the more conservative elements under the Kuomintang banner, should have broken with the Communists as soon as the Yangtze Valley was firmly in their joint grip. The coalition fell apart before the first phase of conquest was completed, and consequently the military unification of China was never fully achieved by the Kuomintang.

In the resulting struggle, Chiang had one definite advantage over the Communists. He could borrow from Communist doctrine only those techniques and concepts which proved useful, while the Communists were burdened with all the tenets of their faith, however unrealistic some of them were. For example, they tried to put into practice the theory of a proletarian dictatorship by attempting to seize power in the cities through the few industrial workers that China had. The result was not only the crushing of the incipient labor movement but also the complete disillusionment of most industrial workers with communism. They quite rightly felt that their own interests had been ruthlessly sacrificed on the altar of Communist ambition, and thereafter what few industrial workers there were in China paid little or no attention to the Communist movement, until the peasant armies of Mao eventually marched into the industrial cities.

The Communist movement collapsed almost completely under the weight of Chiang's superior military power and their own doctrinaire rigidity. In fact, communism might have virtually disappeared from China at this time if some of the younger Communist leaders had not been realistic enough to drop the hopeless effort to win power through a tiny city proletariat and shifted their efforts to the peasantry. This was heresy for a Communist at that time, but certainly made good political sense in China. Although Mao Tse-tung and the others who adopted the new approach managed to keep their movement alive only in out-of-the-way mountainous areas, they at least survived on Chinese soil, while their more orthodox Russian and Chinese colleagues had to flee to the Soviet Union.

Mao's heresy produced a curious situation in Chinese politics which has continued up to the present: the Western political faiths borrowed by the Chinese have survived as practical political movements only after important modifications of the original creeds. Those who had chosen the pattern of democracy survived only by adopting some of the non-democratic techniques and theories of communism, just as the Communists themselves survived only after reversing a major Communist doctrine. Of course many idealistic Chinese intellectuals remained true to the more orthodox concepts of Western democracy, but these men, though later dignified by the misleading title of "the third force," never exercised any political power and were usually the objects of persecution from both sides, carried out sporadically by the Kuomintang but thoroughly and ruthlessly by the Communists when their time came. There were also orthodox Chinese Communists, but they too remained entirely powerless until the triumph of Mao's tactical heresy enabled them to return to China on his coattails. Thus in China we find a particularly clear example of the inapplicability to Asia of Western political models until substantial accommodations have been made to local conditions.

The elimination of the Communists from the revolutionary coalition left Chiang effectively in control of most of China and enthusiastically supported by the majority of the nationally aroused citizens. The prospects looked rosy for the complete unification of the country and the creation not only of a respectably strong China but of conditions that would lead to the eventual inauguration of democratic government. But none of these goals was achieved. Chinese military power increased rapidly but not fast enough to repulse Japanese invaders; some peripheral zones were never brought fully under Chiang's government at Nanking; and the progress through tutelage toward democracy was more impressive on paper than in reality. While making a much better showing than the first republican government, the Kuomintang fell far short of its objectives.

There were probably two major reasons for the Kuomintang failure. An obvious one was Japanese aggression against China. The Japanese, moved in part by fear of what might happen if China did become fully united and strong, started in 1931 a limited war in which they seized Manchuria, the economically most promising part of China, and destroyed part of the city of Shanghai. Then after slower and somewhat more disguised encroachments in north China, they started what was meant to be a second limited war in 1937. But this time the Chinese refused to accept limited losses from a limited war. The fighting continued, and the Japanese kept seizing more and more of China in an effort to force the Chinese to capitulate. Chiang was driven out of all his principal industrial cities and chief areas of agricultural production and was forced back into the mountains of western and southern China. The economy of China was shattered and the Kuomintang regime completely disrupted. These protracted and devastating wars forced on the Chinese by Japan are in themselves certainly ample explanation of the failure of Chiang's regime to accomplish its aims.

There was, however, perhaps another and more fundamental reason for the failure of the Kuomintang. This was the very magnitude of the task it faced and the difficulty for any one group to achieve the whole of it. To the extent that the Kuomintang succeeded, it created a confirmed and privileged leadership that looked on further changes with growing mistrust and distaste. As the years went by, the Kuomintang increasingly came to represent the *status quo* and thus began itself to stand in the way of progress. This natural process seems to have been much accelerated by the wars with Japan, which forced the Kuomintang to rely on groups not in sympathy with its original objectives and to make many compromises of principle that might otherwise have been avoided. Under these conditions the natural slowing down of the Kuomintang movement turned into an open rout in the early postwar years, as corruption and inefficiency undermined the government from within and made it incapable of coping with mounting economic chaos.

In any case, whatever may have been the basic reasons for Kuomintang failure, there can be no doubt that Chiang's regime began to appear in Chinese eyes to be, not the wave of the future, but a wave of the past that was starting to recede. Increasing numbers of younger nationalistic Chinese gave up hope that the Kuomintang would build a strong China capable of winning equality with the West and started to cast about for some new way of achieving this goal, just as their elders had done two or three decades earlier. The disenchantment started with the intellectual classes, which had for long been attracted by Communist ideology, but it spread rapidly to other groups during the latter part of the war and the early postwar years.

The alternative to the Kuomintang that naturally came to the Chinese mind was communism, because the Communist approach now appeared much more promising than it had in the 1920's. For one thing, Mao had by trial and error perfected his heresy into an effective, operating system. He had learned to utilize land reform as a method of winning mass support in rural areas, and on the basis of this support he had built an efficient Communist regime in northwest China, consisting of an educated elite operating through an indoctrinated peasantry.

Mao and his generals had also developed a technique of guerrilla warfare which admirably fitted military conditions in China. The Japanese invaders had destroyed much of the city-based and more formally organized military power of the Kuomintang, but could not strike as effectively at the more elusive Communist guerrillas. The role of the Chinese Communists in resisting the Japanese has often been grossly exaggerated, but to most Chinese and particularly to those in Japanese-occupied areas it appeared that the Communist guerrillas, man for man, were accomplishing far more against the Japanese than were the larger Kuomintang armies, which had to fight pitched and therefore usually losing battles with the Japanese, often in areas quite remote from the centers of Chinese population. For this reason, too, many Chinese began to think of the Communists rather than the Kuomintang as the chief hope in China's attempt to achieve equality with the outside world.

And then finally, during the Second World War, the success of the Soviet Union in stopping and eventually rolling back Hitler's mighty war machine greatly enhanced the prestige of Communist Russia. To the Chinese of the 1940's the superiority of democracy was no ·longer something to be taken for granted, as it had been by their predecessors in the early years of the century. New generations of Chinese who had grown up since then as well as disillusioned older Chinese found no difficulty in shifting their allegiance from democracy to a new hope. In increasing numbers they embraced communism, not because it was intellectually convincing, but because their emotional response to profoundly unsatisfactory conditions in China made them anxious to believe that Mao's so-called New

Democracy provided a better means of achieving China's national objectives. Communism did not conquer Chinese minds; rather the Chinese seized upon communism as the most obvious and available panacea to replace political dreams that had faded with time.

This is not to say that the majority of the Chinese consciously chose the Communist side in preference to the Kuomintang. Many simply jumped on the Communist band wagon when they saw who was winning, and still more were only pawns. But a sufficient number did consciously choose the Communist side to tip the scales in that direction, and once the scales had started to tip, the imbalance became greater and greater. The Communists pushed forward with confidence that victory would be theirs; the Kuomintang soldiers fought with fast-diminishing enthusiasm, and growing numbers deserted to the enemy. It is conceivable that before the scales had tipped too far against the Kuomintang, the United States by wise and determined action might have had some influence on the outcome of the war in China, but a point was eventually reached at which American intervention aided the Communists more than the Kuomintang. American arms and supplies quickly found their way into Communist hands, and the presence of American planes and soldiers in China, instead of bolstering the Kuomintang, was used as an effective argument to discredit Chiang in Chinese eyes as the tool of "American imperialism."

This seems to be the essence of the tragic China story, and if it is indeed the correct interpretation, then we face a far more frightening situation than the one most alarmists point to. If the real reason for China's espousal of communism had been the traitorous conniving of a few Americans, then the prevention of similar disasters in the future would be relatively simple. Even if the main reason had been some subtle trickery on the part of the Russians, it should not prove difficult to devise countermeasures. But to combat what really seems to have happened in China is a much more complicated problem. The steps by which the Chinese came to communism are distressingly logical, given Chinese conditions, and practical alternatives are not easy to formulate, much less to put into effect.

Certainly anyone who believes in democratic equality cannot cavil at the original objectives of the Chinese. Nor do we have any magic formula by which we can make democracy work under conditions like those which existed in China. Tutelary preparation for democracy by those who understand for those who do not would seem to be inevitable. But once the concept of tutelage has been adopted, it is extremely difficult under Asian conditions to devise democratic methods of tutelage by persuasion that will prove as quickly effective as simple compulsion. And once a government has adopted the Communist formula of tutelage through ruthless force and thought-control, there may be no turning back. There is no reason to believe that the Chinese Communists will not follow the Russian precedent and lose sight of the original aims of the tutelary phase in their efforts to preserve their own rule.

What happened in China was certainly a uniquely Chinese story in its details, but in broad outline it takes on more general significance. The basic conditions that existed in China and led to the triumph of communism there are to be found in most of Asia—the same goals, the same inapplicability of democratic techniques of government, the same need for tutelage of the many by the few, the same impatience with the slowness of results in the drive to achieve equality. Only China so far has followed this particular historical line of development the whole way, but many other Asian countries appear to be in one or another of the stages through which China passed. It is improbable that the China story will repeat itself in specific detail in any other part of Asia, but one cannot but wonder whether the general stages of recent political developments in China and the final outcome will not prove typical for Asia as a whole.

Many people, and particularly Asian leaders themselves, would reject this possibility offhand. Some would claim that there is really little resemblance between conditions in China and the other countries, but such a position, unfortunately, is more the product of hope than of an objective study of realities. Others would raise the more valid objection that the sad outcome in China has little significance for the rest of Asia, since it was the result of a mistaken formulation of the political problems facing the Chinese. They would argue that the Chinese, by limiting the choice of political patterns to Western democracy and modern totalitarianism, forced upon themselves the disastrous choice of the latter, whereas the real alternative to communism should have been the development of some native political answer to China's problems.

This is a naturally attractive idea, but unfortunately there is little evidence to support it. It is true that both democratic and Communist ideas were changed to fit Chinese realities, but these were still Western theories modified to fit local conditions, not Chinese traditions modified to fit the new age. The Kuomintang in its later years did lean increasingly on Confucian ethics, but this compromise with the past, far from strengthening the Kuomintang, seems to have contributed to its downfall. It is unlikely that any Asian country will develop political patterns that exactly parallel those of any part of the West. There is sure to be a large traditional component influencing the pattern and making it unique in its details. But this does not alter the fact that all Asian lands, to the extent that they have become modernized, have adopted the fundamental political forms of the contemporary West.

As we have seen, political institutions, not only in China but throughout Asia, have been the first major casualties of the Western impact. Monarchy, which is the traditional political pattern of Asia as of most of Europe, has proved almost as defenseless in the face of modern technology there as in the Occident, where it has virtually disappeared. In any industrialized and modernized Asian country traditional aristocratic forms of government appear to be no more viable than in the contemporary West, and the basic political choice seems to be limited, as it so clearly is for us, to the freedoms and equality of democracy on the one hand or the common slavery of totalitarianism on the other.

No one can either prove or disprove this conclusion, but we have a great deal of evidence in support of it in recent political developments in the many Asian lands that are beginning to modernize. In this connection the experience of the Japanese over the past century is particularly illuminating. It is a very significant fact that the whole modern history of Japan, the most thoroughly industrialized country of Asia, suggests very clearly that the choice between democracy and totalitarianism facing the industrialized West is a choice that Asians too must make if they are to build industrialized societies.

Starting their period of rapid modernization well back in the nineteenth century, the Japanese felt no need to borrow the whole of any specific Western political system and, as time went on, became increasingly insistent that they were holding to a peculiarly Japanese policy. The farther the Japanese went in developing this supposedly unique system, however, the clearer it became that it had certain close parallels to both of the two conflicting Western political patterns, democracy and totalitarianism, and the more probable it seemed that one or the other of these Western patterns would win out completely. The Japanese, unlike the Chinese, refused to choose either pattern, but the greater their progress in industrialization, universal education, scientific knowledge, and the other more technical aspects of modern civilization, the weaker became native political traditions and the more inevitable the choice between either a full-fledged democratic system or a full-fledged totalitarian regime.

Until the past century Japanese political traditions had always been authoritarian and aristocratic. In their primitive days as a tribally divided people, the Japanese were ruled over by hereditary high priests and high priestesses. Subsequently the Chinese pattern of absolute monarchy was adopted, and this in time broke down into successive stages of divided feudal rule by hereditary military lords. True feudalism was in turn replaced by the unified Tokugawa regime, which lasted until the middle of the nineteenth century and was characterized by a curious mixture of strong feudal survivals and certain centralized political institutions quite distinct from real feudalism.

The group of young revolutionaries who took over the government from the Tokugawa in 1868 realized clearly that the old feudal disunity must go and some form of completely centralized government must take the place of the half-centralized, half-feudal Tokugawa system. They justified the change on the grounds that they were at last restoring the emperor to personal rule. They also found in the emperor an unparalleled personal symbol for national unity among a people still accustomed to personal bonds of feudal loyalty. For these reasons they naturally made the most of the convenient fiction that their own control of the nation was actually imperial rule. The government they created, however, was monarchic only in theory, and they faced the practical problem of developing new organs of government to replace those they had destroyed.

The chief objectives of the young revolutionaries were the same as those of the Chinese revolutionaries of more recent decades, and they too appeared willing to borrow whatever political institutions would best aid them in reaching these ends. Since the rapidly rising United States and all-powerful Britain both drew strength from democratic forms of government, the Japanese innovators showed a readiness to adopt these if they proved useful, and they actually experimented half-heartedly with bicameral legislatures and semi-representative bodies of one sort or another. Since, however, neither the government nor the people really understood the procedures, much less the philosophy, of democracy, these early experiments proved abortive and were soon dropped. Attempts to restore the institutions of the Chinese-type monarchy of ancient Japan proved equally meaningless. The Japanese leaders, however, were more successful in adopting individual aspects of the centralized nation-states of continental Europe. In the autocratic and aristocratic regimes of Germany and Austria in particular they found models that were more attractive and practical for nineteenth-century Japan than were those provided by the Western democracies or the ancient Japanese monarchy.

As a result of these various borrowings as well as of natural evolutionary development in Japan, a bureaucratic, authoritarian state had taken shape by the late 1880's. The civil government culminated in a Western-type cabinet and the military in the general-staff system of the Germans. The Japanese government as a whole, however, was not patterned on any particular Western state. It utilized techniques of centralized rule as developed by a variety of nineteenth-century Western nations, but at the same time it relied heavily on traditional Japanese attitudes of respect for all authority and of loyal devotion to the personal symbol of rule.

Moreover, the leading revolutionaries themselves had developed into a leadership that was quite distinct from anything to be found in their European models. While working through essentially Western political organs, they had become in essence a loosely organized but extraordinarily effective oligarchy, reminiscent of the committee-type governments and the passion for sharing responsibility which had characterized Japanese political leadership in the past. Individually the oligarchs were also a blend of the old and the new: they continued to be the aristocratic samurai of their birth, but at the same time were the bureaucrats and career generals of the modernized state they had created. The new Japanese government, thus, was a curious patchwork of piecemeal borrowings from the West and native political survivals, but it was amazingly successful and led Japan through the most difficult phase of its great transformation from an isolated and semi-feudal land into a modern world power.

The Meiji oligarchy might appear at first sight to be the peculiarly Japanese form of the native political systems that some people expect to win out in Asia, but it proved to be no more than a passing phase. The amalgam of old and new it represented was adequate for a period of transition but became progressively less practical as the new technology of the West became thoroughly entrenched in Japan. For one thing, the original oligarchy was unable to perpetuate itself under the conditions it had itself created. In fact, its last surviving members had drifted far apart even before the group disappeared entirely through death. Those who had specialized in military careers thought increasingly in terms of strict government controls over society not unlike those of modern totalitarianism. Those who had remained essentially civilians found themselves repeatedly and not always unwillingly compromising between their natural aristocratic tendencies and the growing demands for representative government.

This emerging dichotomy in Japanese politics was even clearer among the people as a whole. As larger and larger groups of Japanese began to feel the impact of the new technology and new ideas, they awoke from their traditional political apathy, but they did not all react in the same way. While most shared a declining respect for traditional authority and hereditary rights, some showed this by espousing democratic ideals and others by turning to totalitarian doctrines, which by then were beginning to take shape in Japan as well as in Europe.

The Meiji oligarchy was thus essentially a transitional stage bridging the huge gap between the almost purely aristocratic, hereditary rule of earlier days and the new age in which hereditary political power was to play little or no part. And even before the bridge had been fully crossed, it became apparent that two alternative and rapidly diverging paths led from its farther end into the new age of mass action. Some Japanese began to prepare themselves for a semi-democratic future, not fully realizing that this path would lead inevitably to an ever more completely democratic system; others prepared for the continuation of authoritarian rule but without the sanctions of hereditary authority, not realizing that this path led with equal certainty to the as yet not fully formulated totalitarianism of our twentieth-century world. Sometimes progress down these two diverging roads was made alternately, sometimes simultaneously, but in either case the political situation in Japan became year by year more contradictory and compromise between the two groups less possible.

Between 1881 and 1901 the first great strides toward democratic forms of government were made. The oligarchy, against the better judgment of some of its members, promised the people a constitution and a popularly elected parliament. The leaders were persuaded to do this because of popular demand and their own desire for Western approval, but they carefully designed the parliament to be an essentially powerless debating society. When this supposed safety valve for popular dissatisfaction proved to be more troublesome than had been expected, some of the oligarchs found themselves descending from their Olympian heights as unchallenged spokesmen for the emperor to the arena of popular politics. They were forced to seek the support of elected politicians, and some of them even formed political parties themselves in order to achieve their objectives. During these same years, however, others of the oligarchy were making the Japanese armed services independent of effective civilian control, since the civil government, they felt, was now contaminated by democratic institutions. Moreover, all the oligarchs joined in creating through the so-called Peace Preservation Laws legal means of suppressing popular political action whenever desired.

The triumph of the democratic powers in Europe over the autocracies in the First World War gave rise in the following decade to another great surge forward toward democratic government in Japan. In 1925 the suffrage was extended to all Japanese men; at times the cabinet fell under the full control of the Diet; and even the Japanese army seemed for a while subservient to the will of elected politicians. But at the same time the groundwork was being laid for the militaristic form of totalitarianism which was soon to engulf Japan. The Peace Preservation Laws were strengthened; the irrational doctrines of ultranationalism, race superiority, and blind obedience to a mystical concept of the imperial will went unchallenged; and efforts were made to put intellectual blinders on inquiring Japanese minds through the persecution of students and professors for alleged "dangerous thoughts."

Under the leadership of the oligarchy the ambivalence of Japanese political developments had remained beneath the surface, but the last of the oligarchs died in 1924, and by then the growing divergence of the two roads Japan was simultaneously following had stretched Japanese politics to the breaking-point. The oligarchs, however much they differed in personal views or temperament, had all been cut from the same old aristocratic pattern and consequently had been able to take turns at the helm of the ship of state to steer Japan delicately through an intricate course. But now Japan's rulers were either politicians, far from the old aristocratic traditions in their constant concern over ways of winning votes, or else equally unaristocratic professional soldiers, like Tojo, who knew how to rule only through a ruthless military machine. Such men were not united by any common background; they were schooled in entirely different techniques of leadership; they were looking down two different roads. The day of compromise was over. The farther some Japanese had gone toward democracy, the more violent had become the reaction of other Japanese against them. The upsurge of parliamentary government in the 1920's was followed by a sharp about-face in the 1930's as Japan rapidly shifted from incipient democracy to the now familiar pattern of the totalitarian police state.

Even today when the defeat of Japan's armies and the example of American power through democratic institutions has restored democracy to Japan in far greater strength than ever before, the other political alternative is always present in Japanese minds. And this alternative is not oligarchy or any other aristocratic form of government. If democracy again fails in Japan, the Japanese, we can rest assured, will switch to a totalitarian pattern, and this time a much more complete totalitarianism than they had even during the war years under Tojo. Many Japanese, thinking as most people do in terms of their own past experience, visualize the alternative as another semimilitary dictatorship, but obviously under present world conditions a much more probable alternative to democracy in Japan is the Communist variant of totalitarianism.

Unlike the successive waves of Chinese revolutionaries, the Japanese leaders never wholeheartedly embraced any specific foreign pattern; they clung tenaciously to the hope that they could create a uniquely Japanese system of government. During the course of the last half-century, however, it has become increasingly clear that Japan must be essentially a democracy or else a thoroughly totalitarian regime. With each decade any other system or any compromise between these two has become less possible. Thus the Japanese, though trying to avoid the choice between the two basic political patterns of the industrialized West, have found themselves facing this choice just the same.

The development of this political polarization between democratic and totalitarian possibilities in Japan as it modernized itself is perhaps not surprising, for it is characteristic of all the more advanced parts of the West, where, with the fading of traditional hereditary authority, nations have moved either toward an ever fuller democracy or toward totalitarianism at the other end of the political spectrum, while a few less stable lands have fluctuated wildly between the two extremes in the same way as Japan. In fact, the political polarization between democracy and totalitarianism seems to be inherent in the very process of technological modernization.

Modern technology from the start has shown two contrasting, even contradictory, tendencies. On the one hand it has brought with it a rapid centralization throughout society—a marked and steady increase in the unit of economic production and organization, and an equally rapid rise in the possibilities and also the necessity for strong centralized political controls over vast numbers of men. It has, in other words, tended to increase the power of the few in control over the many who must follow. On the other hand, the new technology has required a huge expansion of educational facilities and a rapid rise in individual skills and knowledge. As a result there has been a tremendous increase in the proportion of people capable of effective leadership and still more of those who know enough to question authority and to wish to participate in political control. From this has come in turn a great emancipation of the individual from the restraints of the older societies—an increase in social mobility, a leveling of class differences, and at least in some parts of the world a far greater participation by the general public in political control over the machinery of government. Modern technology thus has at one and the same time increased the powers of those in control and undermined the basis for traditional authoritarian rule.

In the face of this situation the old traditional autocracies have faltered and collapsed. Either they had to bow before the rising knowledge and capabilities of their peoples and give way to increasingly effective democratic controls by the people as a whole over the expanding powers of government; or, if elite rule were to be maintained, then those in power had to devise means of controlling much more fully than ever before not only the actions but also the knowledge and thinking of those they ruled. In other words, they had to move from traditional absolutism, resting largely on the passive acceptance of authority by the ignorant masses, to modern totalitarianism, based on the familiar police-state techniques for assuring submissiveness from the no longer ignorant or naturally passive masses.

All advanced modern nations show to some degree these two contradictory tendencies of the new technology, but never in equal proportion. In the totalitarian states, as in the democracies, we find the opening up of careers to all, the leveling of social differences, and in theory at least an emphasis on the sovereign rights of the people. But centralized control has far overshadowed these factors and has therefore transformed the new freedom into the equal slavery of the masses to the state. In the democracies we find much of the steady increase of government interference in the various aspects of the lives of their citizens that we associate with totalitarianism, but this tendency has been completely overshadowed by the growing participation of all the people in effective control over the government. For instance, we are today witnessing a further extension of popular controls in the United States as our leaders, who at one time were for all practical purposes answerable to the people only at periodic elections, now find it necessary to answer to the public and plead with it almost daily through press interviews and radio and television appearances.

The two conflicting tendencies of the new age are to be found in all of the technologically more advanced nations of the world, but in none of them do we find an equal blending of the two, for apparently either the one or the other must be completely dominant. In other words, there appears to be no middle ground between them. There are, of course, many different combinations of traditional authoritarianism, partial democracy, and totalitarian trends to be found in countries that are not yet thoroughly industrialized or modernized, but it would seem that to the degree a nation becomes fully modernized in its technology these combinations of contrasting political systems become unstable and cannot be maintained. Once thoroughly modernized, a nation apparently must become overwhelmingly democratic or else it will become hopelessly totalitarian. If this situation is essentially the product of the new technology itself, there is no reason why it should not come to be as true of Asia as a whole as it already is of Japan and much of the West.

Viewed in this light, the experience of the Chinese and Japanese in recent decades takes on broader significance. They are the two Asian peoples who at least for the moment seem farthest along the two diverging roads, and the methods by which they chose them illustrate the two possible extremes in approaching the choice. The Chinese rushed to make the choice long before technological advances had made it necessary, and the lack of a sound technological basis for democracy perhaps forced their ultimate selection of totalitarianism. The Japanese avoided and even ignored the choice until the growing rift in the body politic became too wide to be bridged by even their genius for compromise, and perhaps because they had delayed their decision so long they found that technological advances, such as universal education, had made democracy a more practical alternative to totalitarianism than it was in China. But the choice in both countries was between the same two possibilities, and it is this same choice that sooner or later will probably face all the peoples of Asia. Democracy and totalitarianism may be the only possible political systems for modernized nations in Asia as much as in the West. Though to most Asians these two political systems may appear to be merely optional means to already determined ends, it seems altogether possible that the choice Asians make between them will determine the whole future of Asia and perhaps of the world.

9. *Communism and Democracy*

No one would deny the importance of the choice Asians make between democratic and totalitarian forms of political organization, but some may feel that this choice has already been made in most parts of Asia. After all, India, Indonesia, Burma, Pakistan, and many other Asian countries have already chosen democracy. The recent history of China and Japan, however, shows that such choices are not necessarily made for all time. Both the Chinese and the Japanese have changed their minds repeatedly about the specific political organization they wanted, and there is no reason to believe that other Asian peoples will not change their minds too.

Of course, a point of no return is eventually reached. As we all know, a successful totalitarian regime establishes such a strangle hold on its people that nothing but external force seems able to dislodge it. It is not always realized that a successful democracy is equally unshakable, for its hold on the hearts of its people is stronger than any shackles forged by the rulers of the slave states. Certainly the democracies of Great Britain, the United States, and several other lands of the West are as impervious to totalitarian attack from within as the Soviet Union is to democratic revolution. But no Asian regime, whether democratic, totalitarian, or something else, is fully successful today. The Chinese Communists have hardly started to face their real problems. Japanese democracy rests precariously on an extremely shaky economic foundation. And the other lands of Asia are even less definitely committed to any particular political pattern. Their governments are no more than political experiments that are still to be judged. We cannot take for granted that even the Chinese and the Japanese have made their final choice, and it would be entirely unjustified to assume that most of the other peoples of Asia have done anything more than express a provisional and perhaps quite temporary preference.

Among the factors that may shape the choice between democracy and totalitarianism in Asia, one stands out very sharply. The Chinese pattern of conscious choice is far more typical today than the Japanese pattern of ignoring the choice until it could no longer be avoided. In a sense this is unfortunate, for it can be argued that if the decision were delayed until after further technological advances have been made in Asia, democracy would have a much greater chance of working successfully there than it has at present. But this is idle speculation. Throughout Asia today there is a far greater consciousness of the choice between democracy and totalitarianism than existed in nineteenth-century Japan or, for that matter, in any part of the world at that time. Here we see not a difference between the Japanese and other Asians so much as a difference between the nineteenth and twentieth centuries throughout the world. The clock cannot be turned back, and we must assume that most Asians will continue to attempt to make the choice between democracy and totalitarianism before they are technologically ready to carry out either system fully.

A more encouraging factor is that throughout Asia democracy has a far greater theoretical appeal than totalitarianism. There are areas like the Arabian peninsula where traditional concepts have felt little challenge from either of these modern political systems, and in all lands there are masses of people who have not yet been awakened from their age-old political apathy, but in so far as Asian populations have responded to the new age, they have turned with enthusiasm toward democratic ideals of human equality and freedom.

This may seem surprising, since most Asians do not

have the classic experience in limited democracy of the ancient Mediterranean world, nor do they have the strong Christian concepts of individual equality which we associate with the rise of modern political democracy in the West. But the popularity of democratic ideals is perfectly understandable. Few people sufficiently sophisticated to think in terms of political choice would consciously espouse the slave equality of totalitarianism in preference to the democratic ideals of equality in freedom. This is why the Communists have found it necessary to attempt to disguise the Kremlin's tyranny as the benevolent dictatorship of the proletariat, working toward a Utopian state of complete individual freedom for all. Even the fascistic variation of totalitarianism in Germany and Japan utilized mystical concepts of equal participation by the whole national group in what was in fact the ruthless exploitation of the many by the few. And in both the Communist and Fascist forms of totalitarianism the rulers have found it expedient to placate the masses with some of the outward trappings of democracy in rubber-stamp parliaments and single-list or *"Ja"* elections. It is only human nature to prefer freedom to slavery, and this is as true in Asia as it is in the West. It is therefore entirely natural that wherever in Asia colonial rule or internal revolution have broken the political links with the past, the peoples have turned first to democracy rather than to totalitarianism for their new political pattern.

We of the free world can be profoundly thankful that in much of Asia and particularly in the huge and densely populated zone from Pakistan eastward to the Philippines the choice has gone to democracy. We should not forget, however, that the Chinese too, when they first broke politically with the past, chose republican democracy but found in it only the first step of a seemingly natural progression toward communism. Might not the same happen

in India and these other new Asian democracies of today?
This is the biggest question we face in our appraisal of
the situation in Asia.

Many Asians would probably be outraged by the
question, since there are certain very obvious differences
between China in 1912 and the newly established democracies in contemporary Asia. One is that much has
happened throughout the world in the intervening four
decades, and as a result the Asians who recently chose democracy did so with very much less naïveté than did the
Chinese revolutionaries who overthrew the Manchu dynasty. Men like Nehru have a far deeper understanding of
the principles of democracy and a much greater practical
acquaintance with its techniques of operation than Sun
Yat-sen and his associates had. In the Philippines and the
former British colonial possessions in particular, the past
several decades have been a period of clear and conscious
tutelage for democracy. Through education and still more
significantly through practical experience with the legal
bulwarks of individual freedom as well as the representative institutions of democracy and sometimes even its electoral procedures, the peoples of these lands have acquired
an incomparably sounder knowledge of the theory and
practice of the political pattern they have adopted than
the early Chinese republicans possessed.

While the Chinese Republic hardly got beyond the
drafting tables before it disintegrated into complete futil-
ity and sham, the new democracies of Asia have been functioning with considerable success for several years. They
apparently are well beyond the Chinese problems of 1912.
But they are still far from having established successful
democratic governments that can meet the multitudinous
problems of the modern world over a prolonged period of
time. Their accomplishments to date are extremely gratifying, but there is no reason to relax into easy optimism or

to conceal from ourselves the long and hazardous road that lies ahead of them.

A major reason for the relative success of the new democracies of Asia has unquestionably been the running start they received from the colonial regimes that they replaced. This was particularly true in India, Pakistan, and Ceylon, where there had been no interregnum of Japanese conquest, and in the Philippines, where, despite Japanese rule, the Filipinos readily agreed to a gradual and planned transfer of authority from the United States to an independent Philippine government. In these countries the colonial regimes had built up legal institutions and civil bureaucracies of a type suited to democracy. In other words, some of the elements of a democratic system were already in being, and the problem was merely to keep these going and to add to them the other necessary features of democracy. This was a very different situation from that in China in 1912, where there were no elements of democracy in operation and all that the revolutionaries had to start with were the largely unsuitable and, in any case, collapsing institutions of the old empire.

The importance of this running start can be seen in the less happy experience of the Burmese and the Indonesians, who began without it. Japanese conquest in Burma made necessary a precipitate transfer of authority from the British to the new independent regime at a time when the country was still politically and economically disrupted. As a result, the Burmese government has not yet been able to assert its authority fully over the whole area it is supposed to control, and the general political situation remains somewhat precarious. In Indonesia the less advanced state of legal and administrative institutions developed by the Dutch, the Japanese conquest of the entire area during the war, Dutch reluctance to grant immediate independence to the Indonesians, and the resultant civil war and administrative disruption of the country all militated against the success of the new regime. Consequently it has not yet been able to bring the whole of its vast domain under effective control or to stamp out military revolts of one sort or another, and Indonesia has lagged behind India and some other Asian countries in developing the mechanisms of democratic government.

Another advantage of some of the new Asian democracies was the established native political leadership that they inherited from colonial days. For example, India, at the time it won its independence, already had a relatively old and tried group of leaders. These men were thoroughly versed in the theories and procedures of democracy and, through their long and well-publicized fight for independence, had won general recognition both at home and abroad as India's rightful leaders. In Burma and Indonesia the new leaders were much younger, less experienced, and less well known. This may be one of the reasons for the relative weakness of the regimes in these lands, though even here the leadership antedated the creation of the new democratic governments.

Countries that have recently regained their independence and are just beginning to introduce democratic forms of government have naturally had no time to develop a leadership through democratic procedures. The older leaders of India and some other countries, as well as the younger leaders of Burma and Indonesia, are not men who have achieved positions of authority because they have been selected for this purpose by their compatriots. They are men who gained general prestige because of their revolutionary activities and won power as largely self-appointed leaders of revolutionary groups. In Indonesia the leadership at the end of 1954 had still not been put to the test of national elections of any sort. In a more politically advanced country like India, the self-appointed leaders have had their positions confirmed by elections. This is certainly all that could be expected in so short a time. However, the confirmation through electoral processes of the authority of men like Nehru and his colleagues in the Congress Party who had already won recognition as India's leaders long before national elections were held, is a very different matter from choosing between rival would-be leaders, none of whom has overwhelming prestige because of past leadership. The Filipinos met a situation of this sort in the autumn of 1953 and by electing Magsaysay through orderly, democratic procedures showed themselves capable of surmounting this hurdle. Such a choice, however, is yet to face the peoples of the other new democracies of Asia.

Still another reason for the relatively good start of the new democratic regimes was the high degree of unity of purpose and attitudes which they inherited from the preceding colonial period. Western imperialism had unified the peoples of these nations in one overriding ambition, the restoration of independence, and the long fight for freedom had drawn the political leadership together in close camaraderie. This unity was not so much an agreement on positive programs for the future as a negative reaction against colonialism. With independence already achieved and colonialism fast receding into the past, this primary unifying force will most certainly weaken. For the original revolutionary leaders who themselves achieved independence, it may continue to be a firm enough basis for co-operation, and it will probably remain a strong emotional factor in the dealings of these nations with the West, but in domestic politics the once all-absorbing goal of national independence is likely to become overshadowed in time by newer and more controversial problems. The democracies of Asia have yet to prove that they can hold together and solve their problems by democratic means when the old leaders are gone and independence is so taken for granted that it alone is no longer an adequate basis for political unity.

There is perhaps some analogy with the situation in Meiji Japan, despite the great and obvious difference in time and political climate. The young men who seized the government during the period of political transition in Japan soon had won such power and prestige that their leadership was never successfully challenged. And during their period of rule, all politically conscious Japanese were unified by the continuing effort to achieve legal equality with the West. Since the leaders were young men when they came to power and the fight to get rid of the unequal treaties with the West was not fully won until the early years of the twentieth century, this phase of established leadership and unified purpose in Japan lasted from the early 1870's until the First World War. But with the achievement of full equality with the West and the disappearance of the original revolutionary leadership, Japanese political unity rapidly disintegrated. There was no longer any agreement over internal political structure, economic policies, or foreign relations. There was even less agreement over leadership itself. At this point it became necessary for the Japanese either to develop an effective method of choosing their leaders through popular democratic procedures or else to decide such matters through a cruder interplay of brute force.

In India and some of the other new democracies the leadership is very old compared with that of early Meiji Japan, and for all of them the fight for full independence has been won suddenly and dramatically. The unity of leadership and purpose carried over from colonial days, therefore, is likely to disappear much more rapidly. It may not be many years before India and these other lands will be forced to put their still novel and in some cases completely untried popular electoral procedures to the acid test of deciding between conflicting national policies and between rival leaders of approximately equal prestige and power.

We often take for granted the possibility of referring such crucial problems to the general public for ultimate decision, without realizing how relatively new and restricted this procedure is in the world. Equal franchise for all adults goes back only a little over three decades anywhere, and equal franchise for all adult men not much over a century. Even in our country this fundamental procedure of democracy broke down into a disastrous civil war less than a century ago, and in many parts of the West it has never been successfully applied when critical differences of opinion arose within a country.

We cannot simply take it for granted that Asian democracies will find it feasible to leave the ultimate decision to the general public when major divisions of opinion and rivalries for leadership arise, as they certainly will within a decade or two. The new Asian democracies are striving to create the electoral procedures and the informed public necessary for the successful operation of such a system, but none, with the possible exceptions of the Philippines and Turkey, has as yet shown itself capable of carrying out such a system. In this sense, they might best be thought of as countries trying to develop democratic systems of government rather than countries that have already done so.

Unfortunately there are greater obstacles in the path of democracy in Asia than in the West. In fact, the hazards appear considerably worse than in even those countries of the West that have not been able to create effective democratic governments themselves. Perhaps the most serious obstacle is the general economic situation. Some historians have argued that without the rapid rise of living standards in recent times in the West, modern democracy could never have developed. Some go so far as to attribute the rise of modern democracy specifically to the economic well-being and increased individual freedom which resulted from the expanding geographic frontiers of the West. Asia, however, has few expanding frontiers, and, as we have seen, there is little likelihood of much economic advance for the masses, at least in the more heavily populated countries. Living standards in Asia are incomparably lower than living standards in the successful democracies of the West and show little promise of rising appreciably in the foreseeable future.

While it may be true that modern democracy could not have developed initially without a tremendous advance in living standards, such as occurred in the modern West, this does not mean that once the pattern of modern democracy has been developed, it cannot be borrowed by peoples who have not themselves undergone a similar economic process. One could point to a comparable situation in the economic field. The initial development of industrialized economies undoubtedly depended on the prior development of many political, sociological, ideological, and economic factors in Europe, but once this modern industrial pattern had been established, Asian peoples proved themselves capable of borrowing it without passing through all the preparatory phases themselves.

Japan is a good case in point for both industrialization and democracy. The Japanese apparently were beginning to pass through a few of the early preparatory phases that the West experienced on its way to industrialization, but when they became aware of the more advanced Western pattern, they found it possible to skip the rest of the preparatory process entirely and to go immediately into full industrialization. The Japanese have also gone a long way toward the creation of a successful democratic system without the benefit of any native democratic traditions, without much aid from expanding frontiers, and without achieving living standards at all comparable to those of the Western democracies.

The Japanese, however, did not make this progress toward democracy while living at economic levels like those found in the south Asian democracies or in most of the other lands of Asia. Japan for at least the past century has had a considerably higher standard of living than most other Eastern countries. The economic gap between Japan and the West is of course much larger, but the gap between Japan and most of the rest of Asia might represent the crucial difference between a minimal and a wholly inadequate economic foundation for democracy. To close even this gap will take Herculean efforts on the part of the new Asian democracies, and even if this is accomplished, it may not be enough, for there is still considerable doubt whether the Japanese themselves are far enough above this hypothetical economic line to maintain their democracy through the successive crises that plague all modern nations.

Some may feel that there is no such thing as a minimal economic basis for democracy, and indeed there may be no minimal economic level that is equally valid for all societies. There unquestionably has been a high correlation, however, between successful democracies and high standards of living. A modern democracy by its very nature depends on a certain degree of informed interest on the part of a fairly large proportion of its population. No one can define exactly what proportion of the people must show what degree of informed interest, but obviously if most of the people of a nation are so near the starvation level that their chief concern must always be their next meal, one cannot expect them to have an adequate degree of informed interest in the complicated problems of national policy and leadership to serve as the court of last appeal in all controversial matters. Beyond this, it seems doubtful that even a well-fed people could form the basis of a democracy if the great majority of them were illiterate and lacked substitute means of obtaining diverse information on controversial problems. Countries like Germany, Italy, Spain, and Argentina, to say nothing of Russia itself, show that democracy may not work in nations which enjoy very high educational and living standards compared with those of Asia, but we have no historical precedents which would indicate that democracy can work in a country too poor to provide its people with a subsistence diet and fairly widespread educational opportunities.

For the past several decades the Japanese, though desperately poor by our standards, have for the most part been able to look beyond the next meal and have enjoyed universal elementary education as well as a great deal of secondary and higher education. Some of the other peoples of Asia, however, cannot meet even the first test of an adequate food supply, and few can meet the second of adequate educational facilities. The Formosans are not far behind the Japanese in education; the Filipinos, Koreans, and Ceylonese appear to be well on the way toward general literacy; Turkish literacy rates have risen sharply, and those of China, though not definitely known, seem to have improved somewhat in recent decades. But in most of southern, southeastern, and western Asia the percentage of literacy is still extremely low, even though the systems of writing are much more easily mastered than those of China and Japan. In a key country like India the literacy rate is said to be 18 per cent of the adult population; in Indonesia it may be no more than 10 per cent; and it shades off almost to the vanishing-point in countries like Afghanistan and Saudi Arabia.

Although the establishment of a system of universal elementary education may be necessary before a nation can maintain a democratic form of government, it is no easy task for the new Asian democracies to provide even elementary education for all their children. To build the necessary school buildings and to train the necessary teachers would put a heavy drain on their meager resources of money and skills. Unless they win the grim economic race with rising populations, any great increase in educational facilities may be out of the question. And even under the best of circumstances they will be sore put to it to build up their educational facilities rapidly enough to produce an interested and adequately informed public in time to solve by democratic means the clashes on fundamental policy and leadership that inevitably will arise in the not too distant future.

One might ask if the Asian democracies are not attempting the impossible. Or, to put it in terms that Nehru himself likes to use, are they not attempting to run before they have learned to walk? Nowhere in the world has any national group ever been able to pass in one great leap from a non-democratic system of government to a fully developed modern democracy. In the West democratic institutions grew slowly and electorates usually were expanded no faster than educational facilities. Never was a largely illiterate people asked to serve as the interested and informed public on which democracy ultimately depends. Even in Japan, despite all its forced, hothouse growth, it took more than three and a half decades for the electorate to grow from a select few to the whole adult male population. The new Asian democracies might have more hope of succeeding in their great experiment if they were initially a little less ambitious and were willing to limit the franchise to those most capable of using it intelligently.

Such a gradual approach to full democracy, however, though eminently logical, would most certainly not be practical. No Asian people in responding to the challenge of the twentieth-century West is going to be satisfied with eighteenth- or nineteenth-century ways of doing things. It may be unfortunate that in Asia the concept of political equality has gone so far ahead of the technological advances that make it a practical political ideal, but this nevertheless is the situation. The countries of Asia that have consciously posed the choice between democracy and totalitarianism by seeking to adopt the former are forced to achieve democracy in one prodigious leap or else they are not likely to achieve it at all, at least in our time.

The size of most of the Asian democracies also makes their ultimate success more dubious. It is obvious that democracy works most easily in small homogeneous groups. We Americans certainly should be aware of the great difficulties that sectionalism and cultural diversity raise in even our relatively uniform society. With the exception of ourselves, all the larger national groups that have chosen democracy are to be found in Asia. India has more than double the population of the United States; Japan, Pakistan, and Indonesia all have close to twice the population of countries like the United Kingdom and France and are five to ten times as big as most of the other Western democracies.

A democracy inevitably depends on a strong feeling of unity among the people participating in it. With the exception of Switzerland, Belgium, the Union of South Africa, and Canada, four countries of relatively small population, the successful democracies of the West have all had a single national language and usually the homogeneity of culture that a common language implies. The new democracies of Asia, on the other hand, are without exception made up of two or more linguistic groups, and in most of them there is far less cultural unity than is to be found even in a huge geographic unit like the United States, to say nothing of tight little democracies like Sweden, New Zealand, and the United Kingdom.

The problems of cultural diversity are least pressing in Ceylon, the smallest of the new democracies of Asia. About three fourths of the population consists of Sinhalese-speaking Buddhists. There is a large Hindu minority, however, consisting of an old Tamil-speaking population and more recent Indian immigrants, and in addition there are several other smaller ethnic groups.

In the Philippines there are strong cultural contrasts between the Catholic majority and the minority groups composed of Mohammedan Moros and various primitive mountain tribes. A still more serious problem is the welter of languages which has forced the continuation of English as the true lingua franca of the republic.

In Burma we find the Buddhist Burmese themselves almost surrounded by a ring of peoples like the Christian Karens, the Shans, and the Kachins, who feel themselves to be quite distinct from their Burmese compatriots and often have much closer linguistic and cultural affinities with groups beyond Burma's borders. In addition there are large Indian and Chinese minorities whose chief loyalties lie outside of Burma.

In Indonesia we again find a number of different tongues, from which the government is attempting to fashion a new national language. There are also strong regional differences because of the huge and far-flung area that compromises the republic. A tremendous cultural gap exists between the primitive pagan tribesmen of Borneo and the solidly Moslem inhabitants of Java and Sumatra. A much more dangerous cleavage exists between the latter and the linguistically and culturally distinct peoples of the eastern islands, who in some cases find Christianity a further barrier between themselves and the Moslem majority. In addition there is a wealthy and powerful class of Chinese merchants throughout the islands who are by no means exclusively loyal to Indonesia.

In Pakistan we find a Hindu minority in East Pakistan, and there are Baluchi- and Pushtu-speaking minorities on the borders of West Pakistan, whose ethnic affiliations are with similar groups across the frontiers in Iran and Afghanistan. A much more serious division, however, is to be found between the majority groups of the two halves into which Pakistan is divided. These two groups not only speak different languages, Urdu and Bengali; they live under extremely different geographic and climatic conditions; they show great differences in temperament, habits of life, and traditions; and, above all, they live separated from each other by a thousand miles of alien territory. No political regime, democratic or otherwise, has ever succeeded in holding together for long such disparate and far separated elements.

In India the language problem is at its worst. There are no less than eleven major languages, each spoken by upwards of ten million people, and scores of minor tongues. The various languages of India do not even belong to the same general type, for those of the south are not part of the Indo-European family to which those of the north belong. While the people of India are overwhelmingly Hindu, there is a large Moslem minority and considerable numbers of people adhering to other religious communities. Even within the Hindu majority there are great cultural variations over the huge and diverse terrain of India. Moreover, Hinduism, the chief unifying force of India today, is based on a social pattern that can hardly persist unchanged if democracy does win out in India. The caste system is almost the antithesis of the democratic concept of individual equality, and it seems probable that it will crumble to the extent that democracy succeeds. If the caste basis of Hinduism disintegrates, however, one wonders how effective Hinduism will continue to be as a unifying force in the face of the growing significance of linguistic divisions. We have already seen state borders redrawn on linguistic lines in some parts of India. It takes no great insight to perceive that Indian democracy will find at best a narrow passage between a Scylla of caste barriers and a Charybdis of linguistic divisions.

One cannot be dogmatic about the ultimate fate of the new Asian democracies, but one should remember that, though there are significant divisions within some of the Western democracies, none has been forced to face the many and deep cleavages that split up the populations of these Asian countries. It may not be mere accident that in Japan, where democratic institutions have progressed farthest in Asia, the national unit was also an extraordinarily homogeneous cultural and linguistic unit. We need not go to the extreme of categorical predictions of catastrophe for the new Asian democracies, but their profound internal divisions are another factor cautioning us against unthinking optimism.

One other major difficulty facing the new democratic governments of Asia is that they not only must succeed in themselves, but must also succeed in achieving certain other national goals before they will be adjudged satisfactory. The peoples of the new democracies have set out to win full equality with the West, and to do this they plan to modernize and industrialize their economies. Unless their governments are able to make visibly rapid progress in this direction, the people may repudiate them in much the same way that the Chinese shifted their allegiance and hopes from the Kuomintang to the Communists. The Kuomintang showed itself capable of ruling China, and under its leadership the Chinese people turned the corner from supine submission to partially successful resistance against foreign military and economic pressures, but it fell short of what the people believed that the Communist alternative would be able to do. The new Asian democracies, too, will unquestionably be judged by their people not simply against zero but against the hypothetical and therefore perhaps unreasonably high possibilities of this alternative.

Democracy in Asia is being put to a test that it did not have to face in its formative years in the West. It must prove that it can accomplish more in the economic field and in bettering the international status of a nation than a totalitarian regime could. The great political question in Asia, therefore, is not just whether democracy can survive there at all, but whether under Asian conditions it can prove itself as practical a system of political organization as totalitarianism and as capable of producing the desired economic changes. The answer to this question, we must admit, is at best highly dubious.

The totalitarian alternative to democracy in Asia to-day is communism. With the complete downfall of Hitler, Mussolini, and the Japanese militarists still fresh in men's memories and the rapid rise of Soviet power so evident, few Asians are likely to turn under present circumstances to the Fascist variant of totalitarianism, when communism can point to so much more promising a record. But whatever the specific name or form totalitarianism takes, it, too, naturally faces many great difficulties in Asia. It must measure up against democracy, which at least as a theory appeals much more readily to Asians, as it does to all other people. It must deal with the same grave economic problems that make the future of democracy so doubtful; and it, too, must achieve great results if it is to satisfy the peoples of Asia.

In most other respects, however, totalitarianism enjoys tremendous advantages over democracy as a practical system of political organization in Asia. For one thing, the supposedly benign dictatorship of communism forms in some respects an almost perfect continuity of tradition with the supposedly benign autocracies of Asia's past, just as it does with the self-righteous despotism of the tsars in Russia. This continuity of spirit may be particularly true of China, where the transition from the bureaucratic authoritarianism of the old empire to communism was in some ways no step at all. But there is no part of Asia in which democratic methods of organization and control do not represent a far greater and more difficult break with past political practices than does Communist dictatorship.

Communism not only fits in with Asian political traditions; it also fits easily into the existing social situation in much of Asia. Where democracy presupposes a basic equality throughout society, communism or any other totalitarian system is based on the control of the many by the few; in other words, on an elite. And this is exactly what most Asian lands have—a mass of peasants and other ignorant, illiterate, and politically apathetic people on the one hand and an elite of leadership on the other. The elite may be largely one of education, as in China, or of wealth and hereditary prestige as in some other parts of Asia, but in most cases there is a sharp line between those who feel it their right and duty to lead and the others, who have always assumed that they must follow.

Most educated Asians simply take it for granted that they should be and will be leaders. Where we tend to think of political choices in terms of how we individually might fare under different forms of government, the educated Asian assumes with considerable justification that he will be one of the leaders regardless of the system of government adopted. This alone may explain why communism is sometimes more palatable to them than to us. And, as we have seen, the impact of the West has in numerous instances sharpened the dividing line between the many and the few, for new knowledge and skills from the West have set the elite even farther apart from their humble compatriots. The elite leadership that communism presupposes exists in most of Asia; the equality on which democracy depends is still to be developed.

Communism not only fits the social realities of Asia; it also in some ways fits the present political needs. Undoubtedly tutelage of some sort is necessary for the masses in most Asian lands if they are to achieve many of the things they hope to accomplish. But democracy is based on self-improvement, not tutelage. Can a democratic government engage in tutelage without turning information into propaganda and reversing the original meaning of popular political control? Communism faces no such dilemma. It is designed for tutelage through heavy-handed compulsion. The transformation we have already witnessed in China of tutelage in behalf of a would-be democracy into the self-perpetuating slavery of communism may be a natural, even inevitable, progression. There is nothing uniquely Chinese about it. This pattern could recur almost anywhere in Asia.

Another factor that may be favorable to communism in Asia is the great concentration of power and prestige in the hands of the governments. While democracy evolved in the West and even to some extent in Japan as a means of balancing conflicting private interests, private interests are notably weak in most Asian lands. Business enterprises are small and divided, and private entrepreneurial activity extremely feeble. This situation is in part the result of the whole nationalistic response of Asia to the West, for the peoples of Asia face a situation in which they must take action on a national scale if modernization and industrialization are to be achieved. Another reason has been the popular and by no means entirely erroneous interpretation of Western imperialism as the product of Western capitalism. Capitalism is associated in Asian minds with colonialism and the unequal treaties of the past. For many Asians this association alone is adequate proof of the undesirability of capitalism and the corollary superiority of socialism.

The most important reason for the relative weakness of private interests in Asia, however, is the long tradition in many Asian cultures of disrespect for commercial activities. Public service has always seemed a much higher ideal than personal financial gain. As a result, official position has usually carried more prestige than it does in the West and has been offset by none of the half-amused disrespect for political leaders that is so strong a tradition with us and has no doubt contributed to the democratic limitations of government power. Few ambitious young Asians, outside of Japan, think in terms of careers in private enterprise. Government is the natural path to prestige and power. Cabinet position or perhaps the headship of some government monopoly is a much more natural and also realistic goal for an ambitious young man than the presidency of some private corporation. For all these various reasons, power and leadership in most Asian lands are much more fully concentrated in government hands than in our country, and behind this actual situation there exists a strong prejudice against private enterprise and an equally strong penchant for socialism as an economic ideal.

Socialism and communism are, of course, not to be identified. Many of the staunchest democracies of the West are supposedly socialistic in their economic theories. But in all these lands democracy was well established long before socialism was embarked upon, and in any case the socialist democracies have all stopped far short of complete socialism, usually leveling off in a delicate balance between government controls and private enterprise that is not very different from the delicate balance between private enterprise and government controls which is to be found in the supposedly capitalistic democracies. The democratic socialism of the West is a very different thing from complete government initiative in all economic development in a land that has yet to create viable democratic institutions. With so many other factors favoring communism in Asia, it is possible that the heavy concentration of economic initiative and control in government hands may contribute to the development of governments in which everything is controlled from the top downward, and control from the people upward becomes merely an empty theory.

Another factor favoring communism in Asia is the very nature of the economic problem most Asian nations face. We are well aware of the great economic disadvantages of a fully controlled economy as opposed to one that has left wide room for private enterprise, but in Asia these disadvantages may seem much less real or important than the obvious advantages of communism in squeezing needed capital out of an impoverished population. A democracy, both as a matter of principle and for practical political considerations, can scarcely accumulate capital by wholesale confiscation of property, the liquidation of social classes, or planned starvation of a large part of its people. The Communists, however, have shown themselves perfectly ready to adopt these horrible but for them practical economic measures. The Russians did all these things despite reasonably favorable economic conditions in the Soviet Union. It seems inevitable that the Chinese and any other Asian Communists who may come to power will be ready to go at least as far as the Russians in such matters, for the economic conditions they face are much worse. In a large part of Asia the prime economic need is for rapid capital accumulation, primarily by the government, since private saving has shown itself incapable of meeting the need. In such a situation a Communist regime has a definite initial advantage over a democracy.

The final and by all odds the greatest advantage communism has over democracy in Asia is that it is a system which can be applied at once almost anywhere in Asia, whereas democracy requires a relatively long preparatory period in a sort of political purgatory. Most Asian democracies at present face an inner contradiction in their dependence on an elite leadership, some system of tutelage, and a high degree of control downward from the top, offset by little or no effective control by the common people over their government. Communism is in no way embarrassed by these necessities, for they are part and parcel of the Communist system.

Naturally a Communist regime in an impoverished and technically backward Asian land will not measure up to even the relatively low levels of efficiency of the Soviet Union. It can be only as ruthlessly thorough as the economic levels and skills of its people permit, and herein may lie what hope we have that communism, once established in Asia, may prove less durable than in Russia. But a Communist regime in Asia, even though not so efficient as that of the Soviet Union, can apply a fully totalitarian system of control from the start and need not go through a long preparatory phase as a would-be Communist government. In other words, democracy for the time being does not meet communism on even terms in most of Asia, for a somewhat contradictory and far from complete brand of democracy must compete with full-fledged communism.

When listed in this way, the advantages that communism has over democracy as a practical system of political organization in Asia seem almost overwhelming. While the new democracies of Asia today are certainly not to be compared to the Chinese Republic of 1912, the over-all Chinese pattern of the last several decades would seem to be an altogether possible and perhaps even probable pattern for virtually every one of the lands of Asia, whatever its present political status. Exceptions might be found in Japan, Turkey, perhaps even the Philippines, and certainly in Israel, which should hardly be classified as an Asian country in any case, for almost the whole of its leadership and a large proportion of its people are of very recent Western origin. But for almost any other Asian land, it would be hard to refute the defeatist who claims that the China story will inevitably repeat itself in one form or another. We can hope that this will not happen, but a realistic appraisal of the situation can only leave us with the uneasy realization that communism may have a decided edge over democracy throughout Asia.

The possibility of atomic self-destruction is at present, of course, the most pressing danger to us and to all civilized men, but next to this possibility the single greatest danger we all may face is that Asia as a whole will gradually drift toward communism. Beside it the other favorite dangers of the calamity-howlers pale into insignificance. What by comparison is the danger of internal subversion in the United States from a handful of Communist agents and sympathizers who in recent years have shrunk almost to the vanishing-point? Even the difficulties of military defense in Asia seem definitely subordinate to this great political problem, for there is little point in defending countries by arms if they are drifting toward communism in any case. There is a decided possibility, perhaps even a strong probability, that the huge non-Western population of the world will slowly gravitate toward communism and thereby create an overwhelming majority of people against the fraction of the West that remains true to democracy.

This danger is underlined by the history of communism in the West itself. It is certainly no accident that communism has won out or has a broad appeal in most of the technologically more backward parts of the West, but has met with little success, except through conquest, in the more advanced countries of the Occident. Unfortunately almost the whole of the non-Western world is even more backward than even the less advanced parts of the West. If the line of cleavage between the advanced and backward parts of the Occident is extended to the rest of the world, communism may well fall heir to the whole of it. In such a predominantly totalitarian world, democracy might have little chance for survival anywhere.

It would be a mistake, however, to end this brief and very sketchy survey of some of the main aspects of the situation in Asia with the simple conclusion that the cards are stacked completely and irrevocably in favor of communism. There are many factors definitely favoring democracy. As we have seen, the peoples of Asia naturally prefer democracy to communism as a political ideal. One might say that the truth, in terms of fundamental human nature, is on our side. Beyond this, the Communists suffer under the great handicap of their own narrowness and rigidity of thought. Their insistence on a single inflexible answer to each question means that they have far less chance of hitting on the right one than we, who are willing to try many different answers. And then, as has been mentioned before, communism will have no easy task in living up to even a small percentage of its extravagant claims. Popular disillusionment is inevitable in any Communist land in Asia, and the only question is whether this disillusionment will develop fast enough to upset the regime

it hardens into monolithic and apparently inde-
ble solidarity, as in Russia.

The Communists also have a tremendous liability in
being unable to offer Asian regimes full equality with the
Kremlin. The Asian resentment of Western domination in
the past could shift quite easily to the Russians, who are,
after all, white men like ourselves. If Asians once become
fully convinced of the undeniable fact that they have more
to fear today from the new imperialism of communism
than from the nineteenth-century imperialism of the cap-
italist nations, the Communist variant of totalitarianism,
at least, would vanish almost without trace from Asia.

Still another major advantage of the democratic side
in Asia is that the democracies of the West are capable
of giving much greater aid to would-be Asian democracies
than the Soviet Union and its European satellites can give
to China or any future Communist regime in Asia. Even
the problems of transportation are all to our advantage, for
though the Soviet Union is decidedly closer to most of
Asia, it is much easier for us to carry goods to Asia by water
than it is for the Russians to carry them there by land.

There is a real distinction, however, between the potential advantage of these factors to our side and the actual realization of this advantage. We have made larger
investments of goods and skills in Asia in recent years than
have the Russians, but the results have been extremely
meager, especially when compared with the brilliant results for communism of the efforts of a relatively small
group of Communist "missionaries" in China. We face a
major problem in making our potential advantages count
in Asia. They could be important factors, conceivably
the decisive factors, in the eventual outcome. In any case
they are certainly the only factors over which we ourselves
have any control. We must know what we want to ac-

complish and the realities in Asia with which we must deal before we can tell what our advantages really are, but the exploitation of these advantages is itself a problem of strategy, and it is to this aspect of the general problem that we might best turn next.

PART THREE:

10. *The Implements of Policy*

This is not the place for a detailed elaboration of specific American tactics in Asia, for the concrete implementation of policy must be constantly revised to meet changing circumstances. But more important than specific tactics are the general principles of strategy on which they must be based if they are to have much hope of success. Such principles, if rightly conceived, need not change to any great extent unless our objectives are substantially altered or the basic Asian situation itself changes.

We might best start with the means at our disposal

Principles of Strategy

for influencing the course of events in Asia. These implements of policy fall into three major categories: the military, the economic, and what we might call, for lack of a better term, the ideological. Naturally these three fields of activity in actual practice become inextricably intertwined, but they are at the same time three distinct modes or levels for the implementation of policy.

Of the three, the military aspect of strategy is the most clear-cut and understandable. The overrunning of all Asia by Communist arms would be a terrible and perhaps a fatal disaster for the whole free world. Obviously we should defend as much of Asia as we can from Communist aggression. This, as a principle, is clear enough. The problem is that in practice our ability to defend much of Asia by arms is extremely limited. Most of our military potential must be reserved to balance Soviet military might elsewhere, and what we can spare for use in Asia is not always very effective. Moreover, the military implement of policy is by all odds the most costly not only in American lives but even in simple monetary terms. It is also quite clearly the most restricted. To limit policy to the military level would be to maximize costs and minimize results.

All this may be seen in the Korean War. However great the costs and unsatisfactory the outcome, still the war had two important beneficial results for the United States. One was our own awakening from our postwar lethargy. The other was the clear warning to the Communist side that, whatever the indecision and confusion Americans sometimes evince, we are ready to oppose blatant aggression whenever necessary. The Communists as a result are certainly less likely now to attempt aggression of this sort. Our position in Asia would certainly be worse today had we met aggression in Korea only with words and finger-shaking.

Yet the Korean War, even though fundamentally successful, reveals how limited is our military potential when measured against the vast terrain of Asia. No American needs reminding of what it cost us, particularly in that coin we are least willing to pay—the blood of our own men. And what did we achieve at this price? The defense of the southern half of one of the geographically smaller lands of Asia. Perhaps through a more daring use of our land forces or a less limited use of air power we could have driven the Communists farther north in Korea, but even then our achievements would have been very small when seen against the backdrop of all Asia. Take a map of Asia and compare the line running across the narrow waist of Korea with the endless land borders of the Soviet Union, and the limitations of a purely military policy in Asia will become clear. But even this linear comparison does not tell the story adequately.

We have heard a great deal about the special difficulties of fighting in Korea, but actually the type of war we fought there was less difficult in Korea than it would have been in almost any other part of continental Asia, with the possible exception of Turkey. In Korea we had the advantage of a short front line anchored at either end by our overwhelming naval superiority. There are few spots in Asia where as short or neat a defense line can be drawn from sea to sea. And the climate and terrain of Korea, though hardly favorable for military operations from our point of view, are definitely above average for Asia as a whole. Extreme winter cold and torrential summer rains on the barren, precipitous slopes of Korea are not so fearsome as the crushing heat over the marshes and jungle-clad mountains of southeast Asia.

The location of Korea was also a great advantage for us in the war. Again with the exception of Turkey, no part of non-Communist continental Asia is geographically closer to the United States. More important, Korea lies next door to Japan, our only major military base in all of Asia and the only highly industrialized region outside of the Western world. During the Korean War, Japan was our "privileged sanctuary," which was far more valuable to us than Manchuria was to our enemies. Because of the American military facilities in Japan and the reserves of skilled labor to be found there, campaigning in Korea was like fighting in our own back yard, compared with fighting in the really remote parts of Asia from Singapore westward toward Suez.

Finally, the greatest advantage we had in Korea was that much more of the population of the peninsula was determinedly, even fanatically, on our side than supported the enemy. Our troops were matched in numbers by aggressive if not always efficient Korean divisions, and we had behind us a civil population that for the most part supported us with enthusiasm. Without such local backing it would have been much harder and perhaps quite impossible to achieve even the limited success we did achieve. But such local co-operation in the military defense against communism is by no means something that we can always take for granted in Asia. If American armies were forced to campaign in the various other lands of Asia in limited wars comparable to the one in Korea, we could, as things now stand, count on local support such as we received in Korea only in such peripheral areas as the Philippines, Formosa, Japan, and Turkey.

If in our mind's eye we shift the scene of the recent war from Korea to some other Asian countries, the immensity of the problem of defending Asia becomes all too clear. Assume for the moment that American armies were forced to fight in Indochina and to repel enemies as strong as the Communist forces in Korea. What would the problems then be? First, we should discover that the addition of almost two thousand miles to our lines of communication from both the United States and Japan had greatly increased our supply difficulties and correspondingly weakened our punch. Both terrain and climate would be less favorable for us than in Korea, and we should find that whatever our lines of defense might be, they could be anchored by sea power only on the east and would melt away into the jungles and mountains of the interior on the west, where the advantages would lie entirely with the Communist guerrillas. And, worst of all, we should find few Indochinese willing to fight with the ardor of our Korean allies, and at our backs would be a veritable quagmire of civilian apathy or resentment.

Shift the scene but a few hundred miles by land to Burma, and we should find our lines of supply by water extended two thousand miles more, the terrain still less suited to our military capacities, with few possibilities of anchoring a defense line on naval power, and the problems of local support probably no better than in Indochina. Shift the scene across the Bay of Bengal to India, and the problems become greatly magnified by the size of the terrain and the vastness of the population. If Communist aggressors in India had proportionately as much local support as they have had in Korea, to say nothing of Indochina, the defense of India might be entirely beyond our capacities.

Recently the United States has decided to increase its emphasis on strategic air power as the chief deterrent to Communist aggression. This may indeed be the best way to ensure the safety of ourselves and western Europe against Russian military might, but the concomitant reduction of emphasis on conventional land power may weaken our already very feeble military arm in some parts of Asia. The ability to drop atom and hydrogen bombs on enemy targets is a military advantage only when there are suitable targets for such weapons. In fluid guerrilla wars, which seem to be the pattern of Communist aggression in Asia, such targets are usually lacking, and atom bombs are much more likely to alienate the local population from us than to hurt the Communist guerrillas.

Hence the military advantage of the use of atomic weapons in a war like the one in Indochina would be altogether inconsequential when measured against the adverse psychological effect. Many Asians, apparently oblivious of the fact that the atomic bomb was not developed in time for us to use against the Nazis, believe that we dropped it on the Japanese but not on the Germans simply because the former were Asiatics. Nothing would drive the peoples of Asia more quickly and effectively into the arms of the Communists than our use of atomic weapons against relatively ill-armed Asian soldiers or defenseless civilians.

Even in the Korean War the use of such weapons seemed far more likely to produce the world war we were hoping to avert than to settle the limited war in which we were engaged. The sprawling cities of China lay almost defenseless before the terrible forces we control, but the destruction of these cities might not have seriously reduced the Chinese will or ability to fight, while assuredly magnifying the probabilities of global war and alienating the sympathies of the world from us.

Our atomic strength can perhaps deter the Soviet Union from attempting the military conquest of the world; it may help to prevent blatant aggression on a limited scale such as was attempted by the Communists in Korea; it may prevent the Chinese from openly dispatching their armies beyond their borders; but it can do little in civil wars or in aggression through infiltration. In fact, to the extent that the emphasis on strategic air power diminishes our ground strength, we may be even less able to exert military influence in Asia in the future than we have been in the past.

An American defense line the length of Asia is nothing more than a chauvinist's pipe dream. If we were to use our military power with great wisdom, it might suffice for the defense of an occasional spot of maximum significance, such as South Korea. But such external aggression is a far less serious danger in Asia than internal collapse or subversion. The hypothetical American defense line, even if possible, would serve as no defense against these major dangers. In view of Asian sensibilities to Western domination, the presence of American garrisons in most countries would probably do more to increase the already strong internal threat from communism than it would to decrease the external menace.

The very weakness of the military arm of policy has put added stress on the economic. Unless there is considerable economic progress in the various lands of Asia, there obviously will be little to be defended in this area. Nor will democracy interest the minds of men if their stomachs are empty. Substantial achievements on the economic front are prerequisites for any decided stand in the political battle against totalitarianism. Undoubtedly the economic arm of policy operates on the front line of internal defense where American military power does not reach at all. Even on the external front of defense against aggression, economic aid may in the long run prove more effective than our limited and often unwelcome military support. If the economic substructure is sound, an Asian country is likely to have the means and also the heart to withstand aggression; without such solid footing no defense may be possible, with or without our military support.

The American people and their government have shown a real awareness of the economic side of policy and have devoted considerable energy and resources to it. Through Point Four and a variety of other means, we have made a good start on improving economic conditions and helping to lay the foundations for a better future in many parts of Asia. We have supplied the machines and know-how for some great and beneficial undertakings. We have been wise enough to think not only of large and spectacular projects of industrialization but also of increasing the productive capacities of the individual farmer through more scientific knowledge, more effective organization, and better tools.

There is little reason to criticize the type of work we have been attempting to do on the economic front in Asia. Most of it has been soundly conceived and executed with increasing efficiency. On the other hand, our tendency to tie economic aid to political or military commitments by the recipient nations has often undermined our efforts on all three fronts. And the scope of our economic work in Asia leaves much to be desired. It has never been adequate, and recently we have been reducing rather than expanding it. Our efforts on the economic side have been minuscule compared with what we have been willing to expend on the military side. Our total economic investment in all Asia since 1945 amounts to the cost to us of only a few days of the Second World War or a few weeks of the Korean War.

Our reluctance to devote adequate funds to the economic front may be understandable, since the need for economic aid never presents itself as dramatically or pressingly as the need to stop aggression. But it most certainly is not wise. It is here that we have the greatest potential advantage over the Communists. Not to use our economic advantages as effectively as possible is to tie our right hand behind our back.

While we are doing far less on the economic front than we should, we often pin extravagant hopes on what little we are accomplishing. Many Americans, in their frustration over the situation in Asia and particularly over the costliness and ineffectiveness of our military efforts, have turned with sometimes naïve enthusiasm to the prospects of saving Asia from communism by economic and technical aid. This type of activity and its results are deceptively concrete and measurable. They lend themselves to the neat graphs and charts we love so well. We can see at a glance how many new acres were brought under cultivation in region A, how many kilowatt-hours or cotton spindles were added to the economy of region B, how many peasants in region C were inoculated with serum X, were supplied with tool Y, or were taught scientific fact Z.

No one should dispute the desirability, even the necessity, of doing all these things and doing them on a much larger scale than today. But, at the same time, we are deceiving ourselves dangerously if we think that the accomplishment of these tasks will in itself win the battle for democracy. Such achievements will only serve to lay a firmer foundation on which the partisans of democracy can stand. They may be the breastworks of defense, but they will not themselves fight the battle.

We gave much economic aid to China before it went Communist; the Russians gave almost nothing; and yet the decision went against us, and what was left of our economic aid redounded to the advantage of our enemies. Throughout Asia almost all that we are accomplishing through economic and technical aid is exactly what the Communists would wish to accomplish if they were in control. More acres of arable land, more spindles or kilowatt-hours, and better farming techniques are as advantageous to a Communist regime as to a democracy. Economic improvement at these basic levels is itself neutral in the political war.

One could even argue that economic aid to some particularly backward areas may raise economic conditions to levels at which the internal Communist threat will become worse. While almost all the most technologically advanced parts of the world are democratic, the Communist countries come for the most part at the next level of technological advancement, and the truly backward parts of the world are neither democratic nor Communist, nor for that matter much concerned with either ideology. In most of Africa and even in some parts of Asia economic advances may increase rather than decrease the Communist menace. If this is true, our only hope is that still further development will eventually diminish the peril in these areas.

In the lands where the internal threat of communism is already great, as it is in most of Asia, we can perhaps assume that technological advances will serve to lessen rather than increase the danger. On the other hand, we cannot be certain that, even with our aid, these countries will be able to win the race with their populations, and we must realize that in any case the development of an economy capable of providing enough food for all and adequate levels of education will be a long and slow process. Under optimum conditions it may be many decades before a country like Indonesia can achieve living standards and educational levels comparable to those of Japan. Long before any of the new democracies have got that far, even with maximum aid from us, they will have had to face the crucial tests of deciding between rival policies and leaders and perhaps other severe challenges to their shaky democratic institutions. Economic and technical aid alone will certainly not decide the war between democracy and totalitarianism. It can be a potent weapon for the democratic side, but many fateful decisions in Asia will have been made long before it has produced any decisive results.

Since the military arm of policy is so limited in scope and the economic so slow and uncertain in action, we are forced to turn to the third implement of strategy, the ideological. In many ways this is the most important of the three. If the peoples of Asia realized the impossibility of true equality for Asian nations in a Communist world, if they were fully aware of the inevitable slavery of man to the machine of government in any totalitarian system, the problem of defending Asia from communism would indeed be a simple one. In fact, the military and economic arms of policy are in a sense purely subsidiary to the ideological. Through the military arm we can defend some selected spots, but this does us more harm than good if the people in those areas do not elect to use the time bought by our blood to work toward the development of a healthy democracy. Through economic aid we can give the people of an Asian country a better fighting chance to develop democratic institutions, but our economic aid, if they so decide, could be used with equal effectiveness to lay the foundations for a totalitarian regime. Without the support of the military and economic arms, our ideological efforts might prove entirely ineffective, but without the ideological side the other two become almost meaningless.

In the case of China we can see with particular clarity this priority of the ideological over the other two arms of policy. Certainly the Russians exercised much less military power in the Chinese area than we did. This is not to say that their military aid was not of the greatest importance to the Chinese Communists. The Russians permitted their Chinese followers to get hold of the great bulk of Japanese weapons captured by the Soviet forces in Manchuria and Inner Mongolia, and their carefully timed movements in Manchuria were effectively designed to give the local Communists the best possible chance to take over this important region. But Russian military aid to the Communists was in the aggregate much less than the military aid we gave Chiang. In accepting the Japanese surrender we used our forces in a way that would ensure Chiang's getting hold of the vital coastal cities of China; we transported his troops to the north; we trained some of his divisions; we furnished him with military advisers and instructors; and we gave him not only all the Japanese weapons surrendered to us in China but also huge quantities of our own equipment. It is true that subsequently we may have contributed to the collapse of the military efficiency and morale of the Kuomintang by withholding further military equipment, but all in all we exerted far greater military influence in Chiang's behalf than the Russians did in aid of Mao.

On the economic side the situation is even clearer. The economic aid the Soviet Union gave the Chinese Communists before their complete triumph was at best negligible and did not begin to offset the Russian plundering of Manchuria. Obviously underrating their Chinese adherents and expecting the Kuomintang to win out, the Russians decided to strip Manchuria bare of virtually all its movable industrial equipment, even though much of it was of no value when finally deposited in Siberia. Russia thus robbed its Chinese allies of the principal assets of the part of China that fell to them in the scramble following the Japanese surrender and left Mao with a very delicate issue to explain away to his patriotic countrymen. In contrast, we took nothing from China, but poured out literally billions of dollars in goods and financial backing for the tottering Kuomintang, though all to no avail.

We exerted far more military effort in China than the Russians; we gave economic aid, while they were plundering Manchuria; but the Communists outdid us on the third level and won. The ideological war went to them, in large part by default, as more and more Chinese came to the conclusion that communism represented the only or at least the best hope for a united and strong China. While we strengthened the arms of the Chinese and attempted to fill their bellies, the Communists won their minds and of course along with their minds got their arms and bodies too. If countries like India or Indonesia go Communist, it will almost certainly be in the same way. The Russians, even with the support of their Chinese converts, are not likely to surpass us in military efforts in these regions, much less in economic aid. But they have shown themselves all too capable of outdoing us on the crucial level of ideas.

We have not been completely unmindful in recent years of the ideological phase of the problem in Asia. There has been much talk in the United States of psychological warfare, but the term itself is a most unfortunate one and a good illustration of our own ineptness in this field. The aggressive tone of such a term perhaps has done as much to undermine our cause as has been accomplished by the programs under its name.

We seem to have been most successful in the realm of ideas when least self-conscious. Members of technical-assistance missions, as a by-product of their projects, have often done much to foster the growth of democratic ideals and practices, though usually at such low grass-roots levels that their work will affect the central governments only very indirectly and slowly. Even more has been done altogether unwittingly by thousands of unofficial ambassadors of democracy. For example, the strong egalitarian spirit and democratic idealism of the first waves of combat troops we sent into Japan at the close of the Second World War did more to convince the Japanese of the sincerity and strength of our democratic beliefs than did all the preachments of our high command in Tokyo.

Our formal programs designed for the ideological level of the cold war in Asia have been extremely limited in extent and feeble in accomplishment. The Voice of America, even in its heyday in Asia, was of much less value than in Europe. Very few Asians had the short-wave radios with which to listen in, if they had wished, and still fewer were likely to have been influenced by our amateurish efforts. The work of cultural attachés at our embassies has been very restricted and has often received only halfhearted support. This has usually been considered the least important of an embassy's tasks—the diplomatic end of the line.

American libraries in major Asian cities have often been of great value, though they have been little patronized where they were needed most, and their limitation to American authors or American subject matter has created the unfortunate impression that we are interested in the Americanization of Asian lands rather than in their democratization. Worse still, the harm from world-wide publicity given to the purging of allegedly undesirable books in these libraries—that is, "book-burning" in the lurid phraseology of the world press—may have more than outweighed the good they have done over the years.

Something has been achieved in the ideological field through government programs for bringing Asian students to the United States, although technical assistance has usually been our chief motive. Even in this activity, however, the results are probably much more equivocal than is usually supposed. The foreign student anywhere and at any time, if poorly treated or if given a training that fails to meet his needs after he returns home, can easily react against the country where he studied and against its ideals. The ranks of our enemies in Asia are full of returned students from the United States and Europe. On the whole our fellowship programs for Asian students have undoubtedly been a good thing, but they could be made a great deal better if we put a little more effort and imagination into them.

While we have paid lip service to the importance of ideas by creating a few feebly supported and freely criticized programs, we have shown an utter disregard of this arm of strategy in our Asian diplomacy as a whole. We tread unconscionably on toes made sensitive by colonialism and long inequality of status. Some of our senators and congressmen are interested only in making statements that will sound satisfyingly tough to the homefolk, no matter how unsympathetic or idiotic they may sound to Asian ears. Even the members of our State Department, in their understandable though deplorable fear of publicity-conscious members of Congress, have often shown themselves more sensitive to the mere whims of American legislators than to the deepest convictions or most serious prejudices of the Asians with whom they should be dealing. Our net score in the field of ideas is well below zero.

We have been presenting our case in Asia in terms that may be gratifying to the frustrated and somewhat bewildered citizen of Newark or Sacramento and in doing so have often hit upon terms that seem diabolically calculated to alienate Asians from our side. For example, in approaching Asians who are immensely wary about Western domination and almost exclusively concerned with their own tremendous problems, we often imply that they first must pick up a gun and fight on our side before the relationship goes any farther. Because of our order of priority we seem to them callously indifferent to their interests and very possibly bent on creating some new form of military imperialism. It would be hard to find a better way to ensure their unwillingness to stand up and be counted on our side.

Much of the ideological war fought by the Communists in Asia is devoted to defaming us rather than persuading others of the rightness of their cause. It is certainly easier to exploit negative prejudices than to build up positive beliefs. The Communists have done a most effective job in sowing dark suspicions about the United States in Asian minds and in presenting our culture and ideals in the worst possible light. We, on the other hand, have proved very inept at convincing Asians about the terrible realities of the Communist system, perhaps because we have assumed that all this was so self-evident it needed no explanation. Instead we have gone weakly over to the defensive, attempting to explain away in singularly ineffective fashion the Communist charges. Russian cunning and American ineptness made it possible for one shipment of Soviet wheat to have a larger impact on Indian thinking than forty times as much wheat provided by the United States on much more generous terms. We have even allowed the Communists to appropriate the name of democracy for themselves so that to many Asians they seem to be the champions and we the enemies of democracy.

Often enough we have played naïvely into Communist hands. For example, the Indians, who pride themselves on their spirituality, have been given a picture of the United States as the land of mammon, and we obligingly help out the plot with our brash pride in having the tallest buildings in the world, the largest wheat fields, and the most automobiles, without stopping to ask ourselves if this is all we have to offer to countries that may never be able to attain these specific physical assets.

In so far as the ideological war has not gone against us in Asia, it has been despite rather than because of our efforts. In a country like India the ideological strength of democracy is to be attributed largely to the British education of the leadership rather than to anything we have done. Indonesian leaders, who like to think of themselves as the George Washingtons of their country, may at the same time subscribe to the belief that the once admirable American democracy of Revolutionary times has been going steadily downhill ever since.

In America the business of influencing men's minds, particularly to buy cigarettes or cars or some other product, has become a tremendous and presumably successful undertaking. No people in the world show a greater desire to "win friends and influence people." But at the same time no major nation in recent years has been less successful than the United States in communicating information or ideas to peoples beyond its borders. Either we have entirely ignored this problem or, as seems more likely, we have foolishly assumed that techniques that have proved successful for selling toothpaste in America will prove adequate for the ideological war in Asia.

At the ideological level the United States often appears to be engaged in a game of diplomatic giveaway. The Russians with their dogmatic rigidity and the horrible realities of their system are constantly making prodigious blunders that alienate large numbers of thinking Asians. But then we come along, with our complete disregard of the psychology of Asian peoples, and match the Russian blunders with some statement or action which may look good in Peoria but has a very sinister or incredible appearance in New Delhi. The truth is all on our side, and unlike the Russians we need not be fettered by a narrow, rigid orthodoxy of thought. It is indeed disheartening to see us constantly nullifying all these important and conceivably decisive advantages.

We are a practical people, but we have shown our practicality in Asia by a curious inversion of values. The military arm of policy is the most costly and in the long run probably the least effective, but since its accomplishments are easily understood, we have poured most of our energies and resources into this single type of activity. The economic arm also is rather costly and works only slowly and uncertainly, but as it too produces concrete results, we have been willing to devote considerable effort to it, even if not enough. The ideological arm is by all odds the least costly and at the same time probably the most effective, but as its results are hard to measure exactly and always remain somewhat intangible, we have chosen to ignore it almost completely, thereby minimizing the effectiveness of our vast expenditures for the military arm and our large outlays for the economic. All three implements of strategy must be used if we are to have much hope for success in Asia, but of the three the ideological is probably the most essential. We have spent billions of dollars for military activities in Asia and hundreds of millions for economic aid, but we have begrudged a few million dollars for the ideological aspect of strategy and have been even less willing to devote to it the necessary human energy and intellectual effort. If this is practicality, it is the hardheaded practicality of the dinosaur.

11. *Our Arsenal of Ideas*

When Hitler threw down the gauntlet to the democracies in Europe, the arsenal that the United States was forced to prepare to meet this challenge consisted of military weapons. Today in the European sphere of our problems, Moscow's challenge to human freedom has again forced us to build up our military strength. But in Asia, where only a few small sectors along the line of battle can be held by arms, ideas are the most powerful weapons in our potential arsenal of democracy.

It is most unfortunate that we have tended to ignore the ideological arm of strategy in Asia, but it is not surprising. As a people we, like the British, are inclined to approach our problems through pragmatic experiment rather than abstract theorizing. Democracy is not a theory with us so much as a practical way of living. The American feels and acts in an essentially democratic way, but he has little experience in describing his beliefs and feelings in words. If challenged to state his faith, he may resort to certain symbols of it. He might even cite the corner drugstore or hot dogs at a baseball game, for these particular institutions, however mystifying to others, signify for him the democratic equalities and freedoms of American life.

We have no authoritative verbal statements of our modern democratic beliefs and practices. Our great democratic documents date far back in our history, and it is merely practical experience that has kept these documents alive in changing times and has transformed us from a late-eighteenth-century society into a mid-twentieth-century democracy—practical experience in court rulings, in state and national legislation, and most of all in ordinary community living. British democracy exists without any formal constitution describing its nature. What a contrast to Marx's great political bible and the constantly shifting redefinitions of its approved meaning, to which all Communists must blindly adhere, whatever the realities may be! Even the fascist totalitarians of Germany and Japan felt the need for official definitions of their faiths, though they turned out to be peculiarly rambling and self-contradictory.

It is certainly better that most Americans act democratically rather than just talk fluently about democracy. Our innate suspicion of theory and our insistence on practical results have contributed greatly to the strength of our democracy at home. At the same time, these characteristics have sometimes proved to be liabilities abroad. We have overlooked how extremely important words can be to people in some other parts of the world. We have been unable to believe that for many, and especially for the educated elite of Asia, theories may speak more loudly than facts.

The Communists come to Asia with a set of theories to explain away all Asian perplexities; we arrive with complex patterns of action that, instead of being self-ex-

planatory as we assume, sometimes add to the bewilder-
ment. The Communists come with a message of hope: do
these simple things and Utopia will be achieved in short
order. We have an even greater message of hope than
they, but we are more inclined to display our strong pragmatic skepticism to Asians, who in their desperation need
assurance rather than doubt.

Our disregard of ideological factors has often made
us insensitive to the Asian point of view and correspondingly slow to mold our actions to the needs of the situation
there. When we insist, as some of us do, on judging everything, everywhere, on the basis of what people think and
do here in the United States, we are carrying our prag-
matism to a self-defeating extreme. For us at home the
way people think and act in Chicago or Middletown may
count most, but when we come to the problems of Asian
policy, the attitudes and ways of life of the people of Cal-
cutta or the countless peasant villages of Indonesia should
count even more.

Even when we have attempted to employ ideological
weapons in Asia, we have often shown extraordinary ineptness in their selection and use. For example, we appear
to have assumed that our chief objective is to "sell America." The term "sell" is bad enough, for it suggests that
the difference between what we advocate and what is offered by communism is like the difference between brands
of cars or toothpaste, marvelously magnified by smooth
sales talk, but trifling in actuality. Worse, however, is the
assumption that it is primarily America that we are trying
to "sell."

It would naturally be gratifying to have the United
States liked and admired throughout Asia and would
greatly facilitate our immediate relations with that part
of the world, but such popularity would have little meaning if our admirers were at the same time succumbing to

Communist subversion. It would be far better for them to dislike us heartily, if at the same time they had the political and economic strength to resist communism. Anti-American sentiments in England are of small account so long as the British see clearly and realistically the Communist challenge to democracy. Anti-Americanism in France or Italy is chiefly of concern to us because it may further undermine the weak internal resistance to communism in those countries. Similarly the attitude of Asian peoples toward the United States is of major importance to us only in so far as it affects the outcome of the great struggle between democracy and communism. Our goal is not to win an international popularity contest but to preserve from mortal peril the free way of life both for nations and for individuals.

"The American way of life" is a convenient term, especially on the Fourth of July, for suggesting all that we feel to be best in a free society and in democratic political institutions. But it is not an adequate or desirable description of democracy for Asians. Their hope, and ours as well, is that democracy will become as much theirs as ours and will then be best described as "the Indian way of life" or "the Japanese way of life." Under these circumstances "the American way of life" can only signify for them the American departures from what they hope to achieve—in other words, those aspects of American life which are physically unattainable for them or which they feel to be undesirable. What appeal could "the American way of life" have if one chose to equate this term, as many Asians do, with such things as McCarthyism or the less desirable aspects of our race relations, rather than with the many more typical things of which we have a right to be proud.

Actually "the American way of life" is a term used only by the most naïve of our politicians in speaking to

Asians, but what little ideological effort we have made in Asia has often been characterized by an "American way of life" psychology. Our programs have been designed to present the American story to Asians. Our libraries in Asia consist primarily of books by American authors or about America. Naturally the problems and achievements of the United States are a very relevant part of the ideological struggle in Asia. But so also are the terrible realities of life in Communist lands, and perhaps the most relevant body of information may be found in the problems and successes of those democratic nations which do not contrast quite as sharply with Asia in basic economic conditions as does the United States. To the extent that we identify democracy exclusively with the United States, we are actually undermining our cause in Asia, for then we make democracy seem hopelessly unattainable.

There is another good reason for consciously underplaying America in our intellectual dealings with Asians. As the richest and most powerful nation of the world we have inevitably become the primary target for natural human jealousies and resentments. If something is wrong anywhere, it is easiest to blame us. We must accept this situation with what grace we can muster, for it is a natural concomitant of our world leadership. This is something we should be able to understand, since we ourselves found considerable satisfaction not so long ago in criticizing the British Empire, while taking full advantage of the *Pax Britannica*.

The rise of British popularity in the world and the decline of our own are basically a sign of the shifting responsibility for leadership from them to us. We should recognize that the United States cannot expect to be the most appealing symbol of democracy's cause in Asia. The Japanese like to imagine a special affinity with the French, in part perhaps because they can in this way share vicariously in the violent French criticism of the United States. The Indians or Burmese find close association with the British more desirable than with us. We should recognize and accept this situation. Certainly the United Kingdom is an admirable democratic ideal for Indians, and the strong spirit of independence of the individual Frenchman, if not the economics and politics of the French collectively, a desirable pattern for the Japanese. Our ideological efforts in Asia would almost certainly be more effective if we put less stress on ourselves and a great deal more on the other democracies of the world.

The big guns of the democratic arsenal in Asia, however, are not the national patterns of specific Western nations, but the ideals and practices of democracy itself. If we could help Asians to comprehend these fully, the battle would be all but won. Moreover, if we ourselves had a clearer understanding of the basic principles of democracy, we would find it much easier to handle the undeniably ticklish problem of information about America in Asia. No matter how much we underplay the American theme, it will inevitably be a major motif in our intellectual contacts with Asians, simply because basic Communist strategy emphasizes the defamation of the United States through the now familiar technique of the big lie. The attack must be answered and a truer picture of the United States substituted for it.

Our first problem is to answer specific criticisms, which usually are aimed at our weakest points. Take for example the race problem, on which we are very vulnerable in Asian eyes and which consequently is exploited unceasingly by all our enemies. Here undeniably is a gross imperfection in our society. Throughout history serious problems have usually arisen wherever people of different physical type or even of different cultural background have lived together on the same land. This universal human problem has been posed in particularly acute form in the United States, where the white man and the Negro, two radically different physical types, lived together in the relationship of master and slave less than a century ago. In the intervening years we have moved far and fast from this entirely undemocratic relationship between the two races, and our progress apparently has been accelerating in recent decades. Actually the most significant fact about race relations in America is that they have been changing rapidly for the better.

We need not beat our breasts in self-condemnation, particularly before Asians who have often shown comparable racial intolerance. The whole Indian caste system, for example, may well have grown out of some form of racial discrimination; the Chinese have never accepted neighboring peoples as full equals; and the Japanese only recently became absurdly disturbed over the defilement of the Japanese race by a few thousand Eurasian offspring of GI fathers. Race relations undeniably constitute a major weakness in American society, and we have many other imperfections. We should not attempt to conceal these flaws. Instead, we should help Asians see them in proper perspective and in terms of the progress that we are making toward their correction in keeping with democratic ideals. If we could do this, these weaknesses in American society might be turned from major liabilities into virtual assets in our ideological efforts in Asia.

A clear understanding of the basic principles of democracy would also help us to see what in our society we can most validly point to with pride. We have often singled out incidental or purely American accompaniments of our democracy rather than those fundamentals that we share with others. We have been particularly unwise in emphasizing the material wealth of the United States, which we so easily do both with conscious smugness and unconscious arrogance. In a country like India such an emphasis strengthens prejudices against our supposed materialism. Moreover, our wealth is certainly not to be attributed solely to our own virtues. It is in large part due to the natural resources of the land in which we live. In this respect it represents the inequalities of human birth, rather than the equalities on which democracy is based.

What we can be really proud of is not our national wealth as such but its wide and equitable distribution. It is a wonderful thing that most Americans can afford to have vacuum cleaners and washing machines, but we should be proud not so much of the high standard of living these represent as of the reason that lies behind the development and wide use of such household appliances, for they are a clear reflection of the fact that few Americans are so rich or so poor that the one group can hire the services of the other for menial labor.

While the principles of democracy are in themselves potent ideological weapons in Asia, pure theory alone is not enough. Communism too has its allegedly "democratic" ideals, which by departing entirely from Communist realities have maintained considerable appeal for those who do not understand the discrepancy. Communism also offers an immediately practical means of political organization anywhere in Asia, whereas democratic procedures of operation are, for the time being, more or less inapplicable in many Asian lands. It makes little difference that Communist practices will not lead to the achievement of Communist ideals, for the convert may not discover this until it is too late to adopt another course. If we are to meet communism on the ideological plane in Asia, we must have not only high ideals and objectives but also practical means of achieving them.

In the past we have tended to assume that the slow

process of evolution through which we of the West achieved democracy would be satisfactory for Asians too. The Occidental of a generation or two ago, with his supreme confidence in "progress" and his sublime self-assurance, could look with complacency at the prospect of a slow evolutionary development in Asia which might over the centuries bring Asians some of the blessings of Western civilization. It was a long road from Magna Charta to the perfection of late Victorian England or the United States of Teddy Roosevelt. It seemed somewhat presumptuous for Asians, with their serious economic handicaps, to hope to travel the same distance in decades rather than in the seven centuries it had taken us in the West.

Asians today, however, are scarcely satisfied with a vague hope that over some incredibly long time-span they might possibly be able to build a democratic society. If this is the alternative to the Communist gamble, then even the most democratically oriented Asian might decide to take a plunge on communism, for it at least promises quick results.

The greatest task facing the adherents of democracy today is to discover how the ideals of democracy can be translated into realities for Asians in the face of their grim economic conditions and psychological urgencies. The Communists have poured their energies into finding techniques for achieving their relatively simple system of rule in Asia, while we have usually overlooked the much harder task of finding ways to implement democratic ideals. Instead we have taken refuge in a lingering, though often denied, faith in inevitable "progress."

Asian believers in democracy naturally must take the lead in finding practical means of achieving the ideals of a free society in Asia, but we certainly could be of assistance. We show no hesitancy in giving Asians physical things that we have in greater quantity than they, such as arms, machines, or food. We help them with specific technical skills that we have in more abundance than they, such as modern hygienic or scientific farming techniques. The Western world is better supplied than Asia with men possessing the necessary educational backgrounds and technical skills to work realistically on the great problem of developing practical means of achieving democracy in the Asian setting. It is much harder to aid at this level than at the simpler levels of goods and specific technical skills, but it is also far more important. It could be that all our aid at the lower levels may be wasted unless we find some way to help in this more vital task.

But we have not devoted any appreciable proportion of our available manpower to these problems. Extremely few of those able to contribute to their solution have developed enough interest in them and adequate specific knowledge about Asian countries to make their talents and training count. Only an insignificant number of Occidentals have seriously concerned themselves with Asia, and not unnaturally their results have been proportionately as trifling as their numbers.

Another difficulty is that Asians are naturally suspicious and resentful of suggestion, not to say dictation, from Westerners in such matters. It may be possible for American or European medical men or agricultural experts to direct a specific hygienic or agricultural program in an Asian land, but it would be neither practical nor desirable for Occidentals to attempt to master-mind the grand strategy of democracy anywhere in Asia. This Asians must do for themselves. But we could aid them immeasurably if we developed a firm foundation of knowledge and understanding of their problems on which they could stand with assurance while seeking to discover the specific ways to further the democratic cause and the various effective answers to communism.

This is not so intangible and indirect a way of meeting our problems in Asia as it might at first appear. If we in the West should devote that proportion of our intellectual abilities to Asia which its problems merit, we would greatly increase the effectiveness of our more direct and tangible efforts. We would have a much clearer idea of what our real problems in Asia are and how to meet them. We could then more easily avoid self-defeating blunders and perhaps achieve much more with no greater over-all effort than we are expending today. Asian students who come to the West to study would not be forced to apply, within the limits of their own ability and understanding, the evolutionary experience of the West to the intricate and pressing problems of Asia, but would find guidance in this-key problem from capable men who have devoted their lives to its study. Americans working in Asia would not go to their tasks innocently ignorant of the problems they face or the true significance of what they are doing. Most important of all, Asian leaders would find at hand specific information and penetrating interpretations of its meaning that might save them from many dangerous pitfalls and enable them to go farther and more safely in their own thinking than they could without these aids.

It is no simple task for societies that now lack an adequate economic or technological basis for democracy to survive the multiple dangers of economic collapse, internal subversion, and external conquest to become in time healthy members of a democratic world order. This is not a problem that should be left entirely to a few harried adherents of democracy in Asia. They deserve whatever support can be supplied them from the intellectual resources of the whole democratic world. There is little reason for us to devote our attention to the specific problems of Asian defense, living standards, or technical skills unless we are also willing to devote our attention as intelligently and effectively as possible to the broader problems of Asia's future, which no doubt will determine the ultimate meaning of our efforts in these other more limited fields.

Our failure to develop the key weapons for our arsenal of ideas in Asia has been matched by our tendency to approach the whole ideological problem in Asia in the wrong way. To the United States and the healthy democracies of western Europe, communism represents a reversion to less desirable forms of human organization. It means a loss of human freedoms, lower levels of economic existence, and the cruel and on the whole inefficient exploitation of the individual for the sake of the impersonal state. For us to turn to communism would be to turn our backs on hope. Under such conditions it presents little internal danger for us. The menace is largely an external one, posed by the military power the Russians have forged out of human misery. Our own problem, therefore, is essentially one of military defense.

But when we take our predominant emphasis on military defense into the very different conditions of Asia, we put our case in a light that invites defeat. The defensive implies the preservation of the *status quo,* but in few Asian countries do the citizens feel that the *status quo* is tolerable, much less worth fighting for. They are all determined to change existing conditions, not to preserve them. The need for defense against external aggression often seems trifling to them compared to the great offensive that they are waging to change their societies internally. They are looking for something positive, but we seem to offer them an essentially negative policy.

Throughout Asia conclusive evidence is piling up that the defense of the *status quo* is an untenable position for any Asian regime. For the United States a negative, defensive psychology in Asia is even less practical, because to Asians, who have so little to defend, it suggests that we are only interested in the protection of our own soft lives. It is easy for them to interpret our demands for joint defense against a common enemy as a callous willingness on our part to fasten an unsatisfactory *status quo* on Asia in a selfish effort to preserve our own advantageous situation. In fact, American attempts at collective security through joint defense are often misconstrued by them as a new form of imperialistic exploitation, in which Asians are to die so that Americans may live in peace and luxury. A negative and purely defensive strategy in Asia would probably do more in the long run to aid the forces we wish to combat than to thwart them.

No one would deny the effective support we are receiving in our defensive policies from the South Koreans, the Nationalist Chinese on Formosa, the Turks, and the Filipinos. But each of these small nations represents a very special historical or geographical case, and their combined populations add up to a mere four or five per cent of the total population of Asia. They are the exceptions that prove the rule.

And even in the case of these four small nations, a negative policy is certainly not enough. Their defense gains us little in itself, except in Turkey where the defense of Europe is also involved. In fact, throughout Asia the general misunderstanding and suspicion of our relations with the regimes of Chiang and Syngman Rhee may be more of a liability than the soldiers at their command are an asset to our side. Our efforts to defend these countries make little sense and may be doomed to eventual failure unless we also make positive efforts to help them develop healthy democratic governments, securely based on sound economic and social foundations. The development of a successful democratic regime in South Korea, for instance, is incomparably more important to us in the long run than are its staunch fighting men. If South Korea lags economically behind the northern half of the country, if it becomes merely an American stooge, or if it turns out to be a failure as an experiment in democracy, it could do our cause irreparable harm, however well South Korean soldiers may fight on our side.

If a positive policy is so important in the four small nations that are willing to join us wholeheartedly in military defense, it is even more important elsewhere in Asia, where our pleas for an adequate defense against a common danger are so consistently misunderstood. In this part of the world we have most certainly been wrong in putting our chief emphasis on defense; perhaps we have been wrong in putting any emphasis on it at all. If there were adequate internal progress toward the development of prosperous, democratic nations, then external defense might well take care of itself.

Some, however, may raise the question of how our policy can be primarily one of encouraging change, actually revolution of a sort, in other lands. Problems of mutual defense against a common external enemy may be proper matters for our concern, but how can we justify meddling in the domestic affairs of other nations?

Stated bluntly in this way, the question at first seems hard to answer. Certainly it is taken for granted that countries should not meddle in one another's internal affairs. There is a world of difference, however, between meddling by coercion and force and mediating by persuasion and influence. The former spells imperialism— whether of the traditional nineteenth-century type or the newer imperialism of communism—but the latter is a natural concomitant of a democratic system whether national or international because democracy is based on the assumption that there will be a free exchange of information and opinion and that efforts will be made to achieve compromises and agreements through argument and debate.

Communists and other totalitarians raise dikes at home against the inflow of ideas and attempt to pour their poisons abroad through underground channels. The free nations believe in an open and unhampered exchange of ideas and influences. In fact, each diplomat, each missionary or swami, each lecturer or teacher who goes abroad, does so with the express intention of exerting some influence on the people to whom he has gone. Each Point Four dollar is expected to change something in the land in which it is used. We and almost all other peoples are up to our necks in the business of exerting influence internally in other countries, and if we have not realized this before, it is time to give it some clear thought now.

American missionaries have gone in large numbers to Asia for well over a century with absolutely no compunctions about changing the religious beliefs or social customs of the people they found there. Our businessmen have been active for an equally long time in Asia with no thought about the economic dislocations or gradual social changes that resulted from their work. What policy our government has had toward Asia has largely been the insistence that our missionaries and traders should have as wide a scope as possible for their activities. In fact, American naval strength was used to win them this opportunity in Japan, and American marines and naval units were stationed for long in China to protect our citizens in their varied enterprises. In other words, our government has insisted that individual Americans be given every possible opportunity to influence the thought and mores of Asians.

While all this may seem perfectly natural and innocuous to us, probably no other single group of outsiders proved more subversive to the traditional regimes and institutions of Asia than American missionaries. They taught an ethical system that was not compatible with native concepts and institutions; they introduced ideas that were not only subversive to the native political regimes but ate away at the roots of the whole society; on top of this they helped supply the technological foundations for revolution in Asia—English, the language for contact with the outside world, new educational systems, Western medical and scientific knowledge, even such things as improved agricultural techniques. Our missionaries were as much revolutionaries in Asia as any Communist agents, whether they realized it or not. So also were all the other Americans who went to Asia for business, diplomacy, or merely pleasure. Each, whether by undermining the traditional economy, by demonstrating new techniques of operation, by illustrating new social or ethical attitudes, or by advocating new ideas, made his contribution, great or small, to the cataclysmic transformation of Asia.

The Asian revolution is in reality our revolution, fostered, however unconsciously, by the democratic peoples of the Western world. It is our democracy that represents the great challenge to traditional Asian political institutions, not the revived absolutism of communism, which for Asia is the old authoritarian system bolstered up by new and terrible totalitarian techniques. Our free society is the great challenge to traditional Asian society, not the manacled equality and uniformed, strutting hierarchy of Russia. Our concepts of individual prosperity are the great challenge to Asian poverty, not the misery of the Communist masses under the bloated, all-powerful state. Democracy is what Asians hope to achieve. Communism represents the failure of these hopes, a partial reversion to the least desirable aspects of the old system. To put it in the terms of the Marxist, communism is the counter-revolution of the democratic revolution of Asia.

If the alternative to democracy today were some traditional system quite innocuous in itself or to other nations, we might with good reason hesitate to tamper with it. In the nineteenth century, when Asia counted so little in world affairs, we might have paused to consider the desirability of the blatantly revolutionary activity we of the democratic West were conducting in Asia. But in the middle of the twentieth century, when the revolution we heedlessly started is already in full swing and its outcome is so important for the future of all mankind, it will scarcely benefit Asians or ourselves if we now hang back from the battle in self-doubt. The Communists have long since entered it with full consciousness of what they were doing. It is high time we realized that we are on the offensive for democracy and a free society in Asia. We owe it to the Asians as well as to ourselves not to abandon the revolution halfway but to help carry through as vigorously as possible toward its full realization, past the tragic Communist compromise with the past and on to real democracy.

One may wonder why, if we ourselves did so much to start the Asian revolution, it has not always kept closer to our own pattern. The question is frequently phrased in more specific terms by disillusioned Americans: "How could the Chinese have gone Communist after all that our missionaries did for them?" This is an entirely valid question, and the answer to it may have considerable bearing on our position throughout Asia.

The missionary often sought to abstract his religion or more narrowly his theology from the whole society in which he lived. Even this partial presentation of the Western challenge proved extremely destructive to the traditional societies of Asia, helping to undermine essential timbers in the whole structure. The missionary also helped to provide the tools and techniques of the revolution. But he failed to offer an over-all design. Political, social, and economic organization he usually felt to be at most peripheral to his interests. He offered a limited revolution, primarily in religion and secondarily in social organization, education, and sometimes even medicine and agriculture. Asians, however, soon became involved in a total revolution. It is not surprising that most of them accepted many of the elements of the missionary's teaching but looked elsewhere for a more comprehensive plan that embraced the totality of their lives. The missionary's underestimation of what he was doing may explain why the Christian schools of Asia have produced their full share of Communist leaders. We Americans might more validly be blamed for seeking to change too little in Asia than for attempting to change too much.

Much the same lesson can be learned from our recent experience in the occupation of Japan and South Korea. In Japan, because of our exaggerated wartime concept that all Japanese society was thoroughly evil, we showed no reluctance to use our temporary authority to the maximum to mold Japanese society into a more democratic shape. We did not stop at the political level, but wisely decided to delve deeply into the economic and social substructure. For example, we stripped the very wealthy of most of their possessions; we divided the land almost equally among those who actually farmed it; and we insisted on strict legal equality for women and greater freedom for youth. The vigor and thoroughness of our actions were in part the result of misconceptions, and our impatient disregard of certain democratic safeguards was unjustified and unwise. But, despite these mistakes, our strong offensive for democracy proved vastly more successful than our more defensive pose in Japan in recent years. During the early postwar years in Japan, MacArthur played the role not only of the most radical American revolutionary of modern times but also of the most successful.

The case of Korea presents a sad contrast to Japan. Lacking any strong emotional reason for taking positive action, we exercised our authority there with diffidence. The Koreans were in desperate need of leadership and help, and the responsibility for supplying these was ours, since we had freed Korea. But we were slow to develop any positive policies and failed to provide the strong leadership that was needed to help the new nation off to a sound start toward democracy and real independence.

Postwar Korea and Japan, of course, were very unusual cases. Most of Asia consists of independent nations where we have no special responsibilities of this sort and exert no authority. Here we face the problems of relations between full equals, with which we feel more at ease. In these countries there is no call for us to demonstrate the type of forceful leadership we displayed in Japan and failed to provide in Korea, but this does not mean that we need have any compunctions about exerting by persuasion whatever beneficial influence we can.

Actually we cannot help exerting great influence whether we intend to or not. When the Indonesians were struggling with the Dutch for their independence, we at times sought to exert no influence on the outcome, thereby certainly not' aiding the Dutch in their difficult adjustment to the postwar situation and positively harming the Indonesians, who were in sore need of our encouragement and aid. By attempting to exert no influence on the outcome we may in fact have had a generally bad influence on the situation. A nation as powerful as the United States cannot but exert an influence on every issue in the world. It is better that we realize this clearly and then exert our influence positively and wisely.

Some Americans, however, failing to comprehend this point, are subject to a strange embarrassment about seeking to influence others—an embarrassment which, it might be emphasized, the Communist never feels. But this apparent modesty may be merely a form of inverted snobbery, implying either that Asians and we are such different breeds that our respective experiences can be of no value to each other or else that we in our supposed perfection stand so far above them in their imperfection that there can be no comparison between our problems. Both assumptions are of course nonsense and are nothing more than the revival of Kipling's "East is East" in a new guise.

One of the chief appeals of communism in Asia is its recognition that the fundamental problems of human life are the same everywhere. The Communists, however, are entirely wrong in assuming that these problems can be best met, not by a free exchange of knowledge and experience, but by dictation from a single source. And the modest noninterventionist is equally wrong when he looks for independent solutions to the problems of humanity in culturally isolated national units. We are far more likely to achieve satisfactory solutions through a free exchange of ideas and influences than if we all shut ourselves up into idea-tight national compartments. Even if it were theoretically possible today for humanity to withdraw into such mutually exclusive cultural castles, the result would be a stagnating international caste system, not a democratic society of free nations.

There is one thing, however, that no free society, whether national or international, can tolerate, and that is compulsion. This is the most vital line of distinction between ourselves and the Communists. They certainly believe in persuasion, particularly in the form of intellectually numbing propaganda, but when persuasion fails, they insist on using force. In fact, force and persuasion are inextricably intertwined in Communist techniques. It is a particularly absurd mismanagement of our cause that we appear to many Asians to be relying primarily on force and the Communists on arguments.

Our disasters in Asia have arisen in large part from our failure to recognize the potentialities of our influence throughout Asia or to see that we are part of the spearhead of revolution there. Our negative, defensive attitude toward communism has not been simply ridiculous; it has been suicidal. It has contributed to the belief held by many in Asia that the Communists rather than we are the ones who stand for progress toward democracy and prosperity. At the same time it has forced us into an ultimately hopeless reliance on defensive military power. It has led us into the preposterous position of supporting a *status quo* that not only is untenable but often is inconsistent with our own beliefs. It has frequently made us ally ourselves with regimes that have stopped their forward motion and are therefore doomed to collapse. We should stand beside each regime pressing resolutely forward toward democracy; we should stand encouragingly ahead of those peoples whose forward motion toward democracy is faltering; but we should never lag behind with those who have stopped.

If land reform, for example, seems desirable to help lay the basis for a viable democratic society in some Asian country, then let us advocate and support land reform there as persuasively and effectively as possible. In Japan, when we had the authority, we forced through a sweeping, even drastic, land-reform program with tremendous success. Elsewhere we do not have the authority to force such a program on other people, but we certainly have the right to advocate it and exert our influence in its behalf, if this is for our common good.

At home the strength of the American way lies in our

constant push forward toward higher living standards, particularly for those at the lower end of the economic scale, toward constantly widening opportunities for all, toward growing social and economic equality, toward increasingly effective participation in political control by all. No people has been less willing to abide by the *status quo* than we, no people less inclined to stand on the defensive.

Why, then, should we stand in a false defensive position in Asia? We should return consciously and vigorously to the offensive, exerting every ounce of influence we can muster in behalf of democracy throughout Asia, for greater social and economic equality, for greater individual freedoms, for greater economic well-being for all. These are the things we believe in and should be fighting for. Why surrender the offensive to communism? The defensive can never win in Asia; only the offensive can, and, by all that we believe in, it rightly belongs to us.

12. *Problems of Communication*

The need for an arsenal of ideas may be clear enough, but we should not forget that even the best of ideas will do us little good buried in the catacombs of our libraries or left to rattle emptily down the long corridors of Washington. Only when they become active in Asia, when they become part of the intellectual armor of our allies there, will they be effective in the great battle for Asia. In other words, there is the problem of communication.

In dealing with this problem, we must recognize that there are great differences between a country like Korea, where there has been a very real shooting war with communism, and a land like India, where even the cold war appears a somewhat remote and theoretical affair. Most Koreans during the past few years have lived at least briefly under both Communist and non-Communist governments. They have had a chance to see for themselves some of the actual differences between the two, and as a result they appear to be singularly uninterested in the theories professed by either.

Even the simple, uneducated Korean peasant quickly saw that the Communists ruled by threat and force. Today it was a neighbor who ran afoul of the Communist rulers and was liquidated, and it was not hard to see that tomorrow it might be himself. His experience with our side was hardly under auspicious circumstances. The American army, particularly under occupation or combat conditions, is not the best instrument for teaching democracy, and Syngman Rhee's regime is hardly a full embodiment of democratic principles. But the Korean could see that we did not threaten and liquidate and that the South Korean government, despite occasional lapses into coercive action, was not dedicated to that method of operation. Whatever the imperfections of our side and whatever the glittering theories displayed by the Communists, one quick look at Communist methods of control was all that the Korean needed to convince him that communism was not what he wanted.

When the North Koreans invaded South Korea in 1950, a high proportion of the inhabitants of the south either were quite indifferent to the outcome or actually looked forward with hope to a Communist victory. Except for those whose wealth or political position made them marked men, very few Koreans fled from the invading Communists as they overran nearly the whole peninsula. A few months later, after American and South Korean troops had driven up to the northern extremities of Korea and then were pushed southward again by the invading Chinese, the story was entirely different. This time the poor as well as the rich, the unknown as well as the marked men, tried to flee from the advancing Communists. Those in North Korea had lived for several years under Communist rule and had been free from it for only a few weeks; those in the south had been under Communist control only a few months; but either experience sufficed to convince the man in the street or the paddy field that he did not want the Communists. The Korean masses gave an inarticulate but very convincing vote, not so much for democracy as against communism.

The prisoner controversy in Korea was another reflection of the common man's revulsion against communism when he has once experienced both it and a practical alternative. A large proportion of the Chinese and North Korean prisoners of war decided that they did not wish to return to their Communist homelands. For a Chinese soldier to abandon family and home in this way was far more difficult than for an Occidental, with his weaker sense of family and his broader geographic horizons. It is profoundly significant that despite these difficulties some fourteen thousand Chinese prisoners hated the Communists so much that they broke their ties with home for a very uncertain fate. This was a very encouraging sign for us, but at the same time it produced a complex situation that did much to prolong the war.

We had decided after sober second thought that we had betrayed basic democratic ideals of individual freedom when in 1945 we had acquiesced in the return of huge numbers of anti-Communist Soviet prisoners to certain death or persecution in their homeland. We were not willing to repeat this mistake with Koreans and Chinese. On the other hand, the Communists, who dogmatically claim to be the spokesmen for all workers and peasants, could hardly admit that simple peasant conscripts would repudiate communism. The men themselves could hardly have meant much to the Chinese leaders, but their defection undermined the whole basic theory of the Communist dictatorship of the proletariat. The Communists may have been unable to believe this clear contradiction of their dearest dogma, and this may explain their apparent hope that the anti-Communist prisoners could be persuaded to return home and their frenzy when their efforts to convince the prisoners failed so dismally. It was a bitter pill for the Communists to swallow, and although they finally took it, they did their best to conceal it from themselves and their people by raising a constant smoke screen.

This same pragmatic rejection of communism is, of course, familiar in the satellite countries of Europe. It might also become characteristic of Vietnam, if the Indochinese were sure that they need sacrifice none of their nationalism in repudiating communism. But these are exceptional conditions for Asia and cannot become more widespread without a further extension of Communist conquest. Aside from the mainland Chinese, who are for the moment effectively isolated by their masters from the war of ideas, most Asians have had no experience with Communist rule. From Japan through Indonesia and India to the shores of the Mediterranean the choice between democracy and communism does not rest on hard personal experience but belongs to the realm of theory. It is in this part of Asia that the war of ideas acquires its greatest significance and the need for effective communication becomes most acute.

In communication the first problem naturally is that of translating ideas into a form intelligible to the person to whom you wish to communicate them. At its simplest level, this involves the problem of languages. Obviously no one would advocate broadcasting in English to an audience that does not understand the English language. The point is too self-evident to need argument, though we might reflect on some of its implications. For instance, if it is worth while to establish libraries of English books in Asian lands, might it not be even more valuable to establish libraries of similar books in the native languages? Of course, the relative usefulness of English and the local languages varies greatly from country to country in Asia, and in most of them one would first have to engage in a large-scale enterprise of translation and publication before such libraries could be stocked. But effective communication with Asians will increasingly depend on our ability to make use of the native languages, and it is safe to predict that English-language libraries will prove less and less adequate for our purposes in the future.

Another aspect of the language problem is oral communication. The accepted system throughout Asia, inherited in part from the colonial past, is that the Asian must use our language if there is to be any exchange of ideas. It has been up to him to speak English, or in a few lands French or Dutch, not up to us to speak Hindi, Arabic, or Japanese. The system not only has been convenient for linguistically lazy Americans and Englishmen but has given us the apparent advantage of staying safely on our own verbal ground.

In actuality, however, this system has been in part self-defeating. It has limited communication in some lands to a tiny and not at all representative group of persons who happened to be able to speak English. Even in such countries as India and Ceylon, where almost all persons with higher education speak our language, it has limited our contacts to a single class. It has also tended to make communication a one-way current. The Asian, either unable or unwilling to express himself fully in English, often played the role of half-comprehending listener, while we rattled happily along in English, unaware of what was in his mind.

Worst of all, our exclusive reliance on English raises strong psychological barriers to real understanding. I have often noticed that a Japanese speaking to me in his own language talks much more freely and directly than when restricted to English, and that the resultant exchange of ideas is greatly facilitated by increased clarity and also by a greater emotional sense of equality and reciprocity. The same, I feel certain, must be true of all Asians except for the very small number of persons whose education has been primarily through the medium of a Western language. By speaking the Asian's tongue we have not only more chance of achieving an intellectual meeting of minds with him but also, by this demonstration of our interest in him, a better chance of clearing away the emotional barriers between us. Unquestionably we shall be far more effective in communicating with Asians when there are adequate numbers of Americans who can meet them halfway linguistically.

While the language problem itself is difficult enough, a more complex and important problem in communication is that of translating our ideas into comprehensible and appealing idiom, regardless of the language used. As we have seen, "the American way of life" is a good term for describing democracy only in the United States itself. Similarly many other of our pet phrases need something more than simple word-for-word translation before they can be used effectively in Asia.

Take for example the term "free enterprise." For us this implies freedom from the stultifying restrictions of the bureaucratic super-state. It suggests a healthy and altogether desirable freedom for all men on their own initiative to work for their common good and not simply to serve as cogs in a ponderously inefficient machine of state in which only a handful of men at the very top can show any true initiative. Not unnaturally we emphasize the blessings of "individualism" in our war with those political systems that enslave the faceless masses to the will of a few rulers. But both "free enterprise" and "individualism" suggest entirely different concepts to most Asians. These terms raise before their eyes the picture of the ruthless monopolist, the economic gouger, the foreign or native exploiter of the economic ills of colonial Asia. Where we take for granted that free enterprise and individualism will find expression within the necessary limits imposed by law and custom in behalf of the common good, the Asian may assume that they are symbols of the disregard of all social conscience. Obviously terms such as these cannot be used safely in Asia, and the ideas behind them must be translated into some other idiom.

Successful communication, however, is not merely a matter of finding suitable equivalents for our words. Beyond this it requires an adjustment to the ideas in the mind of the other person. In Asia as in Europe a great many people who have little or no sympathy for communism are strong believers in socialism, and in many Asian countries these socialist sympathizers are either the dominant or a very important group in the intellectual and political life of the nation. We shall have small success in communicating with these people if we stick stubbornly to the vocabulary dictated by our own prejudices against socialism. As we have seen, there are many reasons why so many Asians have this theoretical addiction to socialism, and their attitude is likely to change only slowly at best. In the meantime we should certainly attempt to understand their point of view and put our arguments in such form as to be comprehensible and emotionally appealing to them.

When the American public was not yet vitamin-conscious, the advertiser of breakfast cereals could rely on assertions of the yumminess of his product or the delightful sound it made when coming into contact with milk. But when the public became interested in vitamins, the advertiser turned to citing with pride the full list of vitamins and the microscopic quantities of minerals that his product presumably had always possessed. The analogy is admittedly far-fetched, but we might, in the light of the theories and prejudices of the Asian socialist, re-examine democracy as we understand it and as it is exemplified in the United States to see what vitamins of socialistic theory it may possess.

Actually if we were to do this, we might find that we have vastly more to offer the socialist-minded Asian than either he or we have imagined. Take for example the socialist ideal of a classless society. Where does one find the closest approximation to a classless society today? Very probably in the United States, rather than in the various lands of Europe or Asia, whether they be socialist, Communist, or neither.

Despite the great American mixture of races and of peoples with different linguistic and cultural backgrounds, our society has not divided itself up into various clear-cut strata like those of both Europe and Asia. We have our quota of snobs of all varieties, but no category of Americans who are recognized as aristocrats by anybody but themselves. Similarly, except for recent immigrants, we have no large body of Americans who consider themselves a lower class. There are of course great differences in wealth, power, and prestige among individual Americans, but the great majority of them feel no inherent sense of inferiority to any other group and, when asked to classify themselves, have usually considered themselves part of an all-embracing middle class.

The contrast with almost all other parts of the world

is marked. It is hard for Americans to comprehend the strong feelings of class that remain in Europe as well as throughout Asia. We have only to look at the costumes of the Soviet officials and officers to see how strong is the Russian sense of class and how the Communist Revolution has resulted in a reshuffling rather than an abolition of classes. The high proportion of domestic servants in other lands is in a sense a symbol of their class societies. The petty intellectual in Europe or Asia, who may declaim on the merits of the classless socialist society, assumes that he himself will have servants, while the corresponding American, who may declaim as violently against socialism, takes his lack of domestic servants for granted and would be embarrassed to find himself in the position of either master or servant. If a classless society is desirable and Americans have shown by their lives that they believe this far more fundamentally than those who mouth the term most, then America can pride itself on being the country that has come closest to achieving this socialist ideal.

Another basic socialist concept is that individuals should contribute to society according to their abilities and be rewarded according to their needs. It seems doubtful that this particular ideal will ever be fully realized by human beings, but certainly it is not even being approximated in Communist lands, where rigid controls from the top keep all but the most hardy and fortunate from contributing to their full ability, and where the needs of the masses are interpreted by one harsh scale and the needs of the rulers by a much more generous standard.

On the other hand, the United States, without ever using this slogan, has come closer to achieving it than almost any other country. Nowhere in the world is it easier for an individual, regardless of his background, to make his maximum contribution to society, for nowhere else will he find greater educational opportunities and fewer social or economic barriers in his way. And nowhere in the world is there a smaller proportional difference between the rewards accorded the unskilled worker, the skilled worker, the educated technician, and the manager or owner, in ascending order of income. Where the junior engineer, the schoolteacher, or the petty bureaucrat in most of Asia will receive an income much higher than that of the skilled worker and many times greater than that of the unskilled worker, such persons in the United States are lucky to receive anything more than the skilled worker or even an appreciably greater salary than the unskilled laborer.

It is also the American tradition for a man to work harder and longer the higher he stands on the ladder of prestige and power. Regardless of wealth an American who has not reached the age of retirement is ashamed to be without a job. There is probably less leisure per capita among those in the upper levels of our society than among those in the middle or lower levels. This situation, together with our lack of class feeling, has inevitably given to American culture a certain plebeian tone. We have of course music, literature, art, and entertainment designed for the minority with a broad education and cultivated tastes, but this is quantitatively outweighed by music, literature, art, and entertainment designed to meet the needs of Americans of less discriminating tastes. We should be proud of this rather than apologetic. It simply illustrates that leisure for us is not the monopoly of a relatively narrow aristocracy, bourgeoisie, or officialdom. Proportionately the common man plays a much larger role in our culture than in the more aristocratic societies of the rest of the world. Ours is the culture of the classless society. It is an irony that those who are loudest in criticizing it are often those most en' ausiastically dedicated to the creation of that very classless society.

We may have advanced as far as we have toward the achievement of these supposedly socialist ideals because we were largely unconscious of what we were doing. Certainly our progress in this direction owes little to socialist theory and nothing to socialist catch-phrases. On the contrary, we tend to be strongly anti-socialist, because we identify by this term not these commendable achievements but rather a system in which there is so much centralized control that all individual initiative is stifled with red tape.

But this does not mean that we should carry our prejudices against socialism into our dealings with socialist-minded Asians, for whom the term has entirely different connotations. What hope can we have for effective communication with them if we hold doggedly to the words and phrases that we like but that frighten them, while reacting in anger and fear against the terms they cherish? When we do this we are speaking in mutually unintelligible idioms, even if we both are using the same language. In communicating with Asians, we should attempt to use words and phrases according to the connotations and emotional overtones the terms have for them. If in dealing with socialist Asians, for example, we first made clear the excellent claims we have for being regarded in some ways as the leading socialist nation in the world, we might not only establish much more harmonious and satisfying contacts but also have much greater hope of convincing them of the very real dangers of what we mean by socialism.

The use of socialist idiom when necessary is but one example of the many ways in which we must translate our concepts into the native patterns of thought as well as into the native languages. But even supposing an adequate body of ideas and corresponding ability to translate them as required by local attitudes, we still would face the problem of creating adequate agencies for the war of ideas.

While the government, for financial reasons, will undoubtedly have to bear the major burden in communication with Asians, this field above all others is one in which private educational and philanthropic agencies can and must play an important role. In other words, we must rely to a large extent on private enterprise. One reason is the very fact that in many parts of Asia we must couch our arguments in terms that will be understandable to socialist-minded people. In a totalitarian state the government can say one thing at home and the opposite abroad without any fear of undesirable domestic repercussions, but in a democracy even a variation of idiom raises difficulties.

An American can hardly speak intelligibly and effectively to the socialistically oriented Burmese, for example, without becoming correspondingly unintelligible to many of his compatriots at home. But the official representative of a government cannot limit his words artificially to one audience. One can imagine the explosion if a junketing congressman hears an American official in Burma talking of the great "socialist" achievements of the United States. The American people, he might quite reasonably feel, had not paid their taxes to support this sort of treachery. American representatives abroad obviously need not be hobbled so completely as they are today in the war of ideas, any more than they need be surrounded by the present state of fear and demoralization that has undermined their value as reporting officers—that is, as the eyes and ears of the United States abroad. On the other hand, it seems Utopian to hope that Congress and the general public will come to have so thorough an understanding of the ideological problems abroad that they will give our representatives free rein in translating our concepts into the local idiom.

But where the government leaves off in its efforts, private enterprise can begin. Individual Americans or representatives of private foundations can speak with a freedom and therefore with a cogency that representatives of the government can rarely achieve. They can also speak with the diversity of points of view that is the true strength of democracy. There can be a single party line for Communists, but any narrowly defined policy for the representatives of a democracy in the war of ideas is in a sense a falsification of democracy itself and eliminates the rich variation that gives it its flexibility and resilience. The private citizen is needed not only to say what the official representative cannot say for fear of being misunderstood at home, but also to give to our statements the variety that is the only true measure of our views.

The private citizen also has the great advantage in the war of ideas of being in large part free of the natural suspicion with which any people insulates representatives of a foreign government. The private American, while not standing on the elevated stage of official status, finds himself by this very fact closer to the people with whom he wishes to communicate. He can more easily enter into the free and uninhibited give-and-take of ideas on which our whole concept of democratic progress depends.

The work to be undertaken by private groups and individuals in the ideological field is almost endless. We should be trying to establish fruitful intellectual contacts at every possible level. The limitations are purely those of available funds and suitable personnel. The possibilities may best be seen from a consideration of one of the most obvious and important areas of activity—the universities of Asia.

In Asia the individual university plays a more important part than in the United States. While an incomparably smaller percentage of the population attends college, the experience of higher education marks a much sharper dividing line between leadership and the masses than it does with us. The governments of Burma and Indonesia are made up of men who were themselves students in universities just a few short years ago, and throughout Asia it is safe to assume that, in comparison with American students, a much higher proportion of those now attending classes in universities in Asia will be important in the politics of their countries—and much sooner. The intellectual experience of the young men and women of Asia in their college years is a matter of the greatest importance for the future of Asia.

Under these circumstances it is to our interest that the universities of Asia should be as good as possible and that the instruction in them should represent the best in modern scholarship. But this is by no means the fact. In many Asian countries higher education is essentially a matter of prescribed courses leading to prescribed degrees ostensibly leading to specific careers, but having little to do with the great intellectual ferment of our day. Such key subjects as economics and history do not progress far enough into the modern age to have much relevancy for the present situation, and the study of sociology may be entirely lacking. Or the theories and established facts of the modern social sciences may be taught out of textbooks that represent the attainments of a half-century ago. As a consequence, it is not unusual to find an Asian student taking a degree at a university in some stereotyped field of study but receiving his education in the modern world at the nearby Communist bookstall. It is also not surprising to find Marxism considered by Asian students the latest thing in theory, for they are largely unaware of the subsequent information and thought that have relegated Marxism to the position of a stimulating and interesting theory of a century ago, but hardly an adequate system of thought for the mid-twentieth-century world.

We have not been totally unaware of this situation and have done some things to meet it, though with only indifferent success. There are many mission-supported colleges in Asia, which at one time were extremely important in the field of higher education but in more recent decades have often sunk to the status of second-rate institutions when compared with the local government universities. Through such admirable methods as the Fulbright program we have sought to send private teachers to Asia, though only on a trifling scale.

We have had many private or government programs to train Asian students in this country, though here again the scale has been small and the handling of the programs sometimes unwise. In a desire to see that all American states and colleges were proportionately represented in the program, the administering agencies have at times sent Asian specialists to colleges where they found no adequate guidance in their particular fields of study, and those who went to our bigger institutions sometimes found themselves in a coolly impersonal atmosphere, in which unhappy contacts with racially prejudiced landladies sometimes loomed larger than their occasional contacts with the scholars with whom they had hoped to work.

We should be trying to give promising Asian scholars the best training that can be found in the Western world under the most favorable conditions for their particular needs and problems. Beyond this we should be attempting to place the best Western scholars and teachers we can find in Asian universities. Few first-rate scholars are willing to go to Asia under present conditions of extreme financial insecurity and temporary eclipse from the Western scholarly world. But this difficulty could be easily surmounted by making a period of work in an Asian university financially and professionally attractive. If this were done, outstanding scholars could be induced to teach in Asia, where they would find their work immensely stimulating to themselves as well as invaluable to their students. They would find themselves engaged in a dynamic intellectual exchange of a type that can only strengthen free thought and weaken the appeal of dogmatism, whether in the name of Marx or some other modern ism. There would be no need to check on what Western scholars in Asia said or did. They might learn to speak in terms that could not be understood by most Americans or might say things with which some of us would not agree. But if they were true representatives of the best in modern Western scholarship, their influence without doubt would be profoundly beneficial not only for Asians but also for the West.

The field of university teaching is but one of many in which there are great possibilities and a pressing need for free enterprise in the war of ideas in Asia. But this is not to say that the role of the government in the ideological war is unimportant. The government representative can be very influential, for either good or evil, because his words and deeds are watched more closely and judged more severely. Whether we realize it or not, we have an ideological campaign under way wherever a representative of our government can be seen or heard by Asians.

It is perhaps time for us to reconsider the entire nature of our foreign relations and the whole functioning of our foreign service. Diplomatic relations have grown out of the exchange of personal representatives between kings, and they still preserve some of the aristocratic aura of their origin. But diplomatic relations today are not really between individual rulers but between whole peoples of entire nations. Although the American ambassador in any country is in theory the President's personal messenger to the local head of state, he actually is the representative of the American people to the people of that land. The same is true of all the members of the ambassador's staff. Their specific functions are extremely varied, but all play a part in this most important of all public-relations problems in the modern world.

An ambassador stands in a unique position in the relations between two peoples. Ideally, therefore, he should be the embodiment of all that we feel to be best in our society. But usually he is selected for entirely different reasons. His appointment may be a reward for a substantial campaign contribution or a consolation prize for a defeated politician. Preferably, it may be because he is a good housekeeper in administering a complex branch of government or again because he is an astute political reporter or perhaps a skillful negotiator. These are necessary functions in an embassy, but they are specialized duties not differing in type from the specialized functions of military, naval, or commercial attachés. It is a pity to waste the key post of ambassador on a man with only such technical skills.

Actually we have had in recent years a good demonstration of what an ambassador can accomplish in representing the American people to a foreign country. Chester Bowles as Ambassador to India was undoubtedly a happy accident rather than a planned diplomatic triumph. He went to India not because of any perceptive Democratic strategy, but only because he was defeated at the polls, and the President was ready to give him the post he asked for. Not by training or planning but by simple intuition he hit upon the most effective way of representing the

American people abroad. For all its novelty, it was a device ready to hand for any American diplomat—a natural feeling of democratic equality.

Bowles treated the Indians around him as if they had been his neighbors at home in Connecticut, and the results electrified all India. By simply representing in his person American ideals as they are exemplified in ordinary American conduct, he brushed aside innumerable veils of misunderstanding and prejudice between the Indian people and us. Even if Bowles had failed miserably in the more traditional spheres of diplomacy, which he most certainly did not, he could still be counted as by all odds the most successful American Ambassador in any part of Asia since the war.

What is true of our ambassadors in Asia is true to some degree of all the men under them. But the whole system of American government service in Asia puts little emphasis on desirable relations with the people of Asia themselves. The specialist who learns the native language and becomes an expert in the native culture and psychology is likely to find these accomplishments hindrances rather than aids to his promotion. If something goes wrong, as in China, he may be cast to the wolves as a convenient scapegoat, and even if nothing so drastic happens, he may find himself sidetracked in his career because he had been "queer" enough to come to know the local people well. The time he has put into acquiring this knowledge has left him that much less time to develop camaraderie with his fellow American officials on the golf links or to distinguish himself in the indoor sport of cocktail-party repartee. Our foreign service is geared to produce fine mixers with other Americans rather than to produce the all-important contact men with Asians.

When we restrict ourselves to a narrow, traditional interpretation of diplomatic relations, we not only reduce the possibilities for effective communication but also doom ourselves to supporting governments, not peoples. American aid often appears to be aid to a regime rather than to a country. If that regime is on the way out, as is frequently the case in Asia, American support of it can easily be interpreted as an integral part of an undesirable system that the local people are determined to change. When revolution comes, American aid and perhaps all friendly relations with the United States may be scrapped as part of the discarded system. If we could establish our contacts more clearly with Asian peoples as a whole and with governments only as representatives of these peoples, we might avoid the difficulty of having to start our relations with each new regime under the cloud of our association with its discredited predecessor.

Communication, thus, should be established at all possible levels, but we should also remember that, regardless of the level, communication must go in both directions to be truly effective. We shall have small success if we simply attempt to blanket Asia at every possible intellectual wave-length with our own ideas. The Western world, to say nothing of the United States, is certainly not the unique repository of human wisdom. Nor can there be any sort of democratic world order without a successful interchange of ideas between all parts of the globe that participate in it. The degree of success we can achieve in communicating both ways with Asia will be a very real measure of the degree to which Asia comes to participate in such a democratic world order.

The Communist system can tolerate only one-way communication. If Peking is not eventually to try to dictate to Moscow, then Moscow must continue to attempt to dictate to Peking. But democracy suffers from no such weakness. It thrives on two-way communication, not on dictation.

In the historical context in which we live, there is probably more for the West to communicate to Asia just now than there is to be communicated in the other direction. This is something that we Americans should be able to accept with realistic modesty, for it was not long ago that the United States stood in its relations to western Europe in somewhat the same position that Asia now occupies in its relations with the West. Proportionately, however, there is a greater need to expand and improve communications from Asia to the West than in the reverse direction. What flow there has been, though grossly inadequate in itself, has been largely from us to them. We need not be surprised that many Asians fail to see the all-important differences between democratic and totalitarian concepts of a world order, for in our dealings with Asia we have not uncommonly approximated in our own actions the arrogant dictation of the Communists and have ignored the basic democratic ideals of a free exchange of ideas and a reciprocity of influences. Until we come closer to achieving these ideals in our relations with Asia, we not only are failing to create the world order that we seek but are also nullifying one of democracy's greatest advantages over communism.

13. *The Chinese Puzzle*

How do these concepts of communication and the war of ideas apply, if at all, to Communist Asia? In China and other Communist lands an effective wall has been raised against all ideas from abroad, and under present conditions it is idle to think of establishing fruitful communication in either direction or at any level. Perhaps some information and a few ideas could be slipped clandestinely into China, but since the Communists control аи other information and the Chinese are very suspicious of us, any ideological campaign we direct toward China runs the danger of being so distorted as to do more harm than good to our cause.

But we should not conclude that ideological considerations can be overlooked in our relations with China. Our objectives there, if stated in their broadest terms, are fundamentally ideological in nature. Our first hope is that China can be induced to break off its close and exclusive co-operation with Russia, which not only endangers Chinese independence but also increases the strains and perils of the present precarious balance of power in the world. Beyond this we hope that the Chinese can somehow be persuaded to abandon their attempt to create a totalitarian society and instead will undertake the development of a democratic political and social system which will support rather than undermine the democratic world order we envisage.

Although these are basically ideological objectives, our direct ideological leverage on the Chinese at present is nil, or perhaps one might say a negative quantity. Just as Americans tend to view with suspicion anything that Communists are for, the Chinese are inclined to reject anything that Americans advocate. But even this negative influence takes on some significance when we stop to consider the ineffectiveness of our other types of strategy in dealing with China. If we had much hope of exerting influence on China's future through direct military or economic pressure, we might disregard our obviously feeble ideological arm of strategy, but these other two arms appear even less potent.

We do of course have superiority in atomic weapons over China and could wipe out China's cities without fear of comparable reprisal from the Chinese themselves, but this aerial threat, while possibly giving us some negative control over China, gives us no positive influence at all. It may help to deter the Chinese from open aggression against neighboring lands, but at the same time it serves to bind China more closely to Russia, for the Chinese realize that Russian air power and the threat of Russian atomic retaliation are their only effective defenses against American atomic weapons. Unless some tremendous change in Chinese attitudes takes place, American superiority in atomic weapons is likely to continue to strengthen Moscow's control over China rather than weaken it and will give us little influence over China's future, unless we are ready to pass through Armageddon first.

The remainder of our military power is even less effective against China. The Korean War has demonstrated all too clearly that the Chinese are by no means outclassed by the maximum military effort we can safely make on the ground in Asia under present world conditions. In fact, the rapid increase during the past few years in the Russian-supplied equipment of the Chinese divisions and their resultant rise in fire-power and general efficiency would suggest that any future land fighting between Chinese and American troops is likely to be on less favorable terms for us than it was in Korea.

Many Americans have placed great store on Chiang's ability to reverse the course of history and reconquer China from Formosa. This, however, is a mere will-o'-the-wisp, not a reasonable possibility on which we can safely stake our hopes for the future. Some people maintain that if Chiang's forces landed on the mainland, the populace would rise to join him, but there is little objective evidence to support such optimism. Many Chinese, no doubt, are disillusioned with the Communists, but their disillusionment with the Kuomintang is even more profound. Before any appreciable number of mainland Chinese would rally to Chiang's side, he would have to demonstrate definite military superiority over the Communists, and this for the present he cannot do. The human resources at Mao's command outnumber those under Chiang's control by at least fifty to one. The weapons we can provide the Kuomintang armies can be easily matched by the Russians. The Communists have the strong morale of men who only recently whipped their Kuomintang adversaries, while the latter must draw on the morale of desperation. And, finally, the Kuomintang pygmy would have to cross the water and wrest China from the Communist giant by sheer force. Many examples of the "good" triumphing over the "evil" despite such overwhelming handicaps can be found in our comic strips or movies, but not in the annals of military history.

The Kuomintang's only chance of ever returning to power in China rests on the prior collapse of the Communists. If the latter make such colossal blunders that the whole regime falls into chaos, or if the Chinese masses or a significant proportion of the leadership itself should become so disaffected that they wreck Mao's rule, then perhaps the Kuomintang's comparatively slight military strength might again become significant on the Chinese mainland. Thus, in a positive policy toward China the military arm is likely to become significant for us only after tremendous changes have taken place at the ideological level.

If the military arm is so puny in our dealings with China, the economic is even less potent. The Communists fell heir to a China that was living at a mere subsistence level after long years of disruptive warfare during which there had been few economic contacts with the outside world. Unlike the Japanese, who must engage in a tremendous foreign trade to live at all, the Chinese can continue almost indefinitely at this subsistence level without any foreign contacts. Moreover, the Chinese Communists have obviously based their whole strategy on the assumption that they could get along without the economic assistance of the free world. Economic aid from Russia alone, they believe, will be enough for China's industrialization, and they are perfectly willing, if necessary, to have no economic dealings with non-Communist nations.

Under these circumstances our tremendous economic potential exerts no influence on the Chinese at all. They would be chary in accepting our economic aid even if we freely offered it to them. On the other hand, if we insisted on a complete embargo of trade with China by all our allies and we ourselves imposed a rigid naval blockade of the China coast, the chief result would probably be to bind the Chinese all the more closely to the Russians. Of course, the Chinese in time might become dissatisfied with the limited aid the Russians can give them and the unfavorable bargaining position they are in because of their sole reliance on the Soviet Union, or they might become seriously disappointed at the slowness of their economic progress compared with other nations enjoying free contacts with the West. If this should happen, our economic potential might suddenly become an important tool of strategy, but until such changes in ideas take place, it is virtually useless.

China today presents a veritable Chinese puzzle to the Western world. We can see that there are various elements in the situation which could be rearranged with consequent benefit for the whole world, but none of these pieces in the puzzle is easily dislodged. Whenever we have tried to pull one loose, we have found that we were forcing all the pieces more solidly together. Such direct actions are obviously not the way to achieve our ends. Instead we should reconsider the whole problem more closely to see where the puzzle is most likely to come apart and what series of moves is most likely to lead to this result. This is a slower and more painstaking process than the quick, sharp pull we had hoped would solve the puzzle, but we know enough about it now to realize that there is probably no other solution.

Some people have felt that the most likely line of division in Communist China lies between the tolerant traditions and easygoing habits of the common people and the cruel rigidity of their masters. A look at China's past, however, gives no great support to this concept. Throughout history the Chinese ruling class has shown a genius for meticulous organization and sometimes for callous regimentation of the masses. With the aid of modern totalitarian techniques, Chinese rulers are probably as capable of keeping the Communist yoke on their people as Soviet leaders have been of keeping it on the essentially tolerant and easygoing Russians. In any case, this is a possible line of cleavage about which we can do nothing. Any pressures we attempt to put on the Chinese under present conditions are likely not to split them from their government but rather to keep them more closely bound to it by giving credence to Communist claims that we are the external menace.

A second possible line of cleavage is between economic hopes and economic achievements. If the Communists fail miserably in their economic objectives, the leadership itself, if not the common people, will be ripe for new alignments. It would seem advisable, therefore, for us to make no contribution to Chinese economic development unless the advantages to our side for other reasons at least offset the economic gains to Communist China. But actually this too is not a very likely line of major division. Chinese military power and economic production have both increased rapidly under Communist rule. Although the Chinese rate of population growth is apparently less than half that of India, with which the most telling comparisons will undoubtedly be made, the rate of economic growth in China appears to be substantially higher than that of India. Under these circumstances the line between economic hopes and achievements is more likely to become a dangerous rift in democratic India than in Communist China.

A much more probable line of division lies between the proud Chinese and the domineering Russians, for this is a line which coincides with that sensitive frontier of contact between Asia and the West. Mao and his associates are entirely dependent on the Soviet Union for the military weapons and economic aid they must have to develop the type of China they hope to create. At the same time the Chinese can scarcely have overcome their fear of foreign domination or their resentment of the status of superiority assumed by white men during the past several generations. The Russians are unmistakably *ta-pi-tzu,* or Western "big noses," to the Chinese. In addition they are extremely dogmatic and inflexible both in theory and in practice, experienced only in clear-cut relationships of authority and obedience. Even though the Chinese and Russians share the same Communist faith, it would be hard to imagine a more profoundly difficult relationship than that existing between them today.

There has been much talk about possible Titoism in China and more scornful refutation of this idea. The term is at best a poor one. It is true that Tito and Mao are the only two postwar Communist leaders who do not owe their positions largely to Russian military might, but here the comparison stops. Tito was Moscow-trained, and he is a fellow Slav as well; also, he rules over a small country not very far from the main seats of Russian power. Mao is an Asian, received no training in the Soviet Union, and is the master of a people at least twenty-five times as numerous as the Yugoslavs, living three times as far away from the main centers of Russian power. The problems of Soviet-Yugoslav relations can scarcely be compared with those inherent in the relations between the Chinese and the Russians, but only because the latter problems are so much more complex and difficult.

The experience with Tito may have been one of the reasons why the Russians have handled their contacts with Communist China, so far as we can tell, with great tact and care. Another reason may be the object lesson of recent Chinese history. During the last half-century the foreign country most active in China has quickly made itself the most hated symbol of all that the Chinese hoped to change. The British held this dubious honor until the Japanese took it away from them in the 1930's through two ruthless wars. We unwittingly fell heir to the position when we eliminated the Japanese from China. Now the Russians have taken our place as the dominant, in fact the only important, foreigners there. They undoubtedly are doing their best not to succeed us as the chief objects of Chinese hatred, and the Chinese leaders, who are certainly sincere in their Communist beliefs, also must be striving to prevent any rift from developing between themselves and the Russians. But a significant line of division inevitably exists between the emotional structure of China and that of Russia. No crack in the Chinese puzzle gives greater promise than this one of opening wide, and if it does, there might then be some hope of dislodging communism itself from the Chinese scene.

It seems unlikely that we can do much to widen the crack between Chinese sensibilities and Russian habits of dictation. Naturally we should do our best to create situations in which a division of Russian and Chinese interests or opinions would become obvious. The Korean truce negotiations offered many such opportunities, but unfortu-

nately all the important stages of negotiation took place
either at the U.N., with the Chinese absent, or at Panmun-
jom, with the Russians not present, thus permitting the
Russians and Chinese to patch up any possible differences
behind their own closed doors. It might even be possible to
exploit to advantage fortuitous opportunities like that
offered not so long ago by the death of Stalin. But
such positive efforts, however Machiavellian, would be
at best of minor value and somewhat uncertain outcome.

We might make a much greater contribution to the
widening of the rift between the Chinese and the Russians
by simply doing nothing—that is, by relaxing those coun-
ter-pressures that help keep it sealed. Certainly if our military and economic efforts only serve to push the Chinese
toward the Russians, we should give some thought to using
these pressures as sparingly as possible. We could, for instance, give effective protection to Formosa without at the
same time launching an offensive of bold threats against
the mainland. The less fear the Chinese have of an American offensive against their homeland, the less dependent
they will feel themselves to be on Russian weapons. Similarly, we could probably retain those economic embargoes against China that make an appreciable difference in
the Chinese military potential, while striking a much less
menacing economic pose than we now hold. The Chinese
can think in terms of possible alternatives to complete dependence on Russian economic power only if they come to
realize that alternatives actually do exist.

Most important, we might by judicious silence begin
to fade out of the Chinese consciousness as the foreign
bogeyman and leave the field open to the Russians. Any
totalitarian system depends on a supposed external menace to justify its cruel controls at home, and unquestionably the Chinese leaders will continue to cast us in this

role, but at least we need not obligingly help them by trying to make the picture look convincing.

While Americans and Chinese were fighting each other in Korea, there was no hope of demoting ourselves from the spot of public enemy number one in Chinese minds. This situation made the war doubly valuable for the Russians, since the Korean fighting not only whittled away at mobile Western power with immobile and entirely expendable Chinese troops but kept the Chinese all the more closely bound to Russia. This war, however, is over, and so long as we do not have to conduct another campaign to stop Chinese aggression, we have some hope of achieving a gradual fade-out. But to do this we must have the wisdom and self-control to keep our mouths shut at times and to sit on our hands. We need firm declarations of policy that will make our determination to stop Communist aggression unmistakably clear, but beyond this our bellicose denunciations of China, though perhaps consoling to our wounded pride, are of more aid to the enemy than to ourselves. Such shouting appears to be poor strategy unless it is our own nerves rather than the world situation about which we are really worried.

Some may argue that if we do not keep shouting, the South Koreans and Nationalist Chinese will lose heart. But if their hearts are so faint and their desire for freedom so weak that they need, not only our aid and protection, but also a constant din of encouragement, they are going to be small help to us in time of crisis. This whole argument, however, does a gross injustice to these two stalwart allies. They have plenty of courage and determination. What they need is not encouragement so much as sober council that will help turn their minds from now fruitless dreams of military triumph to the serious work of reform and rehabilitation, without which their dreams can never be fulfilled.

This point suggests something very positive that we can do as part of our China policy. The Chinese can scarcely think in terms of a political alternative to communism unless they realize that one exists. But their own recent history apparently has convinced most of them that communism, whatever its drawbacks, is the only practical political system for them. Nothing could aid our cause more than a clear demonstration that democracy can be a practical and desirable system for the Chinese too.

Formosa is the logical place for such a demonstration, and herein lies its real significance to the free world. Its seven or eight million people are overwhelmingly Chinese, and they stand far above the continental Chinese in literacy, technical skills, and living standards, thus providing the Nationalist government with the technological foundation on which democracy can safely rest. But the Nationalists will first have to redirect their interests from military conquest to political growth; they will have to turn their backs more decisively on the totalitarian methods they learned from the Communists; they will have to strive much harder than they have in the past to develop a sound and prosperous society and healthy democratic institutions; and, most important, they will have to integrate the native population with the ruling regime until the Formosans themselves have their rightfully preponderant place in the government. If they would do these things—and all are perfectly feasible—Formosa could develop into a successful democracy that might well point the way to a better system than communism for all Chinese.

For this reason the future of Formosa is a question of vital concern to the whole free world. It also happens to be a problem on which we can exert considerable influence. We should be working for the development of a democratic Formosa with all the economic and political tools at our disposal. A successful democracy on Formosa would unquestionably be of much greater value to our cause than all the soldiers that could ever be marshaled on For-mosan soil.

Another thing that we could do to develop a positive policy toward China would be to start laying the founda-tions for a relationship with the Chinese which might give us some leverage in the war of ideas when the opportunity does arise to exert it. It is essential to re-establish communi-cation of some sort with them, if we are to be ready at that time. In this connection we might take a long second look at the whole question of recognizing Communist China.

Actually the Communist regime has consistently acted toward us in such a way that we could scarcely have recognized it, even if we had wished to. The British did recognize the Communists and found themselves insult-ingly ignored in return. Certainly as long as we were fight-ing the Chinese in Korea there could be no thought of recognition. Our lack of recognition, however, has not been so much a policy as merely an indication of the pro-foundly unsatisfactory relationship that exists between us and the Chinese. The time is coming when we should take a more positive attitude toward the problem. We should at least be thinking about what we would like to see develop in our relations with China and should not just passively accept the situation forced on us by the Communists. We might start by adding up in our minds the respective ad-vantages and disadvantages of formal recognition as op-posed to the continuation of the present situation of theoretical non-recognition but actual dealings around the conference table.

One argument in favor of non-recognition is that, in our frustration, we have found it very gratifying to be able to express our anger by ostentatiously refusing recognition to the Chinese Communists. If we can get over our state of self-debilitating hysteria, however, this particular reason can be discarded as entirely irrelevant. Another argument is that recognition means approval, but this is a complete misconception of the problem. Recognition simply means formal adjustment to a reality, not approval of any sort. Non-recognition on the other hand means the refusal to admit formally that something exists, and if it does actually exist, this position comes dangerously close to willful self-deception.

Still another argument is that American recognition would strengthen the Communist hold on China, but this is entirely false. The Chinese are in no mood to be influenced in their attitudes toward their own government by the stand we take. If American recognition would have any effect within China, it would probably be a favorable one for us, since it might blur the picture of the United States as the great external enemy of the Chinese—a picture that has been very harmful to us and useful to the Communist regime.

A further argument is that recognition would weaken our economic embargoes on trade with China. This seems highly doubtful. Our embargoes of strategic materials can only be maintained with the concurrence of our allies, and since most of them advocate the recognition of Communist China, compliance with their wishes on this matter should not make it more difficult than it is today to win their cooperation in our economic strategy.

The most valid argument against the recognition of Communist China is that it would undermine the will to resist communism in other parts of Asia and would lend credence to Communist claims that they represent the wave of the future. Undoubtedly recognition would have very adverse consequences if it was extended at such a time or in such a way as to suggest that the United States was yielding to Chinese military pressure or was attempting to conciliate the Chinese out of fear or weakness. Recognition at pistol point would seriously undermine the confidence of our Asian allies in us. On the other hand, if the situation in east Asia can be stabilized so that there is no longer any question of Chinese military pressure on us, then this whole argument loses its cogency. Recognition at such a time would not in Asian eyes be yielding to aggression, for even non-Communist Asians for the most part regard Mao's triumph as a matter of Chinese choice rather than external aggression. In fact, if recognition was coupled with clear American commitments to stop aggression in Asia, it would help to clarify for Asians the true principles on which we stand. Recognition at any time would discourage the Chinese Nationalists, but even for them it would have the beneficial effect of turning their energies toward more desirable tasks than arming for a battle they can never fight.

Still another argument against recognition is that the admittance of Communist China to the United Nations, which would probably accompany our recognition if not precede it, would give the Communists greater voting strength in this important international body. This is undoubtedly true, but the consequences of this increase in Communist votes do not seem very important. One veto is all that either side needs in the Security Council, and one additional vote in the Assembly would leave the Communist bloc still overwhelmingly outvoted on all important issues. It might even be possible to deny the Chinese Communists the permanent seat and veto right now enjoyed by Nationalist China in the Council. Moreover, the admission of Communist China to the U.N. would probably be tied in with the admission of several other countries that have been unfairly excluded from it and would presumably vote against the Communist bloc. Formosa itself should be among these new countries, for it is larger and stronger than many nations at present in the U.N.

Actually the Chinese Communist vote in the U.N. might lose us less than we would gain from having the Chinese present at this international forum. During the Korean War, when Peking seemed to be looking with favor on the Indian proposals regarding a truce, the Russians in the absence of their Chinese colleagues were able to kick over the whole applecart. If the Chinese had been there, this could not have been done so easily, and it is not difficult to imagine occasions in the future when the Russians would find it considerably harder to keep Peking in line if Mao's representatives were sitting beside the Russians in New York, observing everything that goes on there.

In fact, it is to our advantage to have as many responsible Chinese government officials as possible out in the free world participating in every possible international conference or committee. Only through contacts of this sort are they likely to learn the falseness of some of their opinions and the alternative possibilities to their present complete dependence on Russia. If the Chinese were simply stooges of Moscow, as are the delegates from the European satellite countries, their presence abroad would mean nothing. But this is not the fact, nor can it ever be, in view of the size of China and the strong racial and historical lines that divide the Chinese from the Russians. Moscow at present dominates Peking, but only because the Chinese think that this is necessary, and the less contact they have with the free world, the less chance there is that they will start thinking otherwise.

It seems altogether probable that the Russians, though forced to pose as the champions of the admission of China to the U.N., wish nothing less than this, unless it be American recognition of the Chinese Communists. It is a very fine arrangement from their point of view to have the United States not only helping to hold up the curtain around the Chinese but also taking most of the blame for its existence. This confirms the Chinese view that America so threatens their independence that they must stick close to the Russians for protection, however obnoxious the latter may become. Our stiff stand on Communist China also appears to most free Asians as the blackballing of Asians by white men. Whatever they themselves may feel about the Chinese, our ostracism of the Chinese touches a most sensitive nerve. The benefits that the Communists have derived both in China and elsewhere in Asia from our adamant stand on recognition seem to have far outweighed any possible advantages to us.

Recognition of Communist China and its admission into the U.N., when such actions become possible, would probably relieve us of a tremendous liability in our dealings with the whole of Asia. These are also the unavoidable first steps if we wish to begin to re-create some system of communication with the Chinese in preparation for the day when we can accomplish something positive through such contacts. The existence of contacts will be no assurance that useful communication will occur, but their absence would be nothing short of tragic if the opportunity arises and we are unprepared to take advantage of it.

American diplomatic missions in China would also have considerable value for us from the point of view of intelligence. For our own security as well as policy formulation, we need more and better sources of information about China. Chinese missions in this country would give the Communists no corresponding gain. Our free system makes information readily available for those who want it, and there would be considerable advantage for us in having this information going directly to Peking without passing in part through Russian filters.

No doubt there are many other considerations that should be added to the balance sheet, and as events unfold, some of these may weight the figures less heavily in favor of recognition. But in any case we certainly should be giving serious thought to the re-establishment of normal diplomatic relations with the Chinese instead of shying away from this possibility in unthinking horror. This does not mean, however, that our government officials should advocate recognition. None is likely to do so in the present climate of opinion in the United States, but wholly aside from this consideration there is good reason for our official representatives to voice continued unwillingness to recognize the Chinese Communists or admit them to the U.N. These are two fine bargaining points, and we should sell them to China, when the proper time comes, for as high a price as possible. We might also see to it that the haggling over them takes place in front of the Russians in order to give the latter as much opportunity as possible to offend their sensitive Chinese colleagues by showing their reluctance to let them out into international society. If we can get some solid concessions on Korea or Indochina in return for recognition or if we could sow some seeds of discord between the Russians and Chinese while negotiating over it, we shall have struck a doubly rewarding bargain.

The approach to our Chinese problem outlined here is at best a roundabout one, and its chance for success may not be very great. But since other approaches, such as direct economic or military pressure, give still less hope of achieving our objectives, we cannot afford to ignore even this small possibility. Whether or not it is a feasible or desirable approach to the question of our relations with China, however, is not the present problem. I am concerned here with principles of strategy, not the specific strategy itself, and this brief outline of some aspects of the problem will at least show that even in this case, in which virtually no communication exists between us and the

Chinese, the ideological side of the problem overshadows both the economic and the military.

14. *Nationalism and Internationalism*

In considering the means of achieving our aims in China or any other Asian country, we should not lose sight of one fundamental principle. American objectives have no real chance for ultimate success unless they are in line with what the peoples of Asia themselves desire. If our objectives ran counter to the basic hopes and aspirations of Asians, we might best retire into "fortress America" and put our reliance, as some apparently advocate, in the grand strategy of sitting quietly by our dry powder with our fingers crossed. Fortunately this is not the case. In terms of fundamental aims, we see entirely eye to eye with Asians. We too look forward to the development of independent and prosperous Asian nations, living as equals with the countries of the West in an international system of law and order. Of all the peoples of the West, we probably have given the most consistent and strongest support to the peoples of the East in their efforts to achieve equality with the rest of the world. Virtually all Americans quite naturally and unselfconsciously sympathize with Asians who desire to create truly prosperous and independent nations. What else could one expect when their dream is so much our own and we have played so important a part in inspiring it in them?

The men who founded the new democracies of Asia have often drawn parallels between themselves and our own founding fathers. We should take pride in this analogy, even if it is not a very close one. The leaders of the American Revolution, as full and natural heirs to British democracy, were reacting against colonial rule in a manner wholly consistent with their British background. The new democratic leaders of Asia have faced a far greater task in breaking with their own political traditions at the same time that they were overturning colonial rule. It might be more to the point if the democracies of Asia sought for analogies in our more recent history, in our successful fight to better the lot of the common man, economically, socially, and politically, and in our slow and bitter but essentially hopeful struggle to solve our great racial problems. Here are analogies with the problems of Asia which are certainly as close as the War of Independence and considerably more relevant for the future. But, in any case, many Asians have undoubtedly drawn inspiration from our own fight for freedom, and most Americans give full emotional support to Asians in their hopes for self-respecting independence.

Our sympathy with the basic aims of Asians, however, is not merely a sentimental one born of historical parallels. It is also a matter of clear intellectual conviction. We have stood fast for the ideal of a democratic community of nations. Despite our great military power, we have specifically rejected the Russian technique of creating a power bloc by ruthless centralized control and coercion. We have in fact staked our whole future as a nation on a free association of equal allies and beyond that, on a world order in which democratic procedures of discussion and voting, rather than force, will be used to settle international disputes. Such a world order depends ultimately on the existence of truly independent and stable nations, in Asia as well as elsewhere in the world. What Asians hope to achieve in creating independent nations is an essential part of what we are hoping to achieve. Our aims are fundamentally the same.

The Russians, on the other hand, have consistently

stood in direct opposition to Asian objectives. No European power was more thoroughly imperialistic in Asia than was tsarist Russia throughout its history. The Communist regime in its days of initial weakness appeared at first to turn its back on the imperialist past, but with the restoration of Russian power came a re-emergence of Russian efforts to conquer and coerce neighboring lands.

Communism as a philosophy and as a practical system of organization is based on the assumption that there should be a single source of absolute authority. Human nature being what it is, such authority can be achieved only by force. There may be moments of divided authority even within the Kremlin, such as the brief period when both Malenkov and Beria sought to become Stalin's heir. An even greater division of authority may exist at present between Moscow and Peking, but if it does, it is a contradiction of all Communist theory and practice. There cannot be two different party lines even on minor matters. In the long run, there can be no place of real equality within the Communist system even for China, the colossus of Asia, much less for the smaller Asian countries.

The Russians are ultimately committed to bucking the great nationalist tides of Asia, but like any good navigator, they have sought to use these tides as best they can, even if they trend in the opposite direction. We, on the other hand, have often found ourselves battling these tides, even though they flow in general with us. Asian nationalism is perhaps the greatest potential bulwark against communism and therefore the greatest immediate support of the cause of international democracy. We, instead of the Russians, should be making effective use of these tides.

Indochina is the classic case in which the Communists have utilized nationalism effectively against us. There we find a sobering example of the weakness of defending the *status quo* against the offensive of Communist-dominated nationalism. In Indochina the French empire, the largest remaining traditional colonial power, backed by the financial and military resources of the United States, was pitted in a frustrating and at best indecisive battle against the Communist Vietminh. In recent years large-scale aid from Communist China greatly strengthened the Vietminh forces and tipped the military scales more definitely in their favor, but for a long time before that the Vietminh guerrillas, though an ill-armed, shoestring force, actively supported by only a minority of the people of one of the smaller countries of Asia, were able to fight the French to a standstill.

The cream of French youth from Saint-Cyr, the competent German hirelings of the Foreign Legion, the tough African colonials, and the best of American military equipment were liberally expended in the defense of Indochina and only managed to preserve a precarious hold on part of the country. The French economy, even French morale, were strained to the breaking-point. For years a significant proportion of the total military potential on which the West depended to balance Soviet power was poured down the military rat-hole of Indochina. It was a contest between David and Goliath or perhaps between Jack and the Giant, and the outcome ran close to the Biblical and fairy-tale precedents.

Part of the reason was that the French were committed to the military defense of the cities and areas of major rice production, while the Vietminh, having little to defend, could adopt a mobile and offensive strategy. But a much more important factor was that in the realm of ideas the adherents of Vietminh were on the offensive, while the French basically were engaged in a defense of national pride and the fast dwindling residue of empire. Vietminh long ago made itself the locally recognized champion of complete and unequivocal independence for

Indochina; the French, while periodically forced to promise greater freedom to the local population, inevitably represented in their eyes the visible survival of colonialism. And in the economic field it was the Communists who carried out much-needed land reform for the peasants, while the French did little more than passively accept the results of land reform when retaking former Vietminh territory.

No one could disentangle the Communist fanaticism of the Vietminh leaders from their national ardor, and among the rank and file these ideological strains may be even less distinguishable. The whole history of the Communist Vietminh revolt against the French, however, indicates that from the start it has rested more heavily on nationalism for its mass support than on Communist dialectics. Therefore, in supporting the French in Indochina, we found ourselves attempting to stem this great Asian tide.

Many Indochinese have been willing to fight with fury and to die with heroism for the Vietminh cause, but few have shown a comparable enthusiasm for the French-backed Vietnam regime. Perhaps most Indochinese remain suspicious of both sides, and a majority may fear the Vietminh Communists more than Vietnam and the French. Still, enough have actively joined the Vietminh side to give it a large and strong fighting force, while, despite all the cajoling of French administrators and the support of American equipment, no Vietnamese military units have had sufficient spirit to bear any great part of the load of defense. In essence, the local farm boy, fighting on his own terrain and for his own soil, was pitted against the professional soldier from across the seas. The fallen Vietminh guerrilla was much more easily replaced than his alien adversary. On Indochinese soil Vietminh-dominated nationalism appears to be more than a match for French pride or American dollars.

Even if the defense of Indochina had gone well, its

over-all effect on our cause in Asia might still have been adverse. No Asian can look at Indochina without seeing the picture of fellow Asians, often physically not very distinct from himself, fighting against European and African aliens of very different appearance. Whatever the rights or wrongs of the situation, emotionally he sees himself in the Vietminh guerrilla, fighting for his independence against foreign rulers.

We saw some of these same adverse results even in our more successful war in Korea. Asians by and large seem to have ignored the fact that the majority of the natives of the Korean peninsula were wholeheartedly on our side and that contingents of troops from three other Asian countries came to Korea to aid us. They forgot that because of geographic proximity China, not the United States, has usually represented and will probably continue to represent the greatest external threat to Korean independence. Asians often lost sight of all this and of the very reasons for the war. More important to them was the emotion-charged picture of white soldiers with superior weapons killing Asian soldiers on Asian soil. This may in part explain the curious ambivalence of the Indian attitude toward the war. Intellectually they were far more on our side than with the Communists, but emotionally they found it almost impossible to support the side that depended in large part on white soldiers to fight native Asians.

The most disturbing aspect of the Indochinese problem is that it may now be too late for any really desirable solution. The fighting may have ended, but this will not stop the creeping penetration of communism into South Vietnam, Laos, and Cambodia. It is perfectly possible that if South Vietnam has not already fallen to the Communists, they will take it over through the elections that are to be held within two years after the signing of the truce.

If this happens, Laos and Cambodia can scarcely withstand the Communists for long, and then Siam would be fully exposed to Communist infiltration and pressure. Weak and underdeveloped as it is and honeycombed with a large and influential Chinese population of doubtful loyalty, Siam might fall an easy prey to Communist subversion. This in turn would increase the Communist pressure on the highly unstable democracies of Burma and Indonesia and would give the Communists a land frontier with Malaya. Across this frontier they could easily pour new life into the desperate Communist guerrilla war in Malaya, which the full might of the British Empire has been unable to stamp out completely.

We have already seen that colonial armies cannot stem the Communist tide in southeast Asia. The only hope of halting it and eventually turning it back rests with the people of that area. There can be no secure defense line in Indochina until the inhabitants of South Vietnam, Cambodia, and Laos themselves are willing and able to maintain it, and this in turn seems unlikely until they have achieved real and not merely nominal independence and on the basis of this new freedom have started to develop strong and healthy societies. But is there time at this late date to erect this one and only effective dike against communism in Indochina? Time is running out, and the creation of independent and healthy nations is at best a slow undertaking.

This is the tragedy of the Indochinese situation. If this solution of the problem had been tried ten or even five years earlier, the chances for success would have been infinitely greater than they are today. If we had had the foresight and courage in the early postwar years to persuade the French to extricate themselves soon enough from their untenable position in Indochina, the great force of Indochinese nationalism might not have fallen into

Communist hands and might instead have served as the basis of nationalist regimes that would have been much more effective than the French in halting communism. Independent Indochinese governments, even under the best of circumstances, would probably not have been as stable as that of India, but there is no reason why they could not have been as successful as the Indonesian and Burmese governments, which to date have certainly held communism at bay far more successfully and easily than have the French in Indochina.

It would not have been easy to give independent Indochinese states the economic and political aid they needed to build up a workable alternative to Communist dictatorship. A still more difficult problem would have been their defense during the interim period of several years before they were able to defend themselves. The French were carrying the military load, in part out of unsound economic hopes, but more out of false pride in empire, perhaps made more dogged and unreasonable by their national humiliation in the Second World War. But if the Indochinese states were to be entirely free, would the French have continued their terrible sacrifices simply to pay for past blunders? And if not, were American GI's to take their place in the pillboxes and graves of Indochina? No one would deny the difficulties of the Indochinese situation even a decade ago. The important point, however, is that we still face these same problems today, but with less time to solve them and far less favorable conditions for their solution.

Indochina illustrates the defensive strategy at its worst. It also shows how absurdly wrong we are to battle Asian nationalism instead of aiding it. From the start the offensive was lost to the Communists, and we were forced into an extremely ineffective and ultimately hopeless defense of the *status quo*. Worst of all, we appeared to be defending things that we do not believe in ourselves. Americans would have preferred to see Indochina a truly independent nation or group of nations rather than a colonial or semi-colonial land. We had scant sympathy for French colonialism there even if it had not been the Achilles' heel of our cause. Our failure to help prevent the Indochinese situation from falling into this sorry state is another great failure of foresight, comparable in many ways to our failures in China and Korea.

It might well be asked what right we have to exercise our influence in behalf of freeing colonies from their mother countries. If Churchill was reluctant to preside over the dismemberment of the British Empire, how much less happy most Europeans would be to have us giving away their colonial territories! Obviously we have no right to compel such actions, but we certainly have every right to use persuasion. The clumsiness with which the Dutch finally gave independence to Indonesia has had an unfortunate effect on both American and Dutch relations with that part of the world ever since. The French failure to relinquish Indochina has put a heavy burden on the United States financially and could end by costing us dearly in lives. The remnants of nineteenth-century colonialism, though not our direct responsibility, may continue to prove extremely costly to us as well as to the colonial powers themselves. If badly handled, they can do untold damage to the cause of democracy and world peace. Under such circumstances the United States has not only the right but the duty to exert its influence toward the solution of the remaining colonial problems everywhere in the world.

A more reasonable objection to our championing of independence for colonial peoples is raised by those who fear the adverse effect of such a stand on our relations with our allies in Europe. For example, in the early postwar years government officials who dealt primarily with Asia tended to advocate a clear-cut American stand in favor of Indonesian independence, but were overruled by the preponderant number of officials who looked primarily toward Europe and felt that we should do nothing which might irritate the Dutch or weaken their economic position. The same division has occurred at times in American attitudes toward Indochina and may arise over other colonial problems in the future.

This conflict between our European and Asian interests, however, is more apparent than real. It is highly doubtful that in the long run we aided the Dutch economy or salved Dutch feelings by not taking a more positive stand for Indonesian independence. Instead we may have prolonged the pains and heightened the bitterness of the period of change-over. If we had made efforts to get the French out of Indochina at a time when this would have done some good, it is true that we would have stepped on sensitive French toes, but this could not have done the damage to the French economy and French pride or for that matter to the whole defense of Europe that has resulted from the present situation in Indochina. The easy way out of the colonial dilemma appeared to be to take refuge in a legalistic position of disinterest or at least neutrality, but this has certainly not proved to be the easy way out in the end, in our relations either with the European colonial powers or with Asia.

The colonial problem cannot safely be ignored. If we are to profit from the bitter lesson of Indochina, we must adopt a much more forthright stand on colonialism everywhere. In the really backward areas, such as Borneo, New Guinea, and parts of Africa, this might mean strong American support for the trusteeship concept. According to it, colonial rule is a trust in which the administering authority has the duty to further the best interests of the local people and prepare them as well as possible for complete independence or for autonomy if independence is not feasible. Such a stand would also entail support for the extension of the trusteeship principle to all colonial lands, regardless of their historical origins, and an increasingly close international supervision over all trusteeship territories.

In the case of less backward peoples already capable of self-rule and independence, the American position should be even stronger. For example, the absurd tag ends of the Portuguese Empire in Asia, such as Goa and other spots along the coast of India, are of negligible benefit to the economy or even the prestige of the Portuguese but serve as constant reminders of the European empires of the past. As such they help keep Asian eyes turned toward the humiliating colonialism of the nineteenth century and away from the present dangers of Communist imperialism. We certainly should support the return of these scraps of land to the local peoples who inhabit them and from whose territories they were originally carved.

Malaya and Hong Kong raise more difficult problems. The people of Malaya obviously are technologically ready for self-rule, but their division into three different ethnic groups and the continuation of a small but bitter war by Communist guerrillas on Malayan soil make the granting of immediate independence unwise. In Hong Kong we find another anachronistic survival of nineteenth-century imperialism, originally cut with the sword from Chinese territory and inhabited largely by Chinese. The time will no doubt come when it should go back to China or be internationalized, but this is scarcely the proper moment. Although Hong Kong too is an unfortunate symbol of colonialism flaunted before hostile Asian eyes, it does serve some very useful purposes for the free world in the present highly unsatisfactory state of relations between the West and China. There would have to be profound changes in this relationship and also in the Chinese Communist attitude toward international law and order before we could reasonably support a change in the status of Hong Kong.

A still more complex and far more dangerous colonial problem is presented by the French holdings in North Africa. Tunisia, Algeria, and Morocco lie only across the Mediterranean Sea from metropolitan France, not at the end of the earth, as does Indochina. The combined population of this vast area is considerably less than that of Indochina, and the French economic interests and the permanent European population incomparably greater, the latter amounting to about twelve per cent of the total population in Algeria and seven per cent in Tunisia. The mother country obviously has a much greater hold over this region than over distant Indochina, and Algeria has even been incorporated politically as an integral part of France.

On the other hand the majority of the population consists of Arab-speaking Moslems, who by strong, even fanatic tradition have always held themselves proudly distinct from France and European culture. The appeal of nationalism is as great to them as to any other people in the world. They have behind them the strong emotional support of all the Arab countries of the Near East and the even broader support of the whole Islamic world. The future of North Africa is of vital interest emotionally to a large voting bloc in the United Nations and a huge number of Asian peoples living in a strategically important part of the world.

In Tunisia, Algeria, and Morocco the forces of colonialism are stronger than anywhere else in the world, but so also may be the forces of nationalism, and the geographic setting is strategically very much more important than Indochina. Only a few ripples have as yet broken the surface, but it takes no great familiarity with our twentieth-century world to see that North Africa has all the makings of a tremendous tempest. This is not the sort of problem that we can safely leave to drift until we find ourselves in another situation as insoluble as our dilemma in Indochina and much more crucial. At present the easy thing to do, of course, is to maintain the narrow, legalistic point of view that keeps our eyes conveniently away from North Africa, but in the long run this is not likely to be either the wisest or the easiest course.

Colonial problems affecting us do not lie entirely in other people's empires. We have our own in the Ryukyu Islands. There we rule more than half a million people who are culturally and linguistically very close to the Japanese and would prefer to be an integral part of Japan, as they were before the war. We have departed from our own belief in the basic right of self-determination in this instance, apparently because we felt that our military needs for a great defensive base in Okinawa were more important than the wishes of the local population. There may have been considerable justification for this point of view when the decision was originally made to retain the Ryukyus at the end of the war, but there is much less reason for it now. Our changing plans for defense in the western Pacific have reduced Okinawa to a much smaller role than was originally envisaged, and the Ryukyus have become tied in much more closely than was foreseen with voluntary defense arrangements with neighboring lands. We might well ask ourselves why our bases on Okinawa necessitate colonial rule when even more important bases elsewhere in the Far East can be left to voluntary agreements with independent Asian governments.

Whatever the reasons for maintaining our control over the Ryukyus for the present, there can be no doubt that

American colonial rule over these islands will eventually become both unnecessary and unwise. If the defense of South Korea, Japan, Formosa, or the Philippines should continue to depend for long on an American colonial enclave in the Far East, then we have entangled ourselves in a hopeless position in that whole area. In any case, Ryukyuan and Japanese resentment against our retention of the islands and general Asian concern over this situation are sure to grow in time to dangerous proportions. If we hope to save Asia and not simply a few peripheral islands from communism, we should be sure that in the Ryukyus we do not commit in miniature the same blunders that some of the European colonial powers have committed so disastrously elsewhere in Asia.

In Japan herself we face a much larger and far more delicate problem. Japan has regained her full political freedom, but her continued dependence on American economic aid and military protection casts a very real shadow over her theoretical independence. Treaty arrangements between the two governments now determine the American role in Japan, but the situation is not entirely like that in the nations of western Europe, for the military partnership is much less equal, Japan's economic dependence on us is far greater, and the psychological strains are heightened by traditional Asian fears of Western domination. To the Japanese, American defense garrisons are much too reminiscent of the recent military occupation, and their uneasiness is underscored by the many irritating incidents that inevitably occur between foreign troops and a local civilian population, especially when contacts are complicated by sharp cultural differences. The Japanese, perhaps because they have not emerged entirely from the state of emotional shock brought on by their recent defeat, have not as yet found the situation intolerable. But it is easy to see that it will become progressively less tolerable and, if continued long enough, may eventually pit American defense interests in Japan squarely against the tremendous forces of reawakened Japanese nationalism.

Our interest in the protection of Japan is very clear-cut. Japan is of vital importance to the free world not only because of military and economic considerations but also for political reasons. A democratic system operating successfully in Japan may in time serve as an invaluable precedent. On the other hand, if Japanese democracy collapses, either because of economic instability or through Communist conquest or subversion, its failure may seriously prejudice the chances for democracy throughout the non-Western world. Under these circumstances, we obviously must provide Japan with the military and economic support she needs.

But the United States cannot continue too long its indirect domination of Japan without eventually running afoul of Japanese nationalism. Naturally Americans would in any case much prefer to have the Japanese carry their own economic and defense burdens. These are two responsibilities that we are as anxious to get rid of as the Japanese are to have us relinquish them. The only difficulty is that they must be borne by someone, and the Japanese are as yet unable to shoulder the full economic load and both unable and unwilling to undertake the military.

Because of the strong revulsion against war in any form that has swept the Japanese people, most of them are reluctant to see Japan rearm herself to any appreciable degree, and many fear that a reborn army would be a menace to their democratic institutions. They have an even stronger conviction that a native military force adequate to defend Japan would put an unbearable strain on her already shaky economy. Those elements in Japan which tend to be the most thoroughly committed to democracy have commonly embraced a dreamy pacifism and have committed themselves to the unrealistic hope that Japan can become an Asian Switzerland, forgetting that the Swiss have been able to preserve their neutrality because they have added to their strong natural defenses a proportionately heavy investment in military preparedness. This pacifistic opposition to rearmament in Japan has begun to assume the shape of a nationalistic resistance to American domination. When Americans not unreasonably urge the Japanese to assume their own defense burden, it is not hard for propagandists in Japan to distort such requests into American demands that Japan provide the cannon fodder for American imperialist ambitions.

The United States faces a delicate problem of timing in Japan. If Japan continues to be militarily and economically dependent on the United States for too long a period, we may eventually come so sharply into conflict with the nationalistic feelings of the Japanese that we shall defeat the purpose of our military defense and economic support. On the other hand, we cannot drop this economic support until effective alternatives have been developed for Japan, presumably through expanded foreign trade. Nor can we insist on too rapid a rate of rearmament without running the risk of so alienating the Japanese as to drive them toward communism. We cannot wait too long in transferring the economic and military burden to the Japanese nor can we accomplish this transfer too precipitately. We are forced to feel our way cautiously between the twin dangers of too soon and too late.

One particularly difficult aspect of the problem is that in Japanese eyes the most obvious economic alternative to American aid is trade with Communist China. While an expanded trade with south Asia would benefit all of free Asia as well as help to carry the Japanese economic burden, this does not alter the fact that before the war China and Manchuria constituted vital markets and sources of raw materials for the Japanese and still represent by all odds their greatest potential trading area. It seems altogether possible that the Communists, adopting the strategy of starving Japan economically into submission, may not be willing to trade with Japan on any significant scale, but this does not prevent the Japanese from looking toward China as the green pastures that might free them from dependence on the United States.

If Sino-Japanese trade were likely to be made up of nonstrategic materials, there would be little problem, and the United States might encourage Japan to develop what trade it could with China. But if Japanese exports do go to China in great quantity, they are certain to consist in large part of such items as rolling stock and rails, machinery and machine tools. In other words, the United States will probably face the choice of encouraging or at least permitting a Japanese trade with China that helps build up the industrial and military potential of the Communist regime there, or else of blocking such trade at the risk of turning the forces of Japanese nationalism against us.

This again is a problem that has not yet reached the critical stage, but it is definitely foreseeable. If we are to take to heart the lessons of our lack of foresight in China, Korea, and Indochina, we should certainly be preparing for future problems of this type with every possible care. If we simply wait for this particular problem to come to a head, we may find Japanese passions so aroused as to preclude any satisfactory solution. We must not dally until most Japanese angrily claim, as some do now, that we Americans are willing to sacrifice Japan's economic future to our own narrow defense plans and that we are interested only in whether the Japanese fight for us, not in whether they eat or starve. If this should happen, it may be already too late to find alternative supports for the

Japanese economy or, if necessary, to reconsider an overly rigid policy toward trade with China. Our tendency in recent years to look back at past failures in Asia seems to have faced us in the wrong direction for seeing and avoiding the possible fiascoes of the future.

Actually the dilemma may not be so difficult as it at first appears. While the strengthening of Japan through Sino-Japanese trade would be all gain for our system of international democracy, the strengthening of China might merely heighten the inner contradiction of the Communist system, which cannot tolerate two equal and independent sources of authority. It is commonly assumed that Sino-Japanese trade would tend to draw the Japanese toward communism. There may be some reason for this fear, but a stronger possibility is that such trade would pull the Chinese even harder in the opposite direction. If the Chinese leaders were to discover that they could with complete safety obtain more of what they want through trade with Japan than through complete dependence on Russian industrial power, they might begin to realize the folly and dangers of their present policies. Perhaps we should be working for the development of Sino-Japanese trade rather than attempting to stifle it.

Asian nationalism is a force that creates complex problems for the United States in any colonial land or even in a country in the still somewhat ambiguous position of Japan, but it should raise no great difficulties for us in the greater part of Asia, where the national regimes are fully and indisputably independent. On the contrary, we must look to nationalism as the chief force that can preserve the freedom of these Asian nations and thus help lay the foundations for a democratic world order of independent states. We must also look to nationalism to supply much of the ardor with which Asians must tackle their many serious economic, social, and political problems.

Under these circumstances, it is particularly discouraging to find nationalistic forces and American policy in apparent conflict with each other in many Asian countries. This unhappy situation can be attributed in part to the narrow prejudices and chauvinism that seem to accompany nationalism everywhere in the world, particularly in its nascent days. We see an undesirable side of nationalism in the basic suspicion of us as a Western nation which so complicates our relationship with Asian countries. Nationalism also provides its full share of discord between the individual lands of Asia, and this can all too easily embroil us too. For instance, American aid to either Israel or her Arab neighbors arouses violent condemnation of us from the other side in this unfortunate enmity, and American military assistance to Pakistan stirs up such bitter resentment in India that we cannot but wonder if our aid in this case has not done more harm than good to the cause we wish to further.

American policy in Asia, however, has not run afoul of nationalism simply because of such specific problems. In the eyes of many Asians a much more basic and serious conflict than this exists between American policy and their nationalistic aspirations. Every one of Asia's Communists, for example, has obviously become convinced that the United States represents a greater threat to the independence of his country than does the Soviet Union or the Communist system. What is even more disturbing, millions of non-Communist Asians seem to have come to the same conclusion. In fact, the majority of thinking Indians and Indonesians appear to be genuinely afraid of the United States, even if many of them may fear Russia more. This is, of course, a deplorable situation, and although in most countries it has not yet headed up into a specific crisis, it certainly creates fertile soil for the rapid growth of serious problems.

In the whole sphere of our foreign relations there has been no more tragic or inexcusable blunder than our failure to utilize or at least take necessary cognizance of the tides of nationalism in developing our Asian policies. Nationalism might very well be called the nuclear weapons of the situation in Asia. Why should we be so disturbed about security lapses in the protection of the atom bomb when we have been so indifferent about letting the comparably potent weapon of Asian nationalism fall into Communist hands? Actually we have been worse than indifferent. Often enough in our ignorance we have deliberately handed this weapon over to our enemies.

A good case in point can be found in our attitude toward neutralism in Asia. We realize that for an advanced democratic country communism represents a tragic reversion into hypocritical despotism and into a terrifying brand of savagery, and so we naturally find it difficult to see how anyone can be neutral in the struggle between democracy and communism. We have small patience today with fellow Americans who cannot perceive the distinction between the imperfections in our own society and the total travesty on democracy and justice into which communism has developed.

But this does not mean that we should be equally impatient with Asian neutralists. They do not necessarily identify the cause of democracy with that of the democracies, least of all the United States. In view of the type of information and misinformation they have in their minds, it is unrealistic to expect them to share our views on the folly of neutralism or to take as clear a stand as we have on the Soviet menace.

Our policy has been unrealistic on the emotional as well as on the intellectual plane. When we demand that

Asian nations follow our lead and stand up and be counted on our side or declare themselves even more decisively on the field of battle, we are undoubtedly forcing our way against the emotional currents of Asia. Asians have for the most part only recently freed themselves from Western domination. Following the lead of any Western nation is scarcely appealing to them and may appear to be a dangerous reversion to the past. They like to cite, not without some smugness, George Washington's warning to the young American Republic to avoid foreign entanglements. The parallel is historically false, invalidated by the time differential of a century and a half that has put the contemporary Asian into an entirely different international situation from that which Washington knew. But the analogy is emotionally sound. No one can blame Asians for wishing to avoid involvement in international tensions that seem more remote to them than their own pressing internal problems of economic and political survival. In any case, Asians have no more desire to follow America's lead or, as they might put it, to fight America's battles than we had in our early years as a nation to follow Britain's lead or fight her wars.

But the real tragedy of our attitude toward Asian neutralism is our entire misunderstanding of what it really signifies in the war between democracy and communism. Asian neutralism is in reality a strong assertion of independence. It is so strong as to be ultimately unwise in the world in which we live, but basically it is the assertion of a point of view with which we sympathize wholeheartedly and on which we must place our greatest reliance for the future development of Asia. The democratic world order that we envisage depends upon this strong spirit of independence; communism in the long run can triumph only if this spirit is broken. The real strength of democracy is that anyone who is not specifically against it must ultimately be for it, while communism suffers from the great tactical liability that anyone who is not specifically for it is eventually forced to oppose it. Asian neutralism runs diametrically against Communist concepts of centralized, unified control, but for us it is just one of many variations of the theme of independence that runs throughout all democracy.

Neutralism is very commonly an unconscious reflection of a nation's military weakness. Those countries which have espoused it most enthusiastically have often been those least capable of affecting the world balance of power. Many of them will be making their maximum contribution to the cause of world democracy and world peace if they can simply maintain their own independence and their democratic forms of government. This is true in varying degrees of countries such as India, Indonesia, and Japan, where neutralism is particularly strong. We should not oppose it in these countries. In Japan, for example, we might best encourage the Japanese to be realistic neutralists, capable of defending their own neutralism both externally from conquest and internally from subversion or economic collapse.

We have usually, however, fought Asian neutralism. In doing this we have saved communism from one of its most dangerous enemies and transformed neutralism instead into a potent Communist ally. A little more sympathetic understanding of the reasons why Asians seek to be neutral would do a great deal to undermine communism in any Asian country. It also would probably bring that country far more rapidly to our side both in the United Nations and on the firing line than any amount of pressure we could exert. It is not surprising that we have done so poorly in the great ideological battle in Asia when we have turned some of our best weapons over to the enemy.

The importance of nationalism in the battle of Asia

can hardly be overemphasized, but it would be a mistake for us to base our strategy entirely upon this one factor. Although the Communists have made skillful use of Asian nationalism, one of their chief appeals is their claim to represent a system of international government. Even in nationally aroused Asia, more and more people are looking beyond the ideal of national independence to a still higher ideal of world peace and order. Communism is not just an international conspiracy; it also purports to be a system of international peace. We may not be able to counter the very real dangers of the international conspiracy of the Communists until we have matched their international ideal. We also should not forget that our chief reason for desiring the development of truly independent nations throughout Asia is our hope that they will become healthy members of a democratic world order.

Each time we contribute to international co-operation through democratic means we are helping to build up the democratic answer to international communism. Each time we are forced to take unilateral action we may be increasing the appeal of the Communist claims by demonstrating that a democratic world order does not yet exist. Under present conditions we cannot rely on international action to solve all of our problems in Asia, but we should exert every effort to make our policies and strategy as international as possible. Just as democracy is its own best weapon in winning the war against communism within any Asian country, so the ideal of an international democratic system of peace and justice may be the only effective weapon in combating the Communist attempt to establish a world order of ruthless dictation.

Actually our relations with Asia are in essence merely part of a greater relationship between the whole Western democratic world and the East. The individual Englishman or Dane is as much concerned in the future of Asia

as the individual American. The chief difference is that
there are more Americans than either Englishmen or
Danes and therefore we collectively exert more influence
in this relationship and have a greater responsibility for it.
But it is no more a uniquely American problem than is
that of European defense. There is every bit as much
need for a grand alliance of the Western democracies to
help solve the problems of Asia as there is for an organization like NATO to block the Russian juggernaut.

The United States clearly cannot itself carry the
whole burden of external assistance to Asians. In fact,
much of the burden is already being borne by European
nations. Not only have French and British troops been
fighting on the military battle line in Asia; the United
Kingdom and the British Commonwealth nations are doing excellent work on the economic battle line through the
Colombo Plan, and some other Western nations have at
least small-scale economic endeavors under way. And on
the ideological front we have perhaps been accomplishing
proportionately less of value than have some of our Western allies.

Unfortunately we and our allies have often been
working at cross-purposes. We sometimes say one thing in
an Asian country and the British almost the opposite. The
French have been fighting a valiant military battle in Indochina, but on a political basis that has been defeating not
only themselves but the whole democratic cause. There is
perhaps a greater need for the co-ordination of Western
democratic efforts in the battle of Asia than in the defense
of Europe, just because the battle lines in Asia are less
clearly defined and our weapons so much less certain in
their use.

We should also realize that our Western allies can on
the whole be more effective in Asia than can we. With the
exception of the Philippines, it would be hard to find a

country in Asia in which an individual Swede, New Zealander, or Belgian would not be in a better position to accomplish a job in either the economic or the ideological field than an American of comparable ability. The former would labor under fewer of the suspicions or resentments that are commonly directed toward Americans in Asia. In addition, higher American wage scales and greater opportunities for jobs here make it more difficult to obtain from the United States persons with high qualifications for work in Asia than it is from our Western allies.

An even more important reason for international cooperation in our Asian policies is that prevalent fears of American domination make Asians much more reluctant to accept aid from us than from an international agency. It is true that international agencies are often clumsy and slow-moving, but these drawbacks are more than offset by the simple fact that anything done through an international body in Asia, just because of its international cachet, has more chance of accomplishing its objectives than a comparable effort by the United States alone. Our general rule should be to approach each specific project through as large an international body as seems capable of handling it at all effectively, instead of emphasizing wherever possible the uniquely American character of our actions in Asia.

It would be even more advantageous if such international bodies also embraced all those in Asia who wished to take part. The greatest advantage of the Colombo Plan is that the participating Asian nations meet with the Western members as a council of equals. Such a fully international approach to the problem gives far more promise of ultimate success than a co-ordinated but exclusively Western approach. There are many technical skills to be exchanged between Asian nations, and any agency that could make the great surplus of technical abilities now lying dangerously dormant in Japan available for use throughout Asia would be doing both Japan and the rest of Asia a great service. Even more important than these considerations, the spirit of democratic equality of such a truly international system of Western aid to Asia would itself be an important part of the war of ideas and a significant step toward the development of an effective democratic system of world peace which can match in accomplishments the glittering but false claims of the Communists.

In emphasizing this essential international ideal in our approach to Asia, we should also not forget that America too is part of a now unitary world and that our own successess or failures with democratic institutions are a vital part of the whole battle of Asia. Our enemies have been making most effective use of our shortcomings in domestic matters as well as in international affairs. Americans who disregard normal democratic ideals of fair play and due process of law or who argue that good ends justify dirty means are providing the Communists of Asia with very effective weapons. For each red or pink who may have been uncovered by McCarthyist techniques in the United States, it seems probable that ten thousand Asians have been lost to democracy's cause and many million other Asians nudged a step farther toward the Communist side. This is a miserable exchange of blows for the United States in its war with communism.

The home front is part of the struggle in Asia in still another way. In a democracy like ours, Asian policy is closely linked with the degree of understanding that the American people as a whole have of Asia and its problems. Our government's policy can only be a direct reflection of the wisdom or stupidity of the American public in such matters. We are all in the battle of Asia.

In conclusion, a word of warning. This book does not constitute an Asian policy, even in the most general terms. It is merely an attempt to probe into the problems of an Asian policy from one particular standpoint and with a limited body of facts at hand. There are many other relevant facts and many other possible points of view. We obviously should be studying the question from all standpoints and with all available facts brought to bear on it. But we are not doing this. As a result of irresponsible congressional attacks, many officials have become frozen into a posture of rigid terror when faced with Asian problems. Informed private individuals have often been frightened away from a serious consideration of Asian questions by the brutal treatment of those who in the past have attempted to grapple with them. And the general public has been diverted from the underlying problem of Asia by a few of its more spectacular surface manifestations or by the dragnet operation of congressional committees endlessly pursuing the shadow of the phantom who is supposed to have betrayed America in China.

It has been several years, a full half-decade and more, since the debacle in China. And yet we are today perhaps less prepared to work seriously on shaping an Asian policy than we were then. We take frantic interest in individual crises when they develop, but appear strangely indifferent to the basic ills that have caused them. Worse still, we are easily diverted from our problems in Asia to more trivial matters. Those who have turned the attention of the American public from the great battle with the marshaled forces of communism in Asia to the search for parlor pinks behind the sofa have rendered a great disservice to their country. It is high time that we returned to the real firing line and left the search for internal subversives in the competent hands of the properly delegated authorities.

But the war, of course, cannot be fought without plans, and plans cannot be safely laid without knowledge and thought. The first order of business should be serious study, followed by a great debate in the best democratic tradition. The perils are grave; the time may be short; and the need is clear—

WANTED: AN ASIAN POLICY

Index

A Note on the Type

The text of this book was set on the Linotype in a type face called Baskerville. The face is a facsimile reproduction of types cast from molds made for John Baskerville (1706–75) from his designs. The punches for the revived Linotype Baskerville were cut under the supervision of the English printer George W. Jones.

John Baskerville's original face was one of the forerunners of the type style known as "modern face" to printers—a "modern" of the period A.D. 1800.